Activities FOR STANDARDS-BASED, INTEGRATED Language Arts INSTRUCTION

Deborah A. Ellermeyer
CLARION UNIVERSITY OF PENNSYLVANIA

Kay A. Chick
PENNSYLVANIA STATE UNIVERSITY ALTOONA

Holcomb Hathaway, Publishers
Scottsdale, Arizona

Library of Congress Cataloging-in-Publication Data

Ellermeyer, Deborah A.
Activities for standards-based, integrated language arts instruction / Deborah A. Ellermeyer, Kay A. Chick.
p. cm.
Includes bibliographical references and index.
ISBN-13: 978-1-890871-76-5
1. Language arts (Elementary)-Standards-United States. 2. English language—Study and teaching (Elementary)—Activity programs-United States. I. Chick, Kay A. II. Title.
LB1576.E425 2007
372.6′044—dc22

2006037967

Holcomb Hathaway, Publishers, Inc.
6207 North Cattletrack Rd.
Scottsdale, Arizona 85250
480-991-7881
www.hh-pub.com

10 9 8 7 6 5 4 3 2 1

ISBN 978-1-890871-76-5

CONTENTS

PREFACE

Competent communication skills are indispensable in the twenty-first century. Language arts educators must deliver effective instruction that helps students to develop these skills while also addressing standards, such as the national standards developed by the National Council of Teachers of English (NCTE) and the International Reading Association (IRA). Classroom teachers have additional responsibilities under the No Child Left Behind Act (NCLB) of 2002 as they strive to meet the needs of all learners.

Activities for Standards-Based, Integrated Language Arts Instruction is designed to meet the instructional needs of teacher educators, pre-service teachers, in-service teachers, and elementary students in grades K–6. Special education teachers, along with Title I teachers and literacy coaches, will also find this book to be a useful resource. We designed this text for versatility, so that it can serve as a companion text for existing language arts textbooks in university-level language arts methodology courses or be used independently of other texts as a valuable teacher-resource book.

Beginning with an array of fresh, developmentally appropriate activities, we designed each aspect of the book to help teachers and future teachers supplement their existing curricula and enliven their classrooms with the joyful sounds of literacy and language learning.

- The text is organized around the *six language arts skills,* and for each activity we identify the national standards that the activity addresses.
- The book focuses on providing *hands-on activities,* so that teachers can easily locate activities to support their curricula without scanning through the expository text of a traditional textbook.
- The *integrated activities* provide a convenient way of addressing often-neglected content areas, including social studies and science.
- The *differentiated instructional component* of the activities allows teachers to meet the needs of a variety of individual learners with varied learning styles. We provide suggestions for adapting the activities to foster the language and literacy development of English language learners.
- The *authentic assessments* provided will save teachers valuable time and energy and allow them to track student progress efficiently.
- *Suggestions for family involvement* provide an essential home–school connection that traditional language arts textbooks often lack.

The lessons are intended for teaching to small groups of students or to individual students in one-on-one instructional settings. Suggestions for differentiated instruction will help teachers adapt the activities for a wide variety of students with diverse learning needs.

We designed these hands-on language arts activities to be appealing and engaging for elementary students. These language-rich activities afford students the opportunity to interact with classmates in social learning situations. Our focus on integration throughout emphasizes for teachers and students that the six language arts are an essential part of every content area, as well as a vital tool for everyday communication. Because the activities are adaptable and suitable for a variety of levels and abilities, teachers can actively involve all students in learning. In addition, students will value the opportunities to engage their families in related home–school activities.

Activities for Standards-Based, Integrated Language Arts Instruction is organized according to the six areas of language arts: listening, speaking, reading, writing, viewing, and visually representing. This organization makes locating activities easy. Each chapter begins with background information and a teaching vignette that includes discussion questions. Each activity is aligned with the NCTE/IRA standards and includes:

- Identification of grade level(s)
- Suggestions for differentiated instruction to meet the needs of diverse learners and English language learners
- Teaching objectives
- A list of materials needed
- Clear procedures for implementation
- Suggestions for home–school connections
- Authentic assessments of teaching objectives

Content areas are integrated throughout the various student-centered activities.

We hope you enjoy implementing these activities as much as we enjoyed creating them. Watching children develop mastery in the language arts gives pleasure and satisfaction to parents, teachers, and, most important, the children themselves.

ACKNOWLEDGMENTS

We would like to thank the reviewers, who read this book in earlier drafts and offered suggestions for its improvement. Our thanks to Kathleen Bukowski, Mercyhurst College; Shirley Dahl, University of Mary Hardin-Baylor; Joan Elliott, Indiana University of Pennsylvania; Rose A. Heilman-Houser, Slippery Rock University of Pennsylvania; Holly Lamb, Tarleton State University; Fannye E. Love, The University of Mississippi; Brian E. Maguire, Clarion University of Pennsylvania; Deborah L. Marciano, Penn State Altoona; Deborah A. Pellegrino, Rockhurst University; Donna Rhinesmith, Truman State University; Bobbie Smothers Jones, University of Mississippi; Pamela Solvie, University of Minnesota; and Gary L. Willhite, Southern Illinois University.

—Deborah Ellermeyer, Kay Chick

In loving memory of my furry little friend, Buddy, whom I will always remember with a special fondness. Special thanks to my children, Anna and Jim, for their love and support. Thanks, also, to my ELED 330 students at Clarion University of Pennsylvania for allowing me to do what I love the most.

—D.E.

Thanks to my children, Tyler and Tim, for their patience, understanding, and support during the process of writing this book. Special thanks to my husband, Bill, for starting dinner and throwing in loads of laundry so I could write. I also extend my gratitude to my colleagues and students at Penn State Altoona. Their continued support makes it possible for me to balance a career, my home, and professional responsibilities.

—K.C.

CHAPTER 1

ACTIVELY ENGAGING STUDENTS IN THE LANGUAGE ARTS

INTRODUCTION

The twenty-first century requires that its citizens be highly competent and effective communicators. From e-mail to long distance teleconferencing, the Information Age has heightened the need for individuals to express themselves clearly and effectively in a vast variety of ways. Consequently, demands on educators in the area of language arts instruction have never been as great as they presently are.

Since the dawn of the "Era of Accountability," teachers have been actively seeking developmentally appropriate learning activities that assist them in preparing lessons that address national and state standards, as well as prepare their students to succeed on mandated, norm-referenced achievement tests. The No Child Left Behind Act (NCLB), signed by President George W. Bush on January 8, 2002, with its emphasis on annual yearly progress, has added to pressures on teachers and left them wondering if the lofty goal reflected in the act's title is even remotely plausible. In light of the push to leave no child educationally behind, teachers are in need of integrated, standards-based lessons and activities to assist them in meeting their challenge. Outdated textbooks and traditional basals provide little to no support in meeting current standards-based instructional demands. This text, *Activities for Standards-Based, Integrated Language Arts Instruction,* assists teacher educators and pre-service and in-service teachers in exceeding those demands, while providing enjoyable, actively engaging, and integrated activities for elementary students.

Activities for Standards-Based, Integrated Language Arts Instruction is filled with language-rich, integrated activities that address the six areas of language arts: reading, writing, speaking, listening, visually representing, and viewing. The book incorporates both the constructivist theory of learning suggested by Swiss psychologist Jean Piaget and the sociolinguistic theory of Russian psychologist Lev Vygotsky. Both propose that students learn best when actively engaged in meaningful activities within authentic contexts. They further suggest that language develops naturally through multiple social interactions with others. This implies that language is learned best when students are engaged in using the language arts for meaningful and authentic reasons, such as reading a daily newspaper, writing e-mail messages to other students around the globe, reciting playful poems they have created, listening to evaluate a political candidate's speech, viewing the body language of others, or visually representing what they have learned in social studies through an informational chart. Clearly, a solid foundation in the language arts equips individuals with the skills they need to communicate effectively in everyday transactions with others.

THE LANGUAGE ARTS DEFINED

The language arts were once defined as those subjects whose goal is to develop a student's capacity for use of written and oral language. Traditionally, reading, writing, speaking, and listening were considered the four language modes by which individuals communicate with and receive information from others. In 1996, however, the National Council of Teachers of English and the International Reading Association (Standards, 1996) proposed two additional language arts, viewing and visually representing, as nonverbal methods of communication (Tompkins, 2005). Today, teachers are held accountable for developing students' competence in all six areas of language arts. Consequently, teachers must understand each language arts area in order to teach students effectively to become competent communicators (Farris, 2005).

Speaking, writing, and visually representing are classified as *productive* language arts, because through these arts an individual produces communication for others. The politician who vigorously delivers a passion-filled campaign speech at the national convention, the author who pens a best-selling novel, and the artist who creates a dramatic visual portrait on canvas all aim to communicate their thoughts and ideas with others. Listening, reading, and viewing are considered *receptive* language arts, because the individual engaging in these arts is receiving communication from others. The conference attendee receives the politician's promises for a better tomorrow, the reader understands the twisted plot detailed by the author, and the portrait's owner interprets the effect created by the colorful brushstrokes made on the canvas by the artist.

The six language arts are often categorized in yet another way: as oral, written, or visual. Listening and speaking are considered *oral* communication skills because the spoken word is involved in both processes. Reading and writing are viewed as *written* communication skills, since written text is the vehicle for the communication, and visually representing and viewing are considered *visual* skills because the communication is produced or received through multiple sign systems such as video productions, body language, dramatizations, or illustrations, to name a few (Daniels & Bizar, 1998). No matter how the six language arts are classified, individuals must develop each in order to enhance the communication process.

Listening

Listening has long been distinguished among the language arts, for several reasons. First, researchers have identified listening as the first acquired of the language arts and the one that provides a basis for the other five (Lundsteen, 1979). Research has demonstrated that the ability to hear and recognize sounds is a prenatal development achieved long before the birth of a child (Farris, 2005). Consequently, eager and well-intentioned parents-to-be now recognize the importance of exposing their unborn children to the stimulating sounds of music and words. Second, listening has been identified as "the most used and perhaps the most important of the language (and learning) arts" (Devine, 1982, p. 1). Youngsters and adults alike spend approximately 50 percent of their communication time listening, whereas the other language arts combined account for the remaining 50 percent of communication time (Werner, 1975). Noted language researcher Walter Loban analogized this relationship as follows: "We listen a book a day, we speak a book a week, we read a book a month, and we write a book a year" (cited in Tompkins, 2005, p. 294). Last, listening has been deemed the most neglected of the language arts, because teachers assume that students know how to listen and, therefore, seldom teach listening skills (Strother, 1987). Experts in the field emphasize the need to teach listening strategies appropriate for different kinds of listening (Brent & Anderson, 1993; Jalongo, 1991; Pearson & Fielding, 1982), such as discriminative listening, which is used to distinguish among sounds; aesthetic listening, used for pleasure or enjoyment; efferent listening, used to understand a message; and critical listening, used to evaluate a message (Tompkins, 2005). Active engagement of students in listening instruction is essential if students are to become effective receivers of the spoken word.

Speaking

Most youngsters begin speaking within the first two years of their lives. A child's speaking vocabulary is largely shaped by interactions with people in the environment who read to the child and engage the child in daily conversations. By the time children enter school, most are fluent language users who possess, on average, a 5,000-word vocabulary that will increase yearly by approximately 3,000 new words (Tompkins, 2005). Research has demonstrated, however, that students greatly benefit from participating in talk activities and that talk is a vital component for learning (Smith, 2001; Wells & Chang-Wells, 1992). The quiet, inactive classrooms of the past have been replaced by the bustling sounds of students using talk within a variety of learning contexts for a variety of different purposes.

Tompkins (2005) identifies two types of classroom talk. *Aesthetic talk* is used to respond to literature and deepen comprehension. Students use aesthetic talk to contribute to grand conversations about literature (Eeds & Wells, 1989), engage in small-group discussions, ask questions, tell stories, and participate in readers' theater and choral speaking. *Efferent talk* is used to inform and persuade others. Students use efferent talk to engage in instructional conversations, present oral reports, interview others, debate, and roleplay.

The value of providing students with plenty of opportunities to engage in classroom talk cannot be overstated. Talk is not only a vital part of the language arts curriculum, but it is also necessary for academic success in all content areas (Heath, 1983).

Reading

Reading is an area of language arts instruction currently receiving much attention, especially at the elementary level. The $26.5 billion NCLB Act aimed to make schools more accountable for reading and math instruction. Its primary goal was that every third grade American student would be reading at a third grade level by the year 2008. Teachers and administrators are under an unprecedented amount of pressure to improve students' reading abilities. The best way to accomplish this goal is highly disputed, however, among reading researchers, policy makers, and teachers alike. Some advocate a skills-based, direct instruction approach to teaching reading, while others promote a more comprehensive and balanced approach of blending direct instruction with reading and writing opportunities (International Reading Association/National Association for the Education of Young Children, 1998). The National Reading Panel Report (2000) suggests that a balanced, comprehensive reading program includes instruction in five key areas: phonemic awareness, phonics, fluency, vocabulary development, and comprehension strategies.

Phonemic awareness involves a basic knowledge that spoken language is composed of individual speech sounds, known as phonemes. Yopp (1992) believes that phonemic awareness is an essential foundation for phonics instruction, and Gillon (2004) proposes that it is a prerequisite for learning to read. Children develop phonemic awareness through singing songs, repeating rhymes, and engaging in word play activities led by parents and teachers (Griffith & Olson, 1992). Additionally, teachers can help young students to develop phonemic awareness by providing learning activities that require youngsters to match word sounds, blend sounds to form words, isolate sounds within words, segment words into sound parts, and substitute sounds in words (Yopp, 1992).

Phonics is the study of the relationship between sounds (phonemes) and the letters of the alphabet (graphemes). The English language is difficult to decode because it does not have a one-to-one correspondence between its sounds and letters. For example, /f/ can be spelled in several different ways, as in the words *f*un, stu*ff*, *ph*one, rou*gh*, and sa*fe*. Typical phonics instruction includes study of consonants, vowels, rhyming words, rimes, and useful phonic rules (Tompkins, 2005).

The ability to read with expression and a degree of ease, speed, and accuracy is known as *fluency*. Teachers help students become fluent readers by providing plenty of opportunities for them to practice reading aloud. Repeated readings is a strategy often used to promote fluency, in which the student practices reading the same text aloud many times. Instructional activities that enhance students' fluency skills include choral reading and readers' theater.

Vocabulary development focuses on the study of word meanings. Vocabulary instruction may also include a study of word histories, root words, affixes, compound words, synonyms, antonyms, homonyms, homophones, and figurative language (Tompkins, 2005). Students typically acquire new words through wide reading, firsthand experiences, and direct instruction. Multiple exposures to new words are critical for effective vocabulary acquisition.

Finally, *comprehension* deals with understanding text. Irwin (1991) describes comprehension as an interaction between the reader, the text, and the reader's purpose for reading the text. Teachers typically teach comprehension strategies that enable readers to "break the code" and understand an author's message. Examples of common comprehension strategies include predicting, analyzing parts of words (such as compound words), distinguishing between fact and opinion, finding the main idea, and using picture and text cues.

Writing

Children begin to emerge as writers very early in life, commencing with scribbles on paper and on the pages of favorite storybooks. Although this early writing cannot be read and understood by others, it clearly evidences the child's rudimentary knowledge that writing is a way of communicating. Slowly and gradually, children's writings become readable to others. Atwell (1998) found that in composing their own stories, emergent writers rely on stories they have read, evidencing the critical link between reading and writing.

Teachers teach students to approach writing as real authors do, through the use of the *writing process* (Graves, 1983). In the writing process, writers choose their own topics and are given sufficient time to develop their compositions. Writers engage in *prewriting* activities to identify the purpose of their writing, the audience for whom the writing is intended, and the form that the writing will take. Students learn that writers write for different reasons, including to entertain, to inform, and to persuade. The form varies with the purpose and ranges from friendly letters to poetry, informational reports, literary stories, lists, and journal entries, to name a few. During *drafting*, writers get their thoughts on paper, focusing on content instead of mechanics. Throughout *revising*, writers reread their work and share it with others, such as classmates and the teacher, for constructive feedback. Writers change the content of their writing by adding, deleting, or clarifying their written thoughts. Once the content is revised, writers engage in *editing* as they proofread and correct mechanical errors, such as errors in spelling, capitalization, and punctuation, to produce a final draft. When the final draft is complete, writers often *publish* and celebrate their written work by sharing it with others. Students' work can be published on a bulletin board within the classroom, bound into book version and placed in the classroom or school library, or submitted to a literary magazine for possible publication.

With the introduction of weblogs, or blogs, and wikis, technology has expanded the possibilities for sharing one's writing. Wikipedia, a free online encyclopedia, defines a *blog* as an online journal or diary whose entries are displayed in reverse chronological order. Blogs may contain personal commentary on news or issues relevant to the "blogger," or writer of the blog. A *wiki* is a website that allows users to collaborate on writing projects and edit a composition together. This form of online collaborative authoring effectively removes physical boundaries among writers. Regardless of whether the author chooses to publish "on paper" or online, sharing the finished piece with an audience beyond the classroom teacher validates the writer's efforts and hard work.

Spelling, punctuation, grammar, and handwriting are tools that help writers to express their ideas clearly and effectively. Lucy Calkins (1991) suggests that students learn these skills best within the context of their own writing through mini-lessons regularly conducted by the teacher. A mini-lesson is a short lesson on reading/writing procedures and skills taught based on the perceived need for one. Routman (1996) concurs and adds that excerpts from books that students are reading are another good source of texts for teaching grammar and mechanics. Learning skills within an authentic context, such as one's own writing or reading materials, is more effective and meaningful than addressing the same skills through disconnected worksheets and workbook pages. Students who learn to conference with each other throughout the writing process have many opportunities to apply new skills. The writing process approach has truly revolutionized writing instruction.

Viewing

Viewing has recently become more widely recognized as a visual language art and an important component of literacy. Viewing precedes reading and writing in human development, since youngsters begin gaining information from visual sources long before they can read and write (Cramer, 2004). Visual media are everywhere. Cramer (2004) suggests that viewing is a major part of our daily lives and is more important for today's generation of children than previous generations. Visual media include film and videos, print advertisements and commercials, photographs and book illustrations, video games, the Internet, graphs, diagrams and charts, maps, and graphic organizers. Effective viewing involves the ability to understand and respond to visual messages, and students must become competent at gaining and utilizing information from a variety of media (Strickland, Galda, & Cullinan, 2004). It follows that students need to be taught how to gain and evaluate information from visual sources. Active engagement with various media in meaningful classroom activities is essential for students to acquire critical viewing skills, as well as media literacy (Cox, 2005).

Visually Representing

The old adage that "a picture is worth a thousand words" holds true for the sixth area of language arts instruction. Visually representing thoughts and ideas is another way to teach concepts and communicate information. Cramer (2004) describes this area of language arts as depicting or portraying an image or likeness through arts, crafts, and other forms of image making. Students can visually represent information through drawing pictures, constructing models, making collages or montages, creating video productions, dramatizing, producing posters, or making a Venn diagram, graph, or chart. The task of representing a concept visually improves students' understanding of the concept (Farris,

2005). In addition, visual representations arouse, stimulate, and enhance interest and knowledge. They engage both the mind and body in portraying imaginative ideas. Visual representations augment the growth of language and advance the development of multiple intelligences (Cramer, 2004). Because of the many benefits derived from this area of language arts, teachers need to provide students with ample opportunities to represent learning and ideas visually in the classroom.

The remaining sections in this chapter provide important background for understanding the philosophy behind and design of the activities in the book.

LANGUAGE ACROSS THE CURRICULUM: EXPLORING INTEGRATION

Discussing the six language arts separately suggests a division among them. However, the language arts are interrelated and dependent on one another. Take, for example, a fourth grade class performing readers' theater. Students are not only reading from scripts and speaking the characters' parts, they are also listening to the performance and visually representing the scenes in their mind's eye. Consequently, as a child develops skills in one area of language arts, the other areas are also enhanced (Farris, 2005). The language arts support one another. Indeed, the area of language arts is more than just a subject; it is part of everything that happens in the classroom and beyond. Reading, writing, speaking, listening, viewing, and visually representing are processes that are instrumental to all learning, rather than products that are ends in themselves (Strickland, Galda, & Cullinan, 2004). The language arts are truly essential communication skills.

Research suggests that the language arts are best taught as integrated language modes rather than separate entities (Farris, 2005). An integrated approach immerses students in language use, and as children use language, their language skills increase (Strickland, Galda, & Cullinan, 2004; Johnston & Louis, 1987). Not only should the language arts be integrated with each other, they should be integrated across the curriculum. *Language across the curriculum* means the integration of the language arts with teaching in the content areas, such as social studies, science, math, music, and the arts (Tevebaugh, 2001; Matthews & Rainer, 2001). Integrating the language arts with each other and with subject area content helps to make the learning more purposeful, effective, and, in essence, seamless instead of fragmented (Strickland, Galda, & Cullinan, 2004). Integrated instruction helps students to realize that the language arts are integrally embedded in every area of the curriculum and in everyday communication with others.

Integration requires careful organization, motivation, and engagement to be effective, however (Pappas, Kiefer, & Levstik, 1999). Tompkins (2005) suggests four options for integrating the language arts and making instruction more meaningful: literature focus units, literature circles, reading and writing workshops, and across-the-curriculum theme cycles. Each of these instructional arrangements actively involves students in all six of the language arts. The language activities are meaningful, functional, and genuine in that they involve real-life language usage, instead of contrived and artificial language practice, such as that provided by worksheets. Teachers are encouraged to experiment with each of the integrated models and choose those that best suit the needs of their learners.

Literature Focus Units

With *literature focus units,* students read a common piece of literature, which may or may not relate to other areas of the curriculum about which students are learning. The manner in which students read may vary from independent reading to shared reading, buddy reading, small-group reading, or reading together as a class. As students read, they discuss what they are reading, ask questions, and make connections to their own lives. They also respond to the story by writing in a reading log. Throughout their reading, students participate in teacher-directed mini-lessons for skill development. The lessons might be related to story vocabulary, parts of speech, story elements, mechanics, or a host of other language arts skills. When they have finished reading the book, students create projects that visually represent some aspect of the book. Students view each other's projects and listen to classmates' explanations of how the projects summarize or extend their learning. Rubrics are used to evaluate student work. The teacher typically selects the piece of literature, directs classroom activities, conducts skills mini-lessons, and monitors individual student progress.

Literature Circles

Literature circles involve the class reading different books within small groups. The teacher begins by giving a brief book talk to stimulate interest in a variety of books. Students then choose which book they would like to read and form small groups based on their selection. Books may or may not be related to other areas of the curriculum. Each student is assigned a distinct task to perform within the group. For example, the *discussion leader* keeps the group discussion focused on the book, the *harmonizer* helps the group stay on task and maintain a cooperative spirit, and the *wordsmith* identifies important words in the story and checks the meaning of unknown words (Tompkins, 2005). Jobs are rotated daily so that everyone has an opportunity to participate in a variety of ways. As students read, they discuss and respond to what they are reading, sometimes orally and at other times in writing. Upon completion of the book, students create related story projects and share them with the rest of the class. The teacher is responsible for monitoring the groups, teaching mini-lessons, and providing evaluative feedback to students.

Reading and Writing Workshops

Reading and writing workshops are instructional arrangements in which students read self-selected books and write on self-selected topics with teacher guidance. As the students read, they respond to the book in literature response journals and participate in reading conferences and skills mini-lessons with the teacher. Students use the writing process to revise and edit drafts of compositions that they will later share with the class. Illustrations or other craft projects, such as a book poster or character soap sculpture, serve to represent visually a book or a student's story. Students are made aware of the criteria by which projects are evaluated, and the assessment of their writing takes into account both the process that the student used to develop the piece and the finished product. The teacher manages this very busy classroom by reminding students of what they need to be working on, conducting conferences with students, and teaching reading and writing skills within the context of small-group and whole-class mini-lessons.

Theme Cycles

Theme cycles focus on a particular theme or topic that is extended across the curriculum. For example, a second grade class whose theme is apples might read picture books related to apples, predict and count the number of seeds contained within an apple in math class, sing songs related to apples in music, learn about geographic regions best known for growing apples in social studies, follow directions to make applesauce and listen to tales of Johnny Appleseed in reading, and write five-sense poems about apples. Students learn about the theme through the language arts in each content area. Students create theme-related projects and share them with the entire class to extend their learning and motivation. The teacher is responsible for effectively managing the classroom, providing resources that relate to the theme, teaching literacy skills, and monitoring and evaluating student progress.

In summary, the language arts are interrelated processes that assist student learning in all areas of the curriculum. Teachers can choose instructional arrangements and language activities, such as those included in this book, that integrate the language arts together and across the curriculum while meeting state and national standards. Regardless of the instructional arrangement chosen, the learning environment should provide ample opportunities for meaningful use of all of the language arts (Morrow, 2004).

THE ROLE OF AUTHENTIC, PERFORMANCE-BASED ASSESSMENT

As elementary classrooms become more student centered, the disparity between instruction and traditional methods of assessment becomes greater. Although standardized tests and teacher-made essay and objective measures are often mandated for accountability purposes, schools are at the same time striving toward a closer alliance between instruction and assessment. To that end, teachers are routinely using authentic or performance-based assessment methods to assess students' learning (Chittendon, 1991).

Authentic assessment "requires that students engage with real-life problems, issues, or tasks for an audience who cares about or has a stake in what students learn" (Martin-Kniep, 2000, p. 26). Thus, students are involved in activities that require real reading, writing, listening, speaking, viewing, and visually representing to demonstrate what they have learned. Because authentic assessment necessitates that learners demonstrate their learning and skills, it is often called *performance-based assessment.* Such assessments are ongoing and integrated throughout instruction, resulting in measures that inform teachers about students' performance and the effectiveness of instruction.

Authentic, performance-based assessment is multidimensional, utilizing many different evaluative techniques. Informal methods, such as observations, anecdotal records, and interviews, are open-ended and are essential to the assessment process, especially in the primary grades. Structured strategies, such as checklists, rating scales, self-assessment measures, inventories, and rubrics, are more objective, and they help teachers to gain insight into students' performances on authentic literacy tasks (Chittendon, 1991; Cooper & Kiger, 2005).

Rubrics are now widely used in elementary classrooms as an important tool in the authentic assessment process. *Rubrics* are scoring tools that provide teachers and students with the criteria for an assignment and gradations of quality from excellent to poor (Goodrich, 1996/1997). Unlike checklists and rating scales, rubrics define quality in very specific terms, so that students and teachers are aware of exactly what makes a high-quality performance different from a poor-quality one (Martin-Kniep, 2000). The most striking benefit of using rubrics is that they improve student performance because they provide students with clear expectations for an assignment in advance. Teachers who use rubrics believe that rubrics also reduce grading time because "what counts" in an assignment has been determined prior to the scoring process (Goodrich, 1996/1997).

One distinct benefit of authentic assessment is that it is perfectly suited for diverse classrooms. With a variety of assessment strategies available, teachers can adapt evaluation methods to the individual needs of learners. However, the purpose for assessment remains essentially the same for diverse learners, such as English language learners and students with disabilities, as it does for all other students. The teacher must determine students' current skills in the language arts, as well as what they are ready to do and the type of instruction that would benefit them the most (Cooper & Kiger, 2005).

DIFFERENTIATED INSTRUCTION: MEETING THE NEEDS OF ALL STUDENTS

In traditional classrooms, instruction is often "one size fits all." Students all listen to the same explanation of concepts or skills to be learned, and everyone participates in identical independent practice, extension activities, homework assignments, and projects. Classrooms such as these are standard fare, but they do not always meet the needs of diverse learners. Students with disabilities, English language learners, and those who simply work at a slower pace or learn in different ways may have little success in undifferentiated classroom settings.

Differentiated instruction is, in fact, a way of thinking about teaching and learning. At its most basic level, it requires teachers to always consider the learners and their needs when planning instruction (Heathcox, 2002). In such classrooms, varying approaches to content, process, and products give all students the opportunity to learn and reach high standards. That is, what students learn, the instructional process they experience as they are learning, and the products they create to demonstrate what they have learned, can all be modified to meet and maximize students' success in the language arts (Tomlinson, 2001).

Differentiated instruction can be further understood by examining its characteristics. First, it is proactive. Teachers assume, in advance of planning and teaching a lesson, that students have different learning needs. Therefore, they do not plan just one instructional approach and expect it to work for all learners. Teachers may need to stock their classroom libraries with books of varying reading levels, pair English language learners with a native language learner when completing activities, and consider the multiple intelligences when creating learning centers. Second, differentiated instruction is qualitative, rather than quantitative. Assigning students fewer math problems or spelling words is not as effective as modifying the nature of the assignment. Teachers may need to use different instructional strategies to teach math, have students use calculators or abacuses as math aids, or teach alternative math skills to some learners. Third, teachers integrate assessment with instruction in differentiated classrooms. Waiting until a unit of instruction has ended to assess learning provides little opportunity to modify the content to be taught, the instructional process, or the products that students will create to demonstrate their learning (Tomlinson, 2001). Teachers can use formative assessment measures, such as checklists and observations throughout instruction, in order to adapt instruction and maximize student success prior to final, summative assessment.

The need for differentiated instruction results from student variables, such as level of academic skill (advanced learners and struggling learners both need adaptations), readiness level, learning styles, and cultural influences (Heathcox, 2002). For example, many English language learners struggle academically because they are working to learn the language while also striving to meet high academic standards. The most important variable in the success of English language learners is the overall quality of the instruction they receive. Beyond that, teachers must evaluate the language demands of each lesson, emphasize vocabulary development, assess and build background knowledge, and provide many opportunities for spoken language (Short & Echevarria, 2004/2005).

In a differentiated classroom, teachers act as facilitators of the learning process. While modifying content, process, and products for individual students, teachers must also organize flexible grouping, be adaptable with time constraints, and collaborate and communicate with other teaching faculty and parents. Differentiated instruction is most effective when the teacher accepts differences, affirms strengths, recognizes interests, and supports success. Most important, successful teachers recognize that for classroom experiences to be fair, motivating, and supportive, they often must be differentiated (Heathcox, 2002). Differentiated instruction appropriately replaces the "one size fits all" approach with sensitivity and responsiveness to individual needs.

ADDRESSING THE NEEDS OF ENGLISH LANGUAGE LEARNERS

Elementary classrooms are now more culturally diverse than ever before. Since the early 1990s, the demographics within the United States have changed significantly (Yellin, Blake, & DeVries, 2004). The U.S. Department of Education reports that since 1991, the number of second language learners has increased 95 percent, with a large percentage of English language learners being found in classrooms in Texas, California, Arizona, Illinois, New York, and Florida (U.S. Department of Education, National Center for Education Statistics, 2001). Hoffman and Pearson (2000) project that by the year 2026, English language learners will comprise approximately one-fourth of U.S. school enrollment. These same researchers hypothesize that the number of Hispanic children in kindergarten through eighth grade will increase by 47 percent.

Because the cultural composition of elementary classrooms has changed and will continue to change, non-bilingual teachers now face the challenge of instructing students who are just beginning to learn the English language. Peregoy and Boyle (1997) provide the following list of do's and don'ts for instructing English language learners:

- Do speak a bit slower, but keep the speech natural.
- Do articulate clearly.
- Do repeat key phrases and vocabulary terms so that English language learners have multiple exposures.
- Do use descriptive language.
- Do use visuals, such as illustrations, photos, and graphic organizers.
- Do use gestures throughout instruction to provide visual cues.

- Do connect the new learning to something already familiar to the student.
- Do provide sufficient modeling.
- Don't shout or speak louder to English language learners.
- Don't use figurative language that will be troublesome for English language learners to understand.
- Don't teach isolated words, but do teach meaningful phrases and sentences.

Freeman and Freeman (1993) offer the following additional suggestions for working with English language learners:

- Display plenty of environmental print in students' first languages throughout the classroom.
- Supplement the classroom library with reading materials in students' first languages.
- Encourage writing in students' first languages.
- Employ the assistance of bilingual tutors.

Clearly, as the cultural diversity in elementary classrooms continues to flourish, teachers must be prepared to meet the needs of English language learners. The activities in this book include suggestions for adaptations for English language learners. Following is a list of Internet resources for teaching these students:

Internet Resources

Cerda, N. & Hernandez, C. (2006). Bilingual education. Retrieved August 20, 2006, from www.freewebs.com/cerdahdz/testimonials.htm.

MIND PLAY, Methods and Solutions. (2006). Working with bilingual and ESL students. Retrieved August 20, 2006, from www.myreadingcoach.com/results/myers-y1.html.

Modern English Publishing, Ltd. (2003). ESL Magazine. Retrieved August 20, 2006, from www.eslmag.com/modules.php?name=News&file=article&sid=92.

Reading Rockets. (2006). Becoming bilingual: The challenge of teaching English language learners to read. Retrieved August 20, 2006, from www.readingrockets.org/shows/bilingual.

THE HOME–SCHOOL CONNECTION: PROMOTING FAMILY LITERACY

Considerable evidence supports the belief that parents' attitudes and convictions about reading affect their children's literacy development (Snow, Burns, & Griffen, 1998). During infancy, children begin to learn about the pleasures of reading from both formal and informal experiences at home. They observe parents reading newspapers, making lists, signing documents, and reading restaurant menus. Therefore, the first literacy lessons occur informally, and children begin to perceive whether literacy is deemed important long before they enter school (Watson, 2004).

The term *family literacy* describes all of the experiences and ways that families use literacy in their homes and communities. In most families, literacy is a natural process that occurs through conversation, sharing stories, drawing and painting, viewing wordless picture books, reading, and writing. In any family, the literacy activities that take place are affected by ethnic and cultural factors. In many homes, literacy experiences are intergenerational. For example, grandparents might enjoy sharing family history stories and reading letters from family members to grandchildren. Families may or may not be able to relate to literacy as it is defined in schools, and some families may have limited reading ability or lack a print-rich environment. In some cultures, storytelling plays a primary role in literacy development. Respect for all types of families is critical, and all home–school connections must avoid bias and support a broad range of literacy activities (Morrow, 2003/2004).

No other family activity is as important as parents sharing books and reading with young children (Neuman, 1999). Dickinson and DeTemple (1998) identify three ways that children benefit from parents' reading aloud. First, through the act of reading itself, children learn about print concepts: turning pages, reading from left to right, and using symbols to represent words. Second, children begin to understand that the language used in books is often different from spoken language: books use longer sentences, more formal language, and more complex words than conversation. Third, children develop an understanding of various genres and forms of writing. In addition, children begin to realize that reading is a social activity, resulting in special time with parents and other family members (Barton, Hamilton, & Ivanic, 2000).

Because family reading is so important, schools must make families partners in literacy development. Teachers can share literacy goals and keep parents informed about what is happening in classrooms. Teachers should invite parents to participate in their child's language and literacy development. Activities can be sent home for parents and children to do together, such as reading books, writing stories, cooking, and telling stories. When children come from homes where Standard English is not spoken, it is essential for teachers to model effective use of both oral and written language. Parents may also be invited to assist with literacy activities in the classroom, including reading to children, dictating stories for writing practice, and sharing their careers and cultural experiences (Morrow, 2003/2004).

Home–school connections should always promote literacy as recreational and enjoyable, to encourage children to investigate literacy activities on their own and find pleasure, as well as knowledge. It has long been said that parents are a child's first and best teachers. Understanding this, schools must support collaborative relationships to further the literacy development of all children (Watson, 2004).

THE NCTE/IRA STANDARDS FOR THE ENGLISH LANGUAGE ARTS

In 1996, the National Council of Teachers of English (NCTE), in collaboration with the International Reading Association (IRA), composed a set of National Standards for the English Language Arts (see the box on the following page). The standards were the culmination of a four-year project that involved thousands of researchers, educators, administrators, legislative leaders, parents, and policy analysts in English language arts from across the nation. The purpose of the NCTE/IRA Standards is "to ensure that all students are knowledgeable and proficient users of language, so they may succeed in school, participate in our democracy as informed citizens, find challenging and rewarding work, appreciate and contribute to our culture, and pursue their own goals and interests as independent learners throughout their lives" (Standards for the English Language Arts, 1996).

The idea of creating a set of common language arts goals was first proposed in August 1990 in a letter to Lamar Alexander, U.S. Secretary of Education, from Judith Thelen, president of the IRA, and Shirley Haley-James, president of the

NCTE/IRA Standards for the English Language Arts

Standard 1. Students read a wide range of print and non-print texts to build an understanding of texts, of themselves, and of the cultures of the United States and the world; to acquire new information; to respond to the needs and demands of society and the workplace; and for personal fulfillment. Among these texts are fiction and nonfiction, classic and contemporary works.

Standard 2. Students read a wide range of literature from many periods in many genres to build an understanding of the many dimensions (e.g., philosophical, ethical, aesthetic) of human experience.

Standard 3. Students apply a wide range of strategies to comprehend, interpret, evaluate, and appreciate texts. They draw on their prior experience, their interactions with other readers and writers, their knowledge of word meaning and of other texts, their word identification strategies, and their understanding of textual features (e.g., sound–letter correspondence, sentence structure, context, graphics).

Standard 4. Students adjust their use of spoken, written, and visual language (e.g., conventions, style, vocabulary) to communicate effectively with a variety of audiences and for different purposes.

Standard 5. Students employ a wide range of strategies as they write and use different writing process elements appropriately to communicate with different audiences for a variety of purposes.

Standard 6. Students apply knowledge of language structure, language conventions (e.g., spelling and punctuation), media techniques, figurative language, and genre to create, critique, and discuss print and non-print texts.

Standard 7. Students conduct research on issues and interests by generating ideas and questions, and by posing problems. They gather, evaluate, and synthesize data from a variety of sources (e.g., print and non-print texts, artifacts, people) to communicate their discoveries in ways that suit their purpose and audience.

Standard 8. Students use a variety of technological and information resources (e.g., libraries, databases, computer networks, video) to gather and synthesize information and to create and communicate knowledge.

Standard 9. Students develop an understanding of and respect for diversity in language use, patterns, and dialects across cultures, ethnic groups, geographic regions, and social roles.

Standard 10. Students whose first language is not English make use of their first language to develop competency in the English language arts and to develop understanding of content across the curriculum.

Standard 11. Students participate as knowledgeable, reflective, creative, and critical members of a variety of literacy communities.

Standard 12. Students use spoken, written, and visual language to accomplish their own purposes (e.g., for learning, enjoyment, persuasion, and the exchange of information).

NCTE. Both IRA and NCTE felt that the English language arts standards should be rooted in current research about the nature of language and language learning.

In the fall of 1992, the U.S. Department of Education awarded a grant for the Standards Project for the English Language Arts to educators at the Center for the Study of Reading at the University of Illinois. The award was contingent upon the Center's agreement to work directly with IRA and NCTE to develop the standards. Federal involvement with the project concluded in 1994, and IRA and NCTE funded the project subsequently.

States' systems of education have followed in providing state standards for teachers. Together, these sets of standards serve as a framework for instruction, as well as a means for teacher accountability. Because state standards vary from state to state, the activities contained within this book are aligned with the NCTE/IRA standards, which are shared by all states.

HOW TO USE THIS BOOK

To help you get the greatest instructional value from *Activities for Standards-Based, Integrated Language Arts Instruction,* we provide the following suggestions:

1. Familiarize yourself with the layout and special features of the remaining chapters of the book. Each of the subsequent six chapters focuses on an area of language arts instruction. An introduction, a classroom vignette, and discussion questions are provided at the beginning of each chapter, followed by standards-based, developmentally appropriate language arts activities related to the highlighted area of language arts. Each activity identifies the intended grade level and provides related NCTE/IRA standard(s), activity objective(s), a listing of required materials, easy-to-follow procedures, an authentic assessment device, and suggestions for meeting the needs of students with special needs and English language learners, integrating the language arts across the curriculum, and extending the language arts into the home to promote family literacy. The reproducible activity sheets, family letters, assessments, and related materials help to make the activities easy to implement. Exhibit 1.1, on pages 17–20, provides a quick reference to the activities, indicating literature used, grade level, standards addressed, and the assessment type.

2. Use the informational background material provided at the beginning of each chapter as an introduction to the activities that follow. The background material provided at the beginning of each chapter presents a brief overview of the language arts area and incorporates the views of leading researchers and experts in the field. This information may serve as a springboard for discussion or further independent exploration.

3. Use the classroom vignettes to examine the role of the language arts in elementary classrooms. Each chapter includes a brief classroom vignette featuring the focused area of language arts. These vignettes provide a glimpse into classrooms where students use the language arts to learn and communicate with others. You should recognize through the vignettes that the language arts are interrelated and extend learning in all areas of the curriculum.

4. Use the discussion questions to explore the provided classroom vignettes. Discussion questions related to each vignette are intended to provoke both higher-level thinking and lively discussion. For further discussion, challenge yourself to pose questions of your own that relate to the vignette. Also, we encourage you to compare any related personal experiences you may have had with those presented in the vignette.

5. Adapt the provided activities to meet your needs and the needs of your learners. Activities include some suggestions for adapting them to meet the needs of diverse learners. Activities and assessments are easily modified for students of varying grade levels. A knowledgeable classroom teacher can adapt almost any activity to suit the grade level of the students. For example, a book that is to be *read by* students can be *read to* them by the teacher. The teacher or a classroom aide may transcribe the dictations of students who do not possess adequate writing skills. Younger learners may need more teacher modeling or concrete examples. Descriptors within a rubric can be changed to reflect behaviors that are more suitable for a particular grade level. Children's books or poems have been suggested for use within some activities. In most instances, other similar books or poems can be substituted if the suggested literature is not available or if the teacher wants to adapt the readability of the material to suit the needs of the students.

6. Encourage parent/guardian involvement by using the home–school connection activities to extend meaningful language usage in the home. Extending language learning beyond the classroom and into the home environment of students is essential. Use the Home–School Connection activities to reinforce learning at home. Encourage youngsters to share their home-related experiences in class and to seek feedback from parents.

7. Prior to implementing activities, familiarize students with the criteria that will be used to evaluate them. Before assigning an activity, duplicate the assessment rubric and share it with the students. It is critical that learners know specifically how they will be evaluated. Discuss the expectations for completion of activities, and answer students' questions related to the assessment tool. Assessments may be included in students' language arts portfolios.

CONCLUSION

Teachers who provide effective language arts instruction enable students to become effective and competent communicators. The language arts are interrelated and should be integrated across all areas of the curriculum. Authentic language arts assessment informs instruction, allows teachers to differentiate instruction as needed and helps to address the needs of English language learners. Furthermore, promoting family literacy through home–school activities should be a primary goal of every teacher. The activities presented in this book can help teachers provide meaningful, enjoyable, and engaging experiences in standards-based language arts instruction.

Overview of the activities included in this book, by chapter

CHAPTER	Activity		Genre/Book*	Grade Level	Standards	Assessment Type
2 LISTENING	2.1	Inviting Students to Listen: *Chicka Chicka Boom Boom*	F, *Chicka Chicka Boom Boom*	K	12	Teacher checklist
	2.2	Listening for Pleasure Through Creative Movement	F, *Over in the Garden*	K	12	Observation/ anecdotal records
	2.3	Listening for the Sequence of Events: Circle Stories	F, *Joseph Had a Little Overcoat*	1	1, 4, and 10	Self-assessment checklist
	2.4	Listening Times Two: Listening for Directions and Character Attributes	F, *Tough Boris*	2–3	3	Whole-class checklist
	2.5	Listening for Important Details: Anticipation/ Reaction Guides	NF, *The Flag We Love*	3	1 and 3	Anticipation/ reaction guide
	2.6	Prediction Charts: Listening to Check and Modify Predictions	HF, *More Than Anything Else*	4	2 and 4	Story artifact prediction sheet
	2.7	Visualizing; Understanding a Spoken Message	Either F or NF	4–6	12	Informal observation of students' drawings
	2.8	Compare and Contrast Matrix: The Book vs. the Movie	Either F or NF	4–6	8 and 12	Compare and contrast matrix
	2.9	Connecting with the Speaker: You Say/I Think Note Taking	No text used	4–6	3, 10, and 12	Teacher assessment of student notes
	2.10	Recognizing and Identifying Propaganda Techniques in Advertising	No text used	5–6	3 and 8	Teacher evaluation of student propaganda record sheet
3 SPEAKING	3.1	Enjoying Creative Dramatics: *We're Going on a Bear Hunt*	F, *We're Going on a Bear Hunt*	K–1	12	Anecdotal records—questions provided
	3.2	*Bugs for Lunch (Insectos para el Almuerzo)*	F, *Bugs for Lunch (Insectos para el Almuerzo)*	1–2	9 and 10	Teacher observation of student participation
	3.3	Flannel Board Scenes: Combining Oral Language with Artistic Expression	Either F or NF	2–3	10 and 12	Checklist

*F = fiction, NF = nonfiction, HF = historical fiction

(continued)

Activity overview, continued

Chapter	Activity		Genre/Book*	Grade Level	Standards	Assessment Type
	3.4	Exploring Choral Speaking: The Hamster's on Vacation	Poetry	3–4	4	Self-evaluation checklist
	3.5	Story Pyramid Retellings	F, *My Great Aunt Arizona*	3–4	12	Rubric
	3.6	Exploring Reader's Theater: *Mr. Popper's Penguins*	F, *Mr. Popper's Penguins*	3–4	12	Peer evaluation questions
	3.7	Creating Radio Commercials: Inventions Then and Now	NF	4–6	10 and 12	Checklist
	3.8	A Meeting of the Minds: Reaching Group Consensus	Either, but F is mentioned	4–6	11 and 12	Teacher observation
	3.9	Interviewing to Learn About the Past	No text used	5–6	7 and 12	Interview scoring rubric
	3.10	Involving Students in Research Discussions	NF	5–6	7, 8, and 10	Self and peer rubric
4 READING	4.1	Pick a Stick: Working with Onsets and Rimes	No text used	K–1	3	Observation/ listening
	4.2	Enhancing Vocabulary Development Through Word Sorts	Picture books	1–2	3	Student self-evaluation
	4.3	Using a Word Wall to Enhance Word Recognition and Comprehension	F, *Mice and Beans*	2	1, 3, and 9	Observation/ anecdotal records
	4.4	Developing Sequencing Skills	NF, *Snowflake Bentley*	3	1 and 3	Check sequencing of sentence strips
	4.5	Semantic Character Analysis	F, *Three Pigs* (several versions)	3	1 and 3	Character analysis handout
	4.6	Read It Again	Reading passages provided	4–5	4	Fluency checklist
	4.7	Literature Graffiti	Either F or NF	4–6	1 and 3	Observation/ anecdotal records
	4.8	Newspaper Scavenger Hunt	NF, newspapers	5–6	8	Teacher observation
	4.9	You'll Take to This Like a Duck Takes to Water: Exploring Figurative Language	F, *There's a Frog in My Throat*	5–6	3 and 6	Rubric

(continued)

Activity overview, continued

Chapter	Activity		Genre/Book*	Grade Level	Standards	Assessment Type
	4.10	Vocabulary Cubes: Building Word Meaning and Spelling Skills	No text used	5–6	3 and 4	Teacher-made vocabulary test
5 WRITING	5.1	All About Me Journals	No text used	K–1	3	Checklist
	5.2	Organizing for Writing	F, folktales	K–1	3 and 6	Teacher observation
	5.3	Creating Colorful Word Pictures: Similes	F, *Quick as a Cricket*	2–3	6	Assign points
	5.4	What Am I? Writing Five-Sense Riddles	No text used	2–3	4, 5, and 12	Rubric
	5.5	Creative Coffee Can Tales	No text used	3	6	Rubric
	5.6	Quickwrites: A Technique to Activate Prior Knowledge	Either F or NF	4	10 and 12	Teacher observation
	5.7	Choices in Poetry Writing: Poetry Contracts	Poetry	5	4, 10, and 12	Rubric
	5.8	Students as Reporters: Creating a Classroom Newspaper	NF, newspapers	5–6	4, 6, and 7	Rubric
	5.9	All About Me: Writing Autobiographies	NF, autobiography	6	5 and 6	Student and teacher rubric
	5.10	Back to Nature: Creating Travel Brochures for Our State and National Parks	NF, travel brochures	6	4, 6, 8, and 10	Rubric
6 VIEWING	6.1	Signs All Around the Town	F, *Mr. Pine's Mixed-up Signs*	K–1	1	Observation
	6.2	Reading the Pictures: Wordless Picture Book Interpretation	F, *The Red Box*	K–1	1 and 3	Observation
	6.3	I See What You Mean: Exploring Pantomime	F, *Peck, Slither and Slide*	1–2	4	Student verbal response
	6.4	Who Am I?	Either F or NF	2–3	3 and 9	Observation
	6.5	Talking Hands: Understanding American Sign Language	F, *Moses Goes to School* & NF, *Simple Signs*	2–3	9	Student verbal response
	6.6	A Picture Is Worth a Thousand Words: Analyzing Photographs	NF, picture books about the past	3–4	12	Checklist

(continued)

Activity overview, continued

Chapter	Activity		Genre/Book*	Grade Level	Standards	Assessment Type
	6.7	Viewing and Understanding Comic Strips	F, comic strips	4–6	6 and 12	Observation of comic strips
	6.8	Don't Always Believe What You See: Website Evaluations	No text used	5–6	7, 8, and 10	Website evaluation questionnaire
	6.9	Eyewitness: Did You Really See What You Thought You Saw?	No text used	5–6	11	Eyewitness to the Crime sheet
	6.10	Propaganda Alert!: Analyzing Magazine Advertisements	NF, magazines	5–6	7	Rubric
7 VISUALLY REPRESENTING	7.1	See How I Feel: Expressing Feelings with Others	F, *The Feelings Book*	K–1	12	Teacher observation
	7.2	Beginning–Middle–End Folktale Retellings	F, folktales	K–1	3 and 4	Teacher observation—questions provided
	7.3	Shoebox Theaters	F, picture books	1–2	1, 10, and 12	Checklist
	7.4	Discovering Women's History: Constructing a Baggy Quilt	HF, NF, F	2–3	2, 10, and 12	Self-assessment questionnaire
	7.5	Kate and Jack Climb Up the Beanstalk: Using Venn Diagrams to Compare and Contrast	F, folktales	3–4	3 and 12	Rubric
	7.6	Depicting the Past: Paper Plate Timelines	NF, biographies	3–4	1 and 12	Rubric
	7.7	Plotting the Story: Developing Plot Profile Graphs	F, *Three Billy Goats Gruff*	3–4	3 and 12	Checklist
	7.8	Constructing a Human Bar Graph	HF, *Let Them Play*, or NF, F	4–5	2 and 12	Observation and anecdotal records
	7.9	Sell That Product!: Creating Media Print Ads	NF, magazine advertisements	5–6	12	Rubric
	7.10	Charting Math Results: Discovering Pi	*Sir Cumference and the Dragon of Pi: A Math Adventure*	5–6	7 and 12	Observation and anecdotal records

References

Atwell, N. (1998). *In the middle: New understanding about writing, reading and learning.* Portsmouth, NH: Heinemann.

Barton, D., Hamilton, M., & Ivanic, R. (2000). *Situated literacies.* London: Routledge Press.

Brent, R., & Anderson, P. (1993). Developing children's classroom listening strategies. *The Reading Teacher, 50,* 36–43.

Calkins, L. (1991). When children want to punctuate: Basic skills belong in context. *Language Arts, 57,* 567–573.

Chittendon, E. (1991). Authentic assessment, evaluation, and documentation of student performance. In V. Perrone (Ed.), *Expanding student assessment* (pp. 22–31), Alexandria, VA: Association for Supervision and Curriculum Development.

Clay, M. (1967). The reading behavior of five-year-old children: A research report. *New Zealand Journal of Education Studies,* 11–31.

Cooper, J. D., & Kiger, N. (2005). *Literacy assessment: Helping teachers plan instruction* (2nd ed.). Boston: Houghton Mifflin.

Cox, C. (2005). *Teaching language arts: A student- and response-centered classroom.* Boston: Allyn & Bacon.

Cramer, R. (2004). *The language arts: A balanced approach to teaching reading, writing, listening, talking and thinking.* Boston: Allyn & Bacon.

Daniels, H., & Bizar, M. (1998). *Methods that matter: Six structures for best practice classrooms.* York, ME: Stenhouse Publishing.

Devine, T. (1982). *Listening skills schoolwide: Activities and programs.* Urbana, IL: ERIC Clearinghouse on Reading and Communication Skills and the National Council of Teachers of English.

Dickinson, D., & DeTemple, J. (1998). Putting parents in the picture: Maternal reports of preschoolers' literacy as a predictor of early reading. *Early Childhood Research Quarterly, 13*(2), 241–261.

Eeds, M., & Wells, D. (1989). Grand conversations: An exploration of meaning construction in literature study groups. *Research in the Teaching of English, 23,* 4–29.

Farris, P. (2005). *Language arts: Process, product and assessment.* Long Grove, IL: Waveland Press.

Freeman, D., & Freeman, Y. (1993). Strategies for promoting the primary language of all students. *The Reading Teacher, 46,* 552–558.

Gillon, G. (2004). *Phonological awareness: From research to practice.* New York: Guilford Press.

Goodrich, H. (1996/1997). Understanding rubrics. *Educational Leadership, 54*(4), 14–17.

Graves, D. (1983). *Writing: Teachers and children at work.* Portsmouth, NH: Heinemann.

Griffith, P., & Olson, M. (1992). Phonemic awareness helps beginning readers break the code. *Reading Teacher, 45*(7), 516–523.

Heath, S. (1983). Research currents: A lot of talk about nothing. *Language Arts, 60,* 999–1007.

Heathcox, D. (2002). *Differentiating instruction in the regular classroom: How to reach and teach all learners, grades 3–12.* Minneapolis, MN: Free Spirit Publishing.

Hoffman, J., & Pearson, P. (2000). Reading teacher education in the next millennium: What your grandmother's teacher didn't know that your granddaughter's teacher should. *Reading Research Quarterly, 35,* 28–44.

International Reading Association and the National Association for the Education of Young Children. (1998). Learning to read and write: Developmentally appropriate practices for young children. A joint position statement of the International Reading Association and the National Association for the Education of Young Children. *Young Children, 53,* 524–546.

Irwin, J. (1991). *Teaching reading comprehension processes* (2nd ed.). Boston: Allyn & Bacon.

Jalongo, M. (1991). *Strategies for developing children's listening skills* (Phi Delta Kappan Fastback Series #314). Bloomington, IN: Phi Delta Kappan Educational Series.

Johnston, T., & Louis, D. (1987). *Literacy through literature.* Portsmouth, NH: Heinemann.

Lundsteen, S. (1979). *Listening: Its impact on reading and the other language arts.* Urbana, IL: National Council of Teachers of English.

Martin-Kniep, G. (2000). Using scoring rubrics to support learning. In *Becoming a better teacher: Eight innovations that work* (pp. 34–65), Alexandria, VA: Association for Supervision and Curriculum Development.

Matthews, M., & Rainer, J. (2001). The quandaries of teachers and teacher educators in integrating literacy and mathematics. *Language Arts 78*(4), 357–364.

Morrow, L. (2004). Motivation: The forgotten factor. *Reading Today, 21*(5), 6.

Morrow, L. (2003/2004). Family literacy: Home and school working together. *Reading Today, 21*(3), 6–8.

National Reading Panel. (2000). *Report of the National Reading Panel.* Washington, DC: National Institute of Child Health and Human Development Clearinghouse.

Neuman, S. (1999). Books make a difference: A study of access to literacy. *Reading Research Quarterly, 34*(3), 286–311.

Pappas, C., Kiefer, B., & Levstik, L. (1999). *Integrated language perspective in the elementary school: An action approach* (3rd ed.). Boston: Allyn & Bacon.

Pearson, D., & Fielding, L. (1982). Research update: Listening comprehension. *Language Arts, 59,* 617–629.

Peregoy, S., & Boyle, O. (1997). *Reading, writing and learning in ESL: A resource book for K–12 teachers.* New York: Longman.

Routman, R. (1996). *Literacy at the crossroads: Crucial talk about reading, writing and teaching dilemmas.* Portsmouth, NH: Heinemann.

Short, D., & Echevarria, J. (2004/2005). Teacher skills to support English language learners. *Educational Leadership, 62*(4), 8–13.

Smith, P. (Ed.). (2001). *Talking classrooms: Shaping children's learning through oral language instruction.* Newark, DE: International Reading Association.

Snow, C., Burns, M., & Griffen, E. (Eds.). (1998). *Preventing reading difficulties in young children.* Washington, DC: National Academies Press.

Standards for the English Language Arts. (1996). Urbana, IL: National Council of Teachers of English and the International Reading Association.

Strickland, D., Galda, L., & Cullinan, B. (2004). *Language arts: Learning and teaching.* Belmont, CA: Wadsworth/Thomson Learning.

Strother, D. (1987). Practical applications of research: On listening. *Phi Delta Kappan,* 68, 625–628.

Tevebaugh, T. (2001). Welcome to our website: Integrating subjects through entomology. *Language Arts* 78(4), 343–347.

The National Council of Teachers of English. Retrieved June 8, 2005, from www.ncte.org/about/over/standards/110839.htm.

Tomlinson, C. (2001). *How to differentiate instruction in mixed-ability classrooms* (2nd ed.). Alexandria, VA: Association for Supervision and Curriculum Development.

Tompkins, G. (2005). *Language arts: Patterns of practice* (6th ed.). Upper Saddle River, NJ: Merrill/Prentice Hall.

Vacca, J., Vacca, R., Gove, M., Burkey, L., Lenhart, L., & McKeon., C. (2003). *Reading and learning to read* (5th ed.). Boston: Allyn & Bacon.

Watson, J. (2004). Family literacy: Support for young readers and their parents. *School Library Media Activities Monthly,* 20(8), 24–29.

Wells, G., & Chang-Wells, G. (1992). *Constructing knowledge together: Classrooms as centers of inquiry and literacy.* Portsmouth, NH: Heinemann.

Werner, E. (1975). *A study of communication time.* Unpublished master's thesis. University of Maryland, College Park.

Wikipedia: A Free Encyclopedia. Retrieved August 15, 2006, from http://en.wikipedia.org/wiki/Main_Page.

U.S. Department of Education, National Center for Education Statistics. (2001). *The condition of Education 2001* (NCED 2001-072). Washington, DC: U. S. Government Printing Office.

Yellin, D., Blake, M., & DeVries, B. (2004). *Integrating the language arts* (3rd ed.). Scottsdale, AZ: Holcomb Hathaway.

Yopp, H. (1992). Developing phonemic awareness in young children. *The Reading Teacher,* 45, 696–703.

LISTENING

Developing the Five Types of Listening Skills

INTRODUCTION

The development of the six language arts begins with listening, for listening is the first skill developed in infancy. Infants hear sound and language before they can read, write, or speak, so listening is imperative to early communication. Unlike hearing, which is a physical act, listening is an active mental process. The brain must be involved, which means that children can hear without really listening. The development of listening goes hand in hand with speaking, as homes and classrooms are filled with conversation and instruction.

Both listening and speaking are the building blocks of well-developed literacy skills (Yellin, Blake, & DeVries, 2004).

Freshour and Bartholomew (1989) outline six steps in the listening process. The process begins when children *hear* information. This can be any sound in their environment, including the speech of teachers and classmates. Second, children choose to *attend* to some of those sounds to get more information. Children will not learn information presented by the teacher if they are attending to sounds other than the teacher's voice, such as children talking, noises in the hallway, or a ball game on the playground. *Understanding* is the third step in the listening process. As the brain takes in new information, comprehension begins and reinforces the listener's ability to focus and listen more carefully. Fourth, children begin to think about and *analyze* what they have heard. This analysis helps children to make listening a meaningful process, as they use their prior knowledge to make sense of new information. As comprehension increases, children can begin to *evaluate* the messages they have heard, which further increases their understanding. Finally, children begin to *react* to what they have heard with both physical and mental activity. In order to react, they must remember what they have heard. Thus, memory is a crucial aspect of the listening process.

Teachers must create a positive environment for the development of listening. Gaining students' attention before speaking, attending to the physical arrangement of the room, and reinforcing students as they listen to classmates are all critical to a positive learning environment (Yellin, Blake, & DeVries, 2004). Teachers must also instruct students in the various purposes for listening, integrate listening activities throughout the curriculum, and be good models. Listening skills have been classified in five categories:

1. *Discriminative listening* helps children to notice differences in the sounds they hear.
2. *Purposeful listening* allows listeners to hear information or directions and respond appropriately.
3. *Creative listening* is listening with one's imagination, sensitivity, or emotions.
4. *Critical listening,* a higher-level skill, requires children to understand, assess, and formulate opinions about what they have heard.
5. *Appreciative listening* is listening for pleasure. Teachers must not forget to give students opportunities for appreciative listening (Miller, 2000).

Educators disagree as to whether listening should be taught as a separate skill or integrated throughout the curriculum. The most important thing to remember is that listening is always done for a specific purpose, never in isolation from the other language arts. Cooper (2006) suggests the use of guided listening lessons to increase the benefits of read-alouds. In a guided listening lesson, the teacher introduces the book and students make predictions about what will happen in the story. Students then listen to verify, discuss, and revise their predictions. After the story is read, teachers extend the text with skills and activities. These extension exercises require students to remember what they heard during the read-aloud.

Listening is both a critical and a challenging skill for second language learners. Many English language learners will need weeks or months of listening to the English language before they should be expected or required to speak it. This "silent period" helps these students to increase their receptive vocabulary and provides them with opportunities to respond nonverbally. As English language learners progress, it is important that teachers use simple vocabulary and avoid idioms and colloquialisms. Students may feel more comfortable interacting in pairs or small groups, rather than listening and responding before the entire class (Cruz, Nutta, O'Brien, Feyten, & Govoni, 2003).

This chapter presents activities to promote the five types of listening skills. Primary grade students will enjoy listening for important details in order to complete an anticipation/reaction guide, listening for specific letters of the alphabet in *Chicka Chicka Boom Boom* (Martin & Archambault, 1989), contributing to a collaborative circle story, listening to directions for a paper-folding activity, and performing creative movements while listening to a story. Intermediate grade students will be engaged in listening and identifying propaganda techniques in advertising, learning a note-taking technique to help them make connections with a speaker, using prediction charts to make story predictions, comparing and contrasting books and videos, and visualizing to better understand a spoken message.

Classroom Vignette

Mrs. Porter is preparing her first grade students for a field trip to the aquarium. She begins with her explanation of permission forms, cost, and lunch arrangements, but as she scans the room she suspects that very few students are listening. Sarah is drawing a picture, Ramón is looking out the window, and Jason and LaTessa are chatting in the back of the room. Mrs. Porter stops talking and asks for students' eyes to be focused on her. When everyone is looking, she continues. She then passes out the permission forms and asks only those students with blue tennis shoes to put their forms in their backpacks. Six children immediately jump up, complete the task, and return quickly. "What excellent listeners!" she exclaims. She then asks for those with brown hair to do the same and continues until all the permission forms have been put away. Mrs. Porter explains that they will be seeing many kinds of marine life at the aquarium. She asks her students to listen closely as she reads *Mister Seahorse,* by Eric Carle, and be prepared to name all of the types of sea animals in the story.

DISCUSSION QUESTIONS

1. What does Mrs. Porter do to promote well-developed listening skills in her first grade classroom?
2. What types of listening skills is she reinforcing?
3. How can Mrs. Porter ensure that her students will be good listeners on the field trip?
4. What other strategies might Mrs. Porter use to promote good listening skills?
5. Do you believe that teachers require students to do too much listening and do not provide enough time for speaking? Why or why not?

References

Cooper, J. D. (2006). *Literacy: Helping children construct meaning.* New York: Houghton Mifflin.

Cruz, B., Nutta, J., O'Brien, J., Feyten, C., & Govoni, J. (2003). *Passport to learning: Teaching social studies to ESL students.* Silver Spring, MD: National Council for the Social Studies.

Freshour, F., & Bartholomew, P. (1989). Let's start improving our own listening. *Florida Reading Quarterly, 25*(4), 28–30.

Martin, B., & Archambault, J. (1989). *Chicka chicka boom boom.* New York: Simon & Schuster.

Miller, W. (2000). *Strategies for developing emergent literacy.* Boston: McGraw-Hill.

Yellin, D., Blake, M., & DeVries, B. (2004). *Integrating the language arts* (3rd ed.). Scottsdale, AZ: Holcomb Hathaway.

ACTIVITY 2.1

Inviting Students to Listen

Chicka Chicka Boom Boom

GRADE LEVEL: **K**

OBJECTIVE

- To listen and respond to verbal prompts (purposeful listening)

MATERIALS

- One copy of *Chicka Chicka Boom Boom*, by Bill Martin, Jr., and John Archambault. (See the Children's Literature section at the end of this activity for additional titles.)
- Six-inch uppercase letters of the alphabet cut from cardboard or six-inch stencils of uppercase letters
- Checklist for Listening Skills
- Literacy bag and family letter

NCTE/IRA STANDARD

12 Students use spoken, written, and visual language to accomplish their own purposes (e.g., for learning, enjoyment, persuasion, and the exchange of information).

PROCEDURES

1. Read *Chicka Chicka Boom Boom* aloud to students.
2. Give each student a letter of the alphabet. If there are fewer than 26 students, some may hold two consecutive letters.
3. Explain to students that as you read the book again, they are to listen for their letter. When they hear it, they are to bring their letter to the front of the room, where they will line up in alphabetical order.
4. Read the story again and assist students in lining up in order.
5. Explain to students that when you read, "The whole alphabet up the—Oh no! Chicka Chicka BOOM BOOM!" and all the letters fall off the tree, they are to fall to the floor with their letters.
6. While students are now sitting with their letters, continue reading the story. As the letters are called again (the letters are now getting up), explain to students that they are to jump to their feet.
7. As you read the story multiple times, students will know in advance what they are to listen for in the story and do in response. Students may also enjoy repeating aloud parts of the story such as, "Chicka Chicka Boom Boom!"
8. You may seat students who tend not to listen attentively or who do not consistently recognize the letters close to you so they can be prompted when their letters are called. These students could also be seated beside the person who has the letter preceding theirs, so they are prompted by that student's actions. English language learners will benefit from this kind of support.

ASSESSMENT

For this activity, you may use the Checklist for Listening Skills (Exhibit 2.1.A) to assess each student's listening skills. The checklist can become part of the child's language arts portfolio. By comparing this checklist to similar checklists, parents and teachers will be able to assess a child's growth in listening skills over the course of the school year.

INTEGRATING LANGUAGE ARTS ACROSS THE CURRICULUM

You may choose other quality children's literature to promote listening skills. Suggested titles include: *We're Going on a Bear Hunt* (Rosen, 1989), *Old McDonald Had a Woodshop* (Shulman, 2002), *There Was an Old Lady Who Swallowed a Fly* (Taback, 1997), *The Very Hungry Caterpillar* (Carle, 1969), and *Click, Clack, Moo: Cows That Type* (Cronin, 2000). Most any alphabet book can be used for the activity presented above with *Chicka Chicka Boom Boom.*

HOME–SCHOOL CONNECTION

You may pack a literacy bag with *Chicka Chicka Boom Boom* and stenciled or magnetic alphabet letters. Students can take turns taking the bag home to share with family members. The child can lay the letters out on the floor. Depending on the child's skill in letter identification, the letters may be placed in alphabetical order or a random order. A parent can read the book, while the student and other family members find each letter as it is read. A note to family members (Exhibit 2.1.B) can be included in the literacy bag.

CHILDREN'S LITERATURE

Carle, E. (1969). *The very hungry caterpillar.* Philomel.

Cronin, D. (2000). *Click, clack, moo: Cows that type.* Scholastic.

Martin, B., & Archambault, J. (1989). *Chicka chicka boom boom.* Simon & Schuster.

Shulman, L. (2002). *Old McDonald had a woodshop.* G. P. Putnam's Sons.

Rosen, M. (1989). *We're going on a bear hunt.* Aladdin.

Taback, S. (1997). *There was an old lady who swallowed a fly.* Scholastic.

Checklist for Listening Skills

Chicka Chicka Boom Boom

Name ______________________________ Date ______________

1. Listens attentively as the story is being read	YES	NO
2. Responds quickly when his/her letter is read	YES	NO
3. Listens attentively to directions	YES	NO
4. Responds without prompting during listening activity	YES	NO
5. Repeats familiar parts of the story during subsequent readings	YES	NO

Comments:

EXHIBIT **2.1.B**

Dear Family Members,

Our class has been reading and enjoying *Chicka Chicka Boom Boom* by Bill Martin, Jr., and John Archambault. Enclosed you will find the book and letters of the alphabet. You can use the materials in the bag with your child in a fun activity, which will also help him/her develop listening skills and alphabet knowledge.

To begin the activity, help your child to lay the letters on the floor in alphabetical order. As you read the story aloud, ask your child to listen closely and pick up each letter as it is named. Provide any help that is needed. If your child is already able to identify the letters, you can lay the letters on the floor in a random order. When you read the book again, your child will have the challenge of finding each of the letters that you name.

After your family has enjoyed the book and activities, you may write some comments below on how your child enjoyed the experiences. Please return this note, the book, and the alphabet letters to school in the bag provided so other children can enjoy them.

Sincerely,

Your comments: ______________________________

____

____

____

____

____

Listening for Pleasure Through Creative Movement

GRADE LEVEL: **K**

OBJECTIVES

- To listen for pleasure (appreciative listening)
- To listen for words that suggest actions and perform those actions (purposeful listening)

MATERIALS

- One copy of *Over in the Garden*, by Jennifer Ward (See the Children's Literature section at the end of this activity for additional titles.)

NCTE/IRA STANDARD

12 Students use spoken, written, and visual language to accomplish their own purposes (e.g., for learning, enjoyment, persuasion, and the exchange of information).

PROCEDURES

1. Read the book aloud. Discuss with students the meaning of the action verb in each verse. (Action verbs include *pounce, crawl, zip, slither, buzz, jump, nibble, roll, march,* and *glow.*) Action verbs can be described simply as things the bugs do in the story.
2. Invite a student to demonstrate each of the verbs as they are discussed. Students can simply make the sound for "zip" and "buzz," and open and close their fingers to represent "glow."
3. Move to a space in the classroom that allows for plenty of movement. The gym might even be an appropriate place for this activity.
4. Read the book again, asking students to listen closely for words that tell what the bugs do. Tell them to pretend they are the bugs and must do everything that the bugs do in the story. Ring a bell to signal students to stop their activity and listen as the next verse begins so they will know what to do next.
5. Students who do not remember what movement to do for each action word can be prompted by those around them. The book and directions for this activity could be recorded on tape and replayed for students who might need extra practice in listening and following directions.

ASSESSMENT

During the activity, you may informally observe students' abilities in listening and following directions. Observations can be recorded in anecdotal records. Anecdotal records are defined as "dated, informal observational notations that describe language development as well as social development in terms of the learner's attitudes, strengths, weaknesses, needs, progress, learning styles, skills, strategies used, or anything else that seems significant at the time of observation (Routman, 1991, p. 309). Teachers who keep anecdotal records of literacy activities such as this are able to determine whether students are mastering objectives and meeting academic standards. These records also provide concrete information on the learning process and students' progress over time to share with family members. In this lesson, anecdotal records would focus on students' ability in listening and following directions as well as evidence of their enjoyment while listening to the read-aloud.

INTEGRATING LANGUAGE ARTS ACROSS THE CURRICULUM

Creative movement is a wonderful way for youngsters to make learning more meaningful in content areas of the curriculum. For example, students can perform actions to accompany a weather song, such as simulating rain by raising both hands in the air and moving their fingers, either slowly or quickly to suggest a light rain or a storm, as they lower their hands. Likewise, students can pantomime the many jobs that the Pilgrims performed in order to get ready for their Thanksgiving feast.

HOME-SCHOOL CONNECTION

Children can take turns borrowing the book and/or taped version of the book. Family members can read the book or listen to the tape with their child and participate in the creative movement activities.

CHILDREN'S LITERATURE

Martin, B., & Archambault, J. (1989). *Chicka, chicka, boom, boom.* Simon & Schuster.

Rosen, M. (1989). *We're going on a bear hunt.* Aladdin.

Shulman, L. (2002). *Old MacDonald had a woodshop.* G. P. Putnam's Sons.

Taback, S. (1997). *There was an old lady who swallowed a fly.* Scholastic.

Wadsworth, O. (2002). *Over in the meadow.* North-South Books.

Ward, J. (2002). *Over in the garden.* Scholastic.

Wilson, A. (2000). *Over in the grasslands.* Little, Brown & Co.

Wood, A. (1990). *Quick as a cricket.* Child's Play International.

Wood, A. (2004). *Ten little fish.* Blue Sky Press.

REFERENCE

Routman, R. (1991). *Invitations: Changing as teachers and learners K–12.* Portsmouth, NH: Heinemann.

ACTIVITY 2.3

Listening for the Sequence of Events

Circle Stories

GRADE LEVEL: **1**

OBJECTIVES

- To listen for the sequence of events in a story and put the events in order (purposeful listening)
- To listen to story retellings for pleasure (appreciative listening)

MATERIALS

- One copy of *Joseph Had a Little Overcoat*, by Simms Taback (See the Children's Literature section at the end of this activity for additional titles.)
- Circle Story handout (one per student)
- Circle Story Retelling Self-Assessment Checklist (one per student)
- Family letter (one per student)

NCTE/IRA STANDARDS

1 Students read a wide range of print and non-print texts to build an understanding of texts, of themselves, and of the cultures of the United States and the world; to acquire new information; to respond to the needs and demands of society and the workplace; and for personal fulfillment. Among these texts are fiction and nonfiction, classic and contemporary works.

4 Students adjust their use of spoken, written, and visual language (e.g., conventions, style, vocabulary) to communicate effectively with a variety of audiences and for different purposes.

10 Students whose first language is not English make use of their first language to develop competency in the English language arts and to develop understanding of content across the curriculum.

PROCEDURES

1. Ask students to listen carefully as you read *Joseph Had a Little Overcoat*, so they are able to discuss what happens to Joseph.
2. Read the book aloud and encourage students to discuss all of the changes to Joseph's wardrobe.
3. Have students name the articles of clothing the author describes in the book. Write each word on the chalkboard or on chart paper. Make sure the words are written in a random order.
4. Give each student a Circle Story handout (Exhibit 2.3.A). Have students write the title of the story in the center circle.
5. Ask students to recall how Joseph's clothing changed from the beginning to the end of the story. Have students write the article of clothing that he was wearing at the beginning of the story (overcoat) in the square labeled "story starts." Students can then work independently to recall the second article of clothing for box 2 (jacket) and subsequent clothing items in boxes 3–7 (vest, scarf, necktie, handkerchief, button). In box 8, ask students to write the word that describes what Joseph had at the end of the story (nothing). Have students get assistance with remembering the clothing items and their spelling by looking at the words listed on the chalkboard.
6. Have students choose a partner for story retelling. Ask students to listen carefully as their partner retells the story using the Circle Story handout as a prompt. The student who is listening must ensure that the articles of clothing are in the proper order. Partners then change roles.

7. Students with less well developed listening skills may need to have the story reread, perhaps a number of times, to ensure they have the clothing in the correct order. A list of the clothing words could be provided at a child's seat for any student who has difficulty copying from the chalkboard. Students with well-developed writing skills might choose to use complete sentences to describe the clothing changes. English language learners could write the clothing items and retell the story in English as well as their first language.

ASSESSMENT

Check the Circle Story handouts to ensure that students have the articles of clothing in the correct order. In addition, first graders may be able to begin to participate in self-assessment. Provide each student with a Circle Story Retelling Self-Assessment Checklist (Exhibit 2.3.B) and read each question aloud. Have students complete their checklist with feedback from their partner.

INTEGRATING LANGUAGE ARTS ACROSS THE CURRICULUM

Books with social studies, math, or science themes could be used for circle stories in order to help students listen for a sequence of events. *Snow* (Shulevitz, 1998) can be incorporated into a science weather unit, Eric Carle's *Mister Seahorse* (2004) can help students learn about aquatic life, *Who Came Down That Road?* (Lyon, 1992) provides an excellent introduction to historical time concepts, and *A Picture Book of John F. Kennedy* (Adler, 1991) may be used to help students recall important events in the life of this historic figure.

HOME-SCHOOL CONNECTION

Students can take their Circle Story handouts home and retell the story to family members. Inform families of their role in the development of their child's listening skills. You may wish to send a letter home (Exhibit 2.3.C) describing behaviors and activities that family members might do at home to strengthen their child's skills in listening.

CHILDREN'S LITERATURE

Adler, D. (1991). *A picture book of John F. Kennedy.* Trumpet.

Carle, E. (2004). *Mister Seahorse.* Philomel.

Lyon, G. (1992). *Who came down that road?* Orchard.

Shulevitz, U. (1998). *Snow.* Scholastic.

Taback, S. (1999). *Joseph had a little overcoat.* Viking.

EXHIBIT **2.3.A**

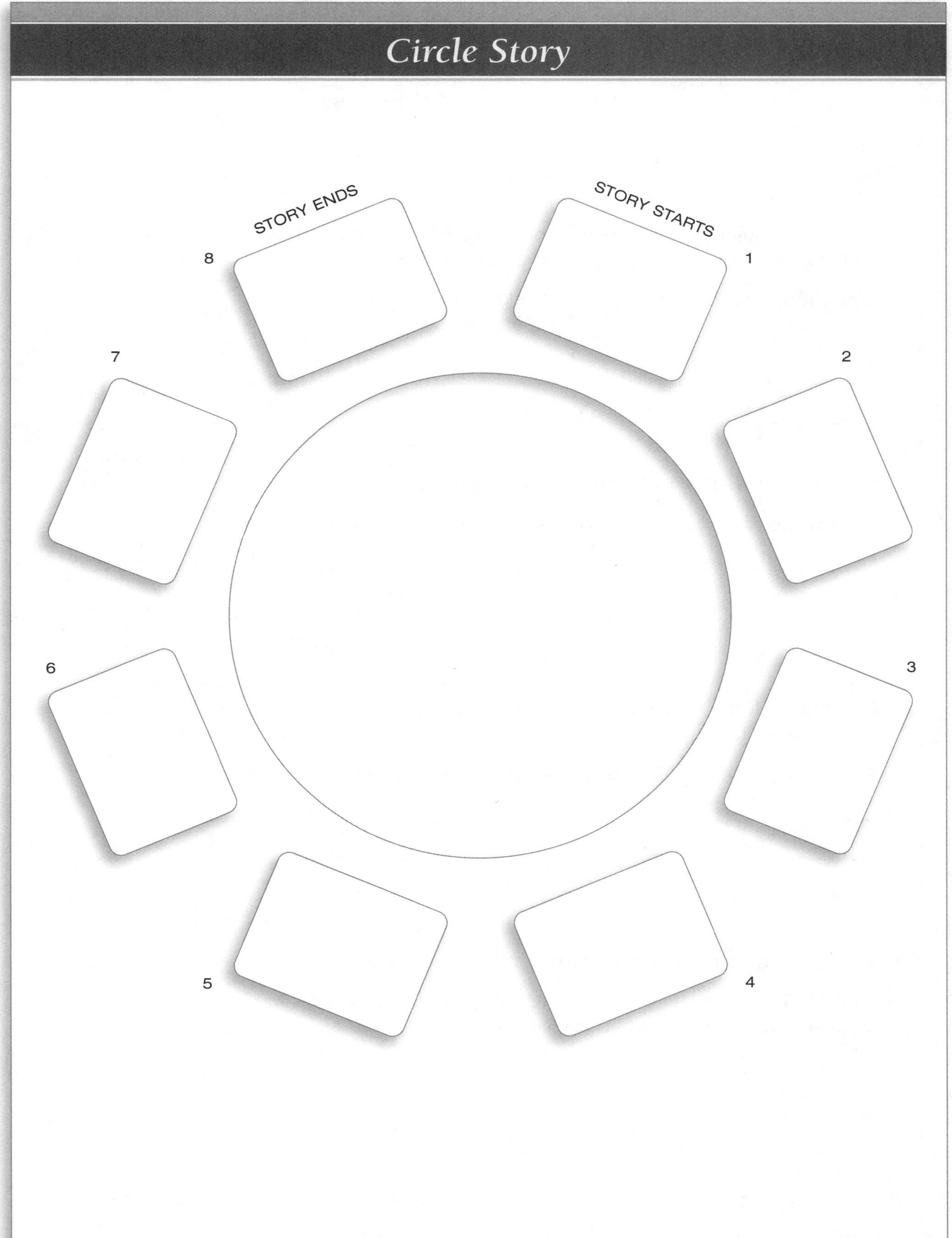

EXHIBIT **2.3.B**

Circle Story Retelling

Self-Assessment Checklist

Name ______________________________ Date ______________

1. Did I listen closely to the story so I could remember all of the clothes that Joseph wore when I told the story to my partner? YES NO

   If my answer was no, which pieces of clothes did I forget?

   ____

   ____

   ____

2. Did I remember all of the clothes in the right order? YES NO

   If my answer was no, which pieces of clothes were out of order?

   ____

   ____

   ____

3. Did I listen closely to the story so I could remember what Joseph had left at the end of the story? YES NO

   If my answer was yes, tell what Joseph had left at the end of the story.

   ____

   ____

   ____

4. Was I a good listener when my partner was telling the story? YES NO

   If my answer was yes, tell why I am a good listener. If my answer was no, tell how I can become a better listener.

   ____

   ____

   ____

Dear Family Members,

Well-developed listening skills are very important for success in school. Family members can have a tremendous influence on the development of the listening skills of children. I would like to suggest that you influence your child's ability to listen well by doing the following:

- Model good listening whenever possible. Look at your child and give your full attention when he or she is speaking. If you are involved in other things and cannot listen attentively, ask your child to wait until you are free.
- Make sure you have your child's attention before speaking.
- Read interesting books to your child and ask questions about the stories.
- Give your child more than one direction at a time to see if he or she is able to remember what to do. For example, you might ask your child to get on his or her pajamas and brush his or her teeth. If your child is able to remember two directions consistently, you can add a third. You can make this fun by asking your child to do silly things, like touch his/her nose, hop on one foot, and bring a banana from the kitchen.
- Ask your child to listen closely to a book that you are about to read. After you've read the book, ask your child to draw a picture of something he/she remembers from the story.
- Put an object inside a shoebox. Give the box to your child, ask him/her to shake it and listen to the sound it makes, and see if he/she can guess what the object is.

Sincerely,

ACTIVITY 2.4

Listening Times Two

Listening for Directions and Character Attributes

GRADE LEVEL: **2–3**

OBJECTIVES

- To listen closely to a story as it is read aloud (appreciative listening)
- To listen for important directions and follow those directions (purposeful listening)
- To listen for words in a story that describe a character's looks, actions, feelings, and personality (discriminative listening)

MATERIALS

- One copy of the book *Tough Boris*, by Mem Fox (See the Children's Literature section at the end of this activity for additional titles.)
- 8 1/2 x 11 sheets of paper (one per student)
- Crayons, markers, pencils
- One sheet of chart paper
- Listening Skills Checklist (one copy)

NCTE/IRA STANDARD

3 Students apply a wide range of strategies to comprehend, interpret, evaluate, and appreciate texts. They draw on their prior experience, their interactions with other readers and writers, their knowledge of word meaning and of other texts, their word identification strategies, and their understanding of textual features (e.g., sound–letter correspondence, sentence structure, context, graphics).

PROCEDURES

1. Introduce the book *Tough Boris.* Ask students to listen closely as you read so they will be able to describe the pirate, Tough Boris. Read the story aloud.
2. Have students brainstorm words from the story that describe Tough Boris's looks, actions, feelings, and personality. As they brainstorm, make a word wall on chart paper.
3. Give each student an 8 1/2 x 11 sheet of paper. Tell students they will need to follow directions closely for a paper-folding and cutting activity. Demonstrate the directions as you say them. The directions are as follows:
   a. Lay paper lengthwise so the 11-inch sides are at the top and bottom.
   b. Fold paper from top to bottom so that it creases in the middle.
   c. Open the paper back up.
   d. Fold in the two 8 1/2-inch sides of the paper until they touch in the middle.
   e. As the two sides touch, crease the paper on each side.
   f. Open the paper back up.
   g. On the first crease that was made in the middle of the paper, cut from each side just over to the second creases.
   h. You should now have four little flaps that open. Fold in the flaps and fold the paper from top to bottom. (Paper should now be one-quarter the size of the original sheet.)

4. Have students write the character's name on the outside cover of the folded booklet. Then have them unfold the paper from top to bottom. Have students number the flaps 1 through 4, beginning in the top left-hand corner. On flap 1, ask students to write words that describe Tough Boris's looks. On flap 2, have them write words that describe his actions. On flap 3, they are to write words that describe his feelings, and on flap 4, words that tell about his personality. See Exhibit 2.4.A. Students may use words from the word wall or other words they might think of.
5. Have students open all of the flaps and draw a picture of Tough Boris in the center half of the paper.
6. Reread *Tough Boris* and allow students to listen again for any other descriptive words they might want to add.
7. The paper-folding portion of this activity may be challenging for some students. Allow those students who finish their folds quickly to help those who need extra support. Less capable students might be paired with those who are more capable, so that those who typically need more help do not become frustrated. Copies of words from the word wall could be provided for students at their seats, for those who have difficulty copying from chart paper. Some students with disabilities may need to dictate words for each flap and allow a peer or teacher to write them.

ASSESSMENT

You may use the Listening Skills Checklist (Exhibit 2.4.B) to guide the assessment process for this listening activity. The rubric is used to assess students' abilities in three areas: listening to the story, listening for directions, and listening for character attributes.

INTEGRATING LANGUAGE ARTS ACROSS THE CURRICULUM

In science and social studies, students can use folded paper activities to enhance their learning. One such activity is a personal K-W-L chart. Students simply fold a blank sheet of paper into three sections that form three columns. The first column is labeled *What I Know,* the second column is labeled *What I Want to Learn,* and the third column is labeled *What I Have Learned.* Before beginning a new area of study, students write what they already know about the topic in the *What I Know* column. In the *What I Want to Learn* column, they write what they want to learn, in the form of questions. As they are listening to class discussion, students record what they learn in the *What I Have Learned* column and check to see if they have learned answers to any of the questions they wrote in the second column. The K-W-L chart is excellent for activating background knowledge, stimulating interest in the topic, and summarizing learning.

HOME–SCHOOL CONNECTION

Suggest that students retell the story of Tough Boris to their families. Using the folded booklet, students can share Tough Boris's looks, actions, feelings, and personality.

CHILDREN'S LITERATURE

Celsi, T. (1992). *The fourth little pig.* Steck-Vaughn.
Coles, R. (1995). *The story of Ruby Bridges.* Scholastic.
Fox, M. (1994). *Tough Boris.* Trumpet.
Gay, M. (2000). *Stella, queen of the snow.* Groundwood.
Kellogg, S. (1986). *Pecos Bill.* Mulberry.
Kellogg, S. (1988). *Johnny Appleseed.* Morrow Junior Books.
McKissack, P. (2001). *Goin' someplace special.* Atheneum.
Pfister, M. (1992). *The rainbow fish.* Scholastic.

EXHIBIT **2.4.A**

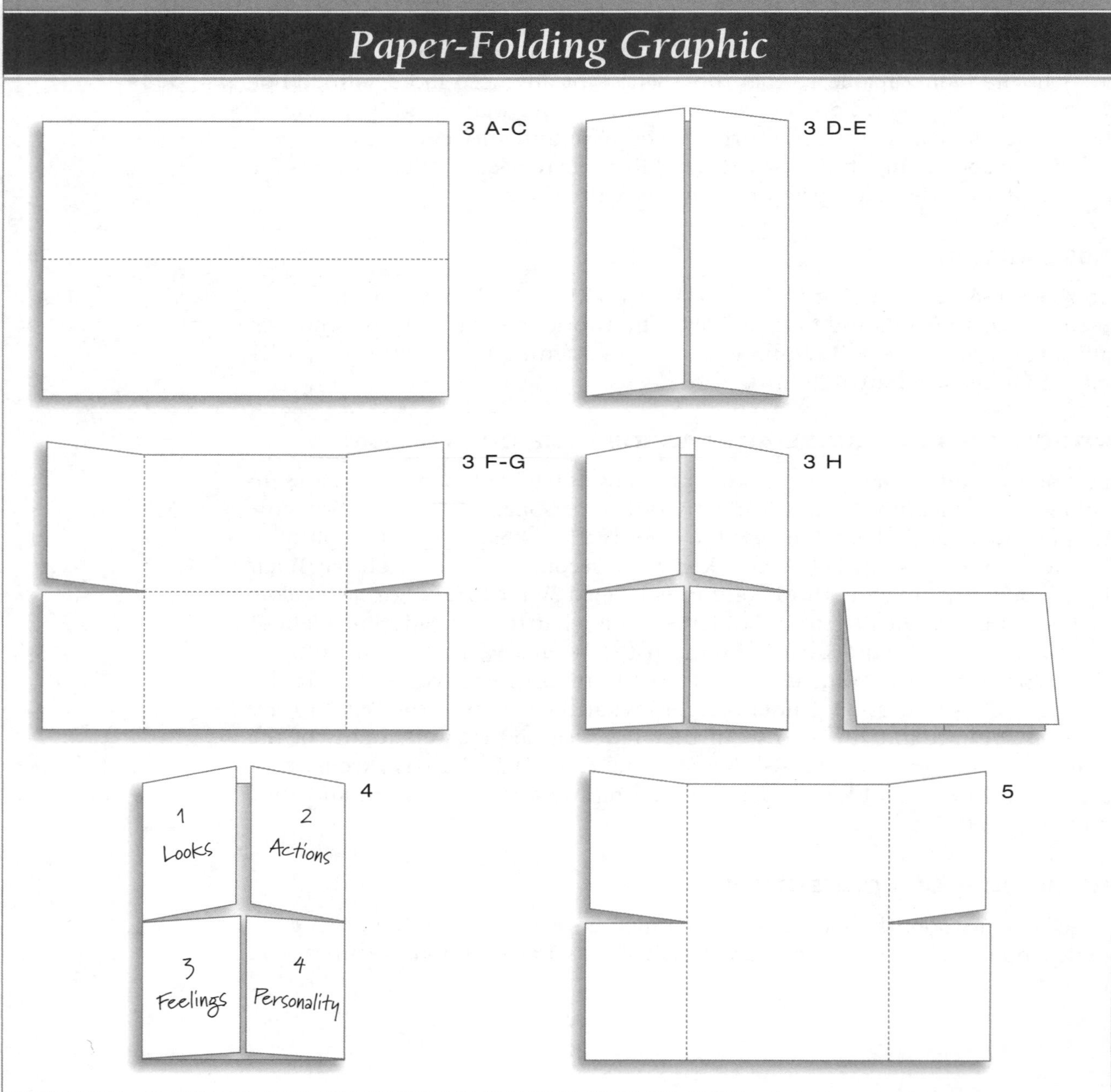

Whole-Class Checklist for Listening Skills

Tough Boris

Date ______________________________ Grade level ______________

KEY: *1 = proficient* *2 = required support or prompts* *3 = not yet capable even with support*

STUDENT NAME	Listens attentively as book is read	Follows directions accurately for paper-folding activity	Uses words from word wall to describe character's looks, actions, feelings, and personality

ACTIVITY 2.5

Listening for Important Details

Anticipation/Reaction Guides

GRADE LEVEL: **3**

OBJECTIVES

- To draw on prior experience and knowledge to make predictions about the truth of statements related to a nonfiction text (critical listening)
- To listen to a nonfiction text to acquire new information (purposeful listening)
- To use listening and comprehension skills to determine the truth of statements (critical listening) related to a nonfiction text that has been read aloud

MATERIALS

- One copy of the *The Flag We Love* by Pam Muñoz Ryan (See the Children's Literature section at the end of this activity for additional titles.)
- Anticipation/Reaction Guide (one per student)

NCTE/IRA STANDARDS:

1 Students read a wide range of print and non-print texts to build an understanding of texts, of themselves, and of the cultures of the United States and the world; to acquire new information; to respond to the needs and demands of society and the workplace; and for personal fulfillment. Among these texts are fiction and nonfiction, classic and contemporary works.

3 Students apply a wide range of strategies to comprehend, interpret, evaluate, and appreciate texts. They draw on their prior experience, their interactions with other readers and writers, their knowledge of word meaning and of other texts, their word identification strategies, and their understanding of textual features (e.g., sound-letter correspondence, sentence structure, context, graphics).

PROCEDURES

1. Duplicate and distribute the Anticipation/Reaction Guide (Exhibit 2.5.A) to students and introduce the book.
2. In the "before" column, have students predict the truth of each statement and write "true" or "false" in the blanks.
3. Tell students that they are to listen closely to the story to determine whether their predictions are correct. As you read the book aloud, have students write "true" or "false" for each statement in the "after" column. Discuss and confirm the correct answers with students, and reread any portions of the book necessary to ensure they understand why each statement is true or false.
4. Have students compare their predictions with the correct answers.
5. As the students make their predictions, you may wish to read the Anticipation/Reaction Guide statements aloud so that struggling readers are able to make informed predictions. The students could also form small groups to make predictions, with one group member reading each statement and then the group discussing whether they believe the statement to be true or false. English language learners might benefit from the small group approach, which would give them the opportunity to have unfamiliar vocabulary words defined.

ASSESSMENT

The evaluation of the Anticipation/Reaction Guide is objective. Answers based on the information in the book are as follows:

1. false
2. true
3. true
4. true
5. false
6. true
7. false
8. true

INTEGRATING LANGUAGE ARTS ACROSS THE CURRICULUM

Use other quality children's books to foster listening skills through the use of anticipation/reaction guides. (See the Children's Literature section at the end of this activity for additional titles.)

HOME-SCHOOL CONNECTION

Students might take a blank Anticipation/Reaction Guide home to share with family members. Family members could make predictions, and then the child could explain the correct answer for each statement and why each is true or false. Students could also take turns borrowing the book to take home, so that family members could listen for correct answers just as the students did.

CHILDREN'S LITERATURE

George, J. G. (1993). *The first Thanksgiving.* Philomel.

Kalman, M. (2002). *Fireboat: The heroic adventures of the John J. Harvey.* G. P. Putnam's Sons.

Maestro, B. (1996). *Coming to America: The story of immigration.* Scholastic.

Martin, J. (1998). *Snowflake Bentley.* Houghton Mifflin.

Ryan, P. M. (1996). *The flag we love.* Charlesbridge Publishing.

EXHIBIT **2.5.A**

Anticipation/Reaction Guide

The Flag We Love

Name ______________________________ Date ______________

BEFORE | | AFTER

______ 1. America's first flags had 14 stars and 14 stripes to represent the 14 colonies. ______

______ 2. The original Pledge of Allegiance was written in honor of the 400th anniversary of Columbus's voyage to America. ______

______ 3. Francis Scott Key wrote our national anthem, "The Star Spangled Banner," as he watched an American flag flying during the War of 1812. ______

______ 4. Flags are flown at half-mast to honor someone who has died. ______

______ 5. On July 4, 1876, the colonies declared their independence from Great Britain. That is why we celebrate the Fourth of July.

______ 6. When a flag is flown upside-down, it is a signal that there is an emergency. ______

______ 7. When the first astronauts landed on the moon, they took two American flags with them. ______

______ 8. The American flag is a symbol of our rights as free people. ______

ACTIVITY 2.6

Prediction Charts

Listening to Check and Modify Predictions

GRADE LEVEL: **4**

OBJECTIVES

- To make predictions based on story artifacts before listening to a story (purposeful listening)
- To modify predictions while listening to a story (critical listening)

MATERIALS

- One copy of *More Than Anything Else,* by Marie Bradby (1995, Scholastic)
- Story Artifact Predictions handout (one per student)
- Story artifacts: table salt, a candle, a twig, a plastic frog, a newspaper, and an alphabet book

NCTE/IRA STANDARDS

2 Students read a wide range of literature from many periods in many genres to build an understanding of the many dimensions (e.g., philosophical, ethical, aesthetic) of human experience.

4 Students adjust their use of spoken, written, and visual language (e.g., conventions, style, vocabulary) to communicate effectively with a variety of audiences and for different purposes.

PROCEDURES

1. Tell students that you will be reading to them a book entitled *More Than Anything Else,* by Marie Bradby. The story relates the tale of how Booker T. Washington learned to read. Before reading the book, however, you will show students some artifacts, or items, related to the book.
2. Pass out the Story Artifact Predictions handout (Exhibit 2.6.A) to students.
3. Show each story-related artifact to students and ask them to predict how it is related to the story to which they will listen. Ask them to record their predictions on the handout in the column labeled "Predicted" and discuss together the possible relevance of each item.
4. Tell students to listen carefully as you read the book to find out how each artifact is actually related to the story. Students should write the actual significance of each item in the column labeled "Actual."
5. After reading the story, have students tally the number of items they predicted correctly and write that number at the bottom of the "Predicted" column. Discuss the artifacts in relation to the role they played in the story.

ASSESSMENT

Collect the completed Story Artifact Predictions handouts and informally assess each student's ability to make reasonable predictions and to modify the predictions accurately after listening to the story. Students can repeat this activity with other books and story artifacts for additional practice.

INTEGRATING LANGUAGE ARTS ACROSS THE CURRICULUM

In content areas such as math, social studies, geography, and history, students can practice their predicting skills by observing artifacts related to the content to be studied. You may display several artifacts related to the topic and ask students to predict what they are going to be studying. Students can confirm or modify their predictions as the lesson unfolds.

HOME-SCHOOL CONNECTION

Encourage students to gather artifacts related to well-known novels or children's stories and bring them to class. Each morning, ask one student to share an artifact, and have the class guess the novel or story to which the artifact is related. The student may then share a brief synopsis of the story so that the rest of the class can confirm or modify their original predictions.

Story Artifact Predictions

More Than Anything Else

by Marie Bradby

Name ______________________ Date __________

STORY ARTIFACT	PREDICTED	ACTUAL
table salt		
candle		
twig		
frog		
newspaper		
alphabet book		
Total Reasonable Predictions		

ACTIVITY 2.7

Visualizing

Understanding a Spoken Message

GRADE LEVEL: **4–6**

OBJECTIVE

- To listen in order to visualize and draw descriptive scenes from literature (creative listening)

MATERIALS

- A level-appropriate story or novel, either fiction or nonfiction, that features descriptive language
- Drawing paper (one per student)
- Colored pencils, markers, or crayons

NCTE/IRA STANDARD

12 Students use spoken, written, and visual language to accomplish their own purposes (e.g., for learning, enjoyment, persuasion, and the exchange of information).

PROCEDURES

1. Select a descriptive paragraph or chapter from a story or novel. Before reading it to students, discuss the fact that good listeners often form mental images in their mind to help them understand and remember the information or story to which they are listening.
2. Ask students to close their eyes, and then read a brief descriptive paragraph aloud. Tell the class to visualize or create mental images about what they are hearing.
3. After reading, have students discuss the mental images they created. Note similarities and differences among the descriptions.
4. Read another passage and ask students to visualize the scene. After the reading, have students draw their mental images on paper. When they are done, have students share their pictures with each other.

ASSESSMENT

You may collect the student drawings and assess the detail included in the individual drawings. A simple rating scale, such as 4 = outstanding, 3 = good, 2 = fair, 1 = poor, can be used to evaluate the accuracy and detail of the drawings.

INTEGRATING LANGUAGE ARTS ACROSS THE CURRICULUM

Students can use visualizing in content areas to better understand and remember the content. Suggest that students close their eyes as the teacher reads content material. Ask them to form mental images and to discuss them after the reading. You may also encourage visualizing skills by reading descriptions of common items and having students visualize the object being described.

HOME-SCHOOL CONNECTION

Suggest that students try closing their eyes as they listen to a movie or a TV program at home, and then to compare their mental images to the actual images to find out how well they were able to visualize the content.

Compare and Contrast Matrix

The Book vs. The Movie

GRADE LEVEL: **4–6**

OBJECTIVES

- To listen attentively to a movie version of a book in order to compare and contrast it to the book (critical listening)
- To construct a compare and contrast matrix that accurately depicts similarities and differences between a book and its video counterpart

MATERIALS

- A level-appropriate novel for which a movie has been produced (For additional suggestions, see the box "Children's Books on Which Movies Have Been Based" and the Internet resource list at the end of the activity.)
- The movie version of the novel (For movies based on children's books, see the list at the end of the activity.)
- Television set
- VCR/DVD player
- Compare and Contrast Matrix student handout (one per student)

NCTE/IRA STANDARDS

8 Students use a variety of technological and information resources (e.g., libraries, databases, computer networks, video) to gather and synthesize information and to create and communicate knowledge.

12 Students use spoken, written, and visual language to accomplish their own purposes (e.g., for learning, enjoyment, persuasion, and the exchange of information).

PROCEDURES

1. Begin by choosing a level-appropriate novel for which a movie has been produced. You might select one from the list of books with movies provided at the end of the activity.
2. When students have finished reading the novel, introduce the Compare and Contrast Matrix student handout (Exhibit 2.8.A). Give each student a handout and explain that they will be comparing the book to the movie.
3. As a class, or in small groups, complete the information related to the book and record this information in the column labeled "Book." Students will write down the book's title and identify story elements, including the setting, main characters, supporting characters, problems, solutions, and ending.
4. Next, ask students to listen carefully to the movie version and record information related to each story element in the column labeled "Movie" on the matrix. Students will compare the book to the movie by placing a plus sign (+) before each similarity and a minus sign (–) before each difference. Have students discuss their observations in class.

ASSESSMENT

You will need to view the movie in advance and record key similarities and differences. A total number of similarities and differences should be calculated and used to assess students' ability to compare and contrast the book and movie.

INTEGRATING LANGUAGE ARTS ACROSS THE CURRICULUM

Students can create compare and contrast matrixes in content areas by comparing and contrasting information presented in their textbook with information presented in a video related to the content. You will need to adapt the provided matrix's main headings to accommodate the materials you have selected. You may use the provided matrix as a guide or create one of your own.

HOME-SCHOOL CONNECTION

After consulting the local television-programming guide, suggest that students watch movies on TV for other books that the class has read or that they have read individually. The day after the broadcast, conduct a brief discussion of the similarities and differences between the movie and book.

INTERNET RESOURCES

Movies and television based children's books. Retrieved October 7, 2005, from www.acs.ucalgary.ca/%7Edkbrown/movies.html.

Children's/family movies based on books. Retrieved October 7, 2005, from http://library.loganutah.org/BOOKLIST/children/videos/books.htm.

Compare and Contrast Matrix

The Book vs. the Movie

Name ______________________________ Date ______________

	BOOK	MOVIE
Title		
Setting		
Main characters		
Supporting characters		
Problems		
Solutions		
Ending		

Children's Books on Which Movies Have Been Based

Abel's Island, by William Steig

Across Five Aprils, by Irene Hunt

The Adventures of Huckleberry Finn, by Mark Twain

Alice in Wonderland, by Lewis Carroll

A Seal Called Andre, by Harry Goodridge and Lew Dietz (*Andre*)

Anne of Avonlea, by L. M. Montgomery

Anne of Green Gables, by L. M. Montgomery

Babe, the Gallant Pig or *The Sheep-Pig* (British title), by Dick King-Smith (*Babe*)

Baby-Sitters Club, by Ann M. Martin

Baker's Hawk, by Jack Bickham

Ballet Shoes, by Noel Streatfield

Bed-Knob and Broomstick, by Mary Norton (*Bedknobs and Broomsticks*)

Ben and Me, by Robert Lawson

Luke Baldwin's Vow, by Morley Callaghan (*Big Henry and the Polka-Dot Kid*)

Big Red, by Jim Kjelgaard

Black Beauty, by Felix Salten

Black Cauldron, by Lloyd Alexander

Black Stallion, by Walter Farley

Borrowers, by Mary Norton

Brave Little Toaster, by Thomas Disch

Bridge to Terabithia, by Katherine Paterson

Caddie Woodlawn, by Carol Ryrie Brink

Call of the Wild, by Jack London

Christmas at Candleshoe, by Michael Innes (*Candleshoe*)

Canterville Ghost, by Oscar Wilde

Captains Courageous, by Rudyard Kipling

Cat in the Hat, by Dr. Seuss

Charlotte's Web, by E. B. White

Chitty Chitty Bang Bang, by Ian Fleming

Hatchet, by Gary Paulsen (*Cry in the Wild*)

Doctor Dolittle, by Hugh Lofting

I Sing the Body Electric, by Ray Bradbury (*Electric Grandmother*)

Eloise, by Kay Thompson (*Eloise at the Plaza*)

Escape to Witch Mountain, by Alexander Key

Finding Buck McHenry, by Alfred Slote

Flight of Dragons, by Peter Dickinson

God and My Country, by McKinley Kantor (*Follow Me, Boys*)

Freaky Friday, by Mary Rodgers

The Westing Game, by Ellen Raskin (*Get a Clue!*)

Ghost of Thomas Kempe, by Penelope Lively

Girl of the Limberlost, by Gene Stratton-Porter

Basil of Baker Street, by Eve Titus (*Great Mouse Detective*)

Grinch Who Stole Christmas, by Dr. Seuss

Harriet the Spy, by Louise Fitzhugh

Harry Potter series, by J. K. Rowling

Heidi, by Joanna Spyri

The Hobbit, by J. R. R. Tolkien

Holes, by Louis Sachar

The Incredible Journey, by Sheila Burnford (*Homeward Bound*)

Indian in the Cupboard, by Lynne Reid Banks

The Iron Man, by Ted Hughes (*Iron Giant*)

The Lost Ones, by Ian Cameron (*Island at the Top of the World*)

James and the Giant Peach, by Roald Dahl

Jumanji, by Chris Van Allsburg

Jungle Book, by Rudyard Kipling

Sign of the Beaver, by Elizabeth George Speare (*Keeping the Promise*)

Kidnapped, by Robert Louis Stevenson

Jane of Lantern Hill, by L. M. Montgomery (*Lantern Hill*)

Lassie Come Home, by Eric Knight

Legend of Sleepy Hollow, by Washington Irving

The Light Princess, by George MacDonald

The Lion, the Witch and the Wardrobe, by C. S. Lewis

The Little Princess, by Frances Hodgson Burnett

Little Women, by Louisa May Alcott

Alias Madame Doubtfire, by Anne Fine (*Mrs. Doubtfire*)

Mary Poppins, by P. L. Travers

Matilda, by Roald Dahl

Mouse and the Motorcycle, by Beverly Cleary

My Dog Skip, by Willie Morris

My Friend Flicka, by Mary O'Hara

My Louisiana Sky, by Kimberly Willis Holt

My Side of the Mountain, by Jean Craighead George

National Velvet, by Enid Bagnold

Neverending Story, by Michael Ende

Pippi Longstocking, by Astrid Lindgren (*New Adventures of Pippi Longstocking*)

Old Yeller, by Fred Gipson

The Phantom Tollbooth, by Norton Juster

Polar Express, by Chris Van Allsburg

Pollyanna, by Eleanor Porter

The Prince and the Pauper, by Mark Twain

The Whipping Boy, by Sid Fleischman (*Prince Brat and the Whipping Boy*)

Prince Caspian and the Voyage of the Dawn Treader, by C. S. Lewis

Princess Diaries, by Meg Cabot

The Rescuers, by Margery Sharp

Ring of Bright Water, by Gavin Maxwell

Sarah, Plain and Tall, by Patricia MacLachlan

Mrs. Frisby and the Rats of NIMH, by Robert C. O'Brien (*Secret of NIMH*)

The Secret Garden, by Frances Hodgson Burnett

Shiloh, by Phyllis Reynolds Naylor

Shrek, by William Steig

Silver Chair, by C. S. Lewis

Sounder, by William Armstrong

Stuart Little, by E. B. White

Swiss Family Robinson, by Johann Wyss

Treasure Island, by Robert Louis Stevenson

Tuck Everlasting, by Natalie Babbitt

Twenty Thousand Leagues Under the Sea, by Jules Verne

Whale Rider, by Witi Ihimaera

Where the Red Fern Grows, by Wilson Rawls

White Fang, by Jack London

Charlie and the Chocolate Factory, by Roald Dahl (*Willy Wonka and the Chocolate Factory*)

The Wind in the Willows, by Kenneth Grahame

The Witches, by Roald Dahl

The Wizard of Oz, by L. Frank Baum

The Yearling, by Marjorie Kinnan Rawlings

ACTIVITY 2.9

Connecting with the Speaker

You Say/I Think Note Taking

GRADE LEVEL: 4–6

OBJECTIVES

- To listen and engage in effective note-taking skills (purposeful listening)
- To react to and connect with a speaker's message (creative listening)

MATERIALS

- Notebook paper (one sheet per student)
- Pencils

NCTE/IRA STANDARDS

3 Students apply a wide range of strategies to comprehend, interpret, evaluate, and appreciate texts. They draw on their prior experience, their interactions with other readers and writers, their knowledge of word meaning and of other texts, their word identification strategies, and their understanding of textual features (e.g., sound–letter correspondence, sentence structure, context, graphics).

10 Students whose first language is not English make use of their first language to develop competency in the English language arts and to develop understanding of content across the curriculum.

12 Students use spoken, written, and visual language to accomplish their own purposes (e.g., for learning, enjoyment, persuasion, and the exchange of information).

PROCEDURES

1. Invite a guest speaker to speak to the class. Possible guest speakers might include a parent to talk about his/her occupation, an area dentist to talk about dental hygiene, another teacher to talk about an area of personal interest, or a local politician to speak about ways that students can get involved in the community.
2. Before the speaker presents, have students fold a piece of notebook paper in half lengthwise. Label the left-hand column "You say . . ." and the right-hand column "I think . . ."
3. Tell students that they are to take notes on what the speaker is saying in the left-hand column. These notes should include the main points of the speech. Across from each main point, students are to react to what the speaker has said. For example, students can agree or disagree with the main point by writing, "I agree!" or "I disagree!" Students can also write questions in the right-hand column if they don't understand the speaker's message or tell how they connected with the speaker's point by briefly jotting down a time when they experienced the same thing or felt the same way. English language learners can be encouraged to transcribe notes in their first language.
4. After the speaker has presented, allow time for students to interact with the speaker by asking questions and sharing their ideas and feelings.

5. Collect the students' notes and assess their ability to listen to the speaker, take notes on the important points, and react to and connect with the speaker's message.

ASSESSMENT

To assess students' note-taking skills, you will need to take your own notes as the speaker is presenting. The number of main points will vary with the speech. Compare your own notes with those taken by each student and score them accordingly. For example, if the speech contained 10 main points and the student identified 8 of these, the student would receive a score of 8/10.

Scoring the students' ability to connect with the speaker is a bit more subjective. To do this, simply note whether the student reacted to each main point written in the left-hand column with an appropriate question or comment. A student who identified 8 of 10 main points and reacted to all of them would receive a score of 8/8.

You may use this assessment to decide which students need additional help with note taking and which require additional assistance interacting with a speaker's message. Teaching the class about graphic organizers may help them to take effective notes. Activating prior knowledge and asking questions before and during a speech will help them become active, engaged listeners.

INTEGRATING LANGUAGE ARTS ACROSS THE CURRICULUM

At the end of each content area class, encourage students to summarize verbally the main points of the lesson and react to the content. To guide students, you might have them summarize several main points of the lesson and ask corresponding questions to stimulate their reactions to the content.

HOME-SCHOOL CONNECTION

Encourage students to watch selected documentaries with their family and discuss them together to discover whether their views and feelings are similar or different.

REFERENCES

Barone, D. (1990). The written responses of young children: Beyond comprehension to story understanding. *The New Advocate, 3*, 49–56.

Berthoff, A. E. (1981). *The making of meaning.* Montclair, NJ: Boynton/Cook.

ACTIVITY 2.10

Recognizing and Identifying Propaganda Techniques in Advertising

GRADE LEVEL: **5–6**

OBJECTIVES

- To identify propaganda techniques (critical listening)
- To recognize propaganda in advertising (critical listening)

MATERIALS

- Videotape/DVD of 10 television commercials
- Television set
- VCR/DVD player
- Propaganda Techniques handout (one per student)
- Propaganda in Commercials Record Sheet (one per student)

NCTE/IRA STANDARDS

3 Students apply a wide range of strategies to comprehend, interpret, evaluate, and appreciate texts. They draw on their prior experience, their interactions with other readers and writers, their knowledge of word meaning and of other texts, their word identification strategies, and their understanding of textual features (e.g., sound–letter correspondence, sentence structure, context, graphics).

8 Students use a variety of technological and information resources (e.g., libraries, databases, computer networks, video) to gather and synthesize information and to create and communicate knowledge.

PROCEDURES

1. Ask students to identify their favorite commercials on television and tell why they enjoy them.
2. After discussing their favorite commercials, tell students that advertisers use propaganda techniques to persuade consumers to buy their products. Distribute the Propaganda Techniques handout (Exhibit 2.10.A) and discuss. Have students give examples of commercials that use these devices. Be prepared to supply examples if students are unable to do so. For more information on propaganda techniques and additional examples, visit http://sourcewatch.org/index.php?title=Propaganda_techniques.
3. Distribute the Propaganda in Commercials Record Sheet (Exhibit 2.10.B) to each student. Tell the class that you will play 10 videotaped TV commercials for them. They are to record the product that is advertised, at least one example of propaganda within each commercial, and the name of the corresponding propaganda technique.
4. Give students time to watch the commercials and complete the Propaganda in Commercials Record Sheet, and then collect their response sheets for evaluation. Replay the commercials and discuss them together.

ASSESSMENT

You may assess students' understanding of propaganda techniques and their ability to recognize the devices in advertising by evaluating their responses on the Propaganda in Commercials Record Sheet. If students correctly identify more than one technique per videotaped commercial, you might award extra credit points.

INTEGRATING LANGUAGE ARTS ACROSS THE CURRICULUM

In social studies, students can identify propaganda techniques in videotaped political speeches. In science, small groups of students can apply their understanding of propaganda techniques by creating original commercials for inventions of the past. The students can present their commercials in class, and peers can identify the propaganda technique(s) used.

HOME-SCHOOL CONNECTION

Ask students to discuss what they have learned about media propaganda with their families. Encourage them to share the Propaganda Techniques handout. As a family, they can look for other examples of propaganda techniques.

REFERENCES

Tompkins, G. (2005). *Language arts patterns of practice* (6th ed.). Upper Saddle River, NJ: Merrill/Prentice Hall.

Source Watch: A Project of the Center for Media and Democracy. *Propaganda techniques.* Retrieved September 18, 2005, from www.sourcewatch.org/index.php?title=Propaganda_techniques.

EXHIBIT **2.10.A**

Propaganda Techniques

1. **Bandwagon:** the advertiser suggests that everyone is using the product, and so should you. ***Example:*** "*2 out of 3* dentists recommend our toothbrush over others."

2. **Card stacking:** the advertiser presents only the favorable effects of the product and ignores the unfavorable effects. ***Example:*** "Evergreen cigarettes *smell like a fresh pine forest.*"

3. **Double speak:** the advertiser presents two contradictory beliefs at the same time. ***Example:*** "*Genuine imitation leather* furniture is half price this week at Fake Furniture Outlet."

4. **Euphemism:** the advertiser uses less harsh words to describe something. ***Example:*** "If your loved one has suffered a *fatal injury*, call our law firm immediately."

5. **Fear:** the advertiser evokes fear within the buyers to get them to purchase the product. ***Example:*** "You can't even see the *millions of deadly germs living on your countertop.* GermFree kills them FAST!"

6. **Glittering generalities:** the advertiser connects to a favorable concept like "motherhood" or "patriotism." ***Example:*** Drive *the American way.* Buy a 2005 Franta truck today."

7. **Name calling:** the advertiser says negative things about another product. ***Example:*** "Why *struggle with inferior plastic wrap like Sticky Wrap?* Wrap Ease is a no-hassle way to store food items."

8. **Plain folk:** the advertiser suggests that the product is preferred by common, everyday kind of people like you. ***Example:*** The advertiser shows *ordinary people* gathered at a backyard barbecue *eating a certain brand of hot dog.*

9. **Rewards:** the advertiser offers a reward for buying the product. ***Example:*** "Get a *$3,000 rebate* today when you buy our car. Offer ends at the end of the month."

10. **Snob appeal:** the advertiser suggests that buyers will become members of an exclusive group if they buy the product. ***Example:*** The advertiser shows *high-society people* at a fancy social gathering *eating a certain brand of butter.*

11. **Testimonial:** the advertiser uses a celebrity to sell a product. ***Example:*** *Fit Fran* says that she *eats Yummy Yogurt* every day.

12. **Transfer:** the advertiser suggests that the buyer will acquire the qualities of the person in the commercial. ***Example:*** The advertiser shows *a beautiful, well-known actress using* a certain kind of *skin cream.*

Propaganda in Commercials

Record Sheet

Name ______________________________ Date ____________

TYPE OF PRODUCT ADVERTISED	EXAMPLE OF PROPAGANDA USED	NAME OF PROPAGANDA TECHNIQUE
1.		
2.		
3.		
4.		
5.		
6.		
7.		
8.		
9.		
10.		

Score: ___________ /30

SPEAKING

Using Oral Language in Authentic Contexts

INTRODUCTION

In years past, it was assumed that the quiet classroom was most conducive to learning. Consequently, students' desks were most frequently aligned in neat and orderly rows facing the teacher at the front of the classroom. The teacher assumed the role of "director of classroom talk," and students seldom spoke unless called upon to answer a question posed by the teacher. Classroom talk primarily consisted of the teacher's voice and students answering sporadic questions throughout the lesson. Students rarely spoke to each other in the classroom; interactive conversation was restricted to the schoolyard at recess.

The "I talk and you listen" mentality appeared to be a most effective behavior management tool, but researchers soon discovered that interactive classroom conversation is a vital component of learning in all curricular areas (Cazden, 1988; Heath, 1983; Wells & Chang-Wells, 1992).

Educators now understand the importance of providing numerous opportunities for language interactions and fostering a language-rich instructional environment in which student voices are central to the learning process (Norton, 2004). Today, classrooms are alive with student talk for interactive, authentic, and meaningful purposes. Straight rows of desks have been converted into group clusters that afford students opportunities to interact and learn together *and* from each other. The teacher no longer "directs" the classroom talk but "facilitates" its occurrence and frequency.

Tompkins (2002) identifies two kinds of talk found in classrooms, which are not mutually exclusive. One type, *aesthetic talk*, is used mainly for the purpose of enjoyment. Examples of classroom activities that employ aesthetic talk include telling stories, reading aloud from literary texts and scripts, choral reading of poetry, discussions of literature, and the use of creative dramatics. The second kind, *efferent talk*, is used primarily to inform and enrich understanding. Instructional conversations, questioning, discussing K-W-L charts, sharing, book talks, content area oral reports, interviews, and debates are a few examples of this second type of classroom talk. Undoubtedly, elementary teachers need to incorporate both kinds of talk every day, since effective oral communication is a valuable life skill.

The activities in this chapter are designed to provide students with opportunities to use oral language in an assortment of authentic contexts and for a variety of meaningful purposes. Primary students will practice reciting poetry using a variety of choral speaking arrangements, retell favorite stories through the use of portable flannel boards, and explore bilingual text while learning to count in both Spanish and English. Intermediate grade level students will participate in a readers' theater presentation and research discussion, retell stories through the use of story pyramids, interview to learn about the past, and use language to reach consensus within a group.

Classroom Vignette

It's a typical Wednesday morning in Mr. Sanchez's second grade classroom. The day begins with morning meeting and opening activities, which include calendar, weather, current events, sharing, and choral reading. Anna begins by telling the class today's date and writing it neatly on the chalkboard. Jim announces the day's weather forecast, records the predicted high temperature on the class weather graph, and calculates the number of days in May that exceeded a temperature of 70 degrees. Tyler and Tim orally share current events taken from the previous night's local newspaper before answering student questions and placing the articles on the Current Events bulletin board located at the side of the classroom. Jenny begins the morning sharing session by telling about her family's plans to go camping in a national park over the upcoming weekend. She answers questions posed to her by Casey and Shawn, and then Jon shares his second place soccer trophy. Following sharing, the class chorally reads a short humorous poem entitled, "The Hamster's on Vacation," which leaves everyone, including Mr. Sanchez, in laughter.

DISCUSSION QUESTIONS

1. How is talk used in Mr. Sanchez's classroom?
2. How is talk used to promote an interactive community of learners?
3. Do you think children should assume the role of "question-asker" at the elementary level? Explain why or why not.
4. What might the students gain instructionally from the choral reading activity?
5. What sort of talk activities do you remember from your elementary school days? Did your teachers encourage a language-rich classroom environment? Explain why or why not.

References

Cazden, C. (1988). *Classroom discourse: The language of teaching and learning.* Portsmouth, NH: Heinemann.

Heath, S. (1983). Research currents: A lot of talk about nothing. *Language Arts,* 60, 999–1007.

Norton, D. (2004). *The effective teaching of language arts* (6th ed.). Upper Saddle River, NJ: Pearson.

Tompkins, G. (2002). *Language arts: Content and teaching strategies* (5th ed.). Upper Saddle River, NJ: Pearson.

Wells, G., & Chang-Wells, G. (1992). *Constructing knowledge together: Classrooms as centers of inquiry and literacy.* Portsmouth, NH: Heinemann.

Enjoying Creative Dramatics

We're Going on a Bear Hunt

GRADE LEVEL: **K–1**

OBJECTIVE

- To use spoken, written, and visual language for learning and enjoyment

MATERIALS

- One copy of *We're Going on a Bear Hunt*, by Michael Rosen (See the Children's Literature section at the end of this activity for additional titles.)
- Word cards for the repetitive verse in the story
- Character drawings on poster board hangers (Characters are drawn on poster board and attached with yarn in the top two corners, so students can hang them around their necks.)
- *We're Going on a Bear Hunt* Journal sheet (one per student)
- Family letter (one per student)

NCTE/IRA STANDARD

12 Students use spoken, written, and visual language to accomplish their own purposes (e.g., for learning, enjoyment, persuasion, and the exchange of information).

PROCEDURES

1. For background information and additional information about creative dramatics, see the Resources for Creative Dramatics and the Internet Resources lists at the end of the activity.
2. Read *We're Going on a Bear Hunt* aloud to students.
3. Read the book again, and during the second reading, ask students to participate by saying the repetitive verse in the story. Gestures can be used to assist English language learners.

   We're going on a bear hunt.
   We're going to catch a big one.
   What a beautiful day!
   We're not scared.

4. Have students choose word cards for each word in the repetitive verse. On the third reading, ask students with word cards to come to the front of the room when the other students say their word. The students in the front of the room "write" out the repetitive verse. After the verse is complete for the first time in the story, the students take their seats. They repeat this process each time the repetitive verse is read.

5. Ask for volunteers to choose characters from the story and hang the appropriate poster board drawing around their neck. During the fourth reading of the story, have students with poster board drawings of the characters come to the front of the room. These students role-play the story as the teacher reads it and say the repetitive verse at the appropriate times. Students can take turns playing the characters in the story for subsequent readings. Fluent readers could assist with the repeated readings of the story.
6. Students who need additional readings of the story in order to learn the repetitive verse could listen to the story on tape before or after the first class reading. Struggling readers and English language learners could benefit from prompts or cues so that they know when to bring their word card to the front of the room.

ASSESSMENT

Creative drama allows teachers an opportunity to observe students in the learning process and to utilize informal methods of authentic assessment, such as anecdotal records. In this lesson, anecdotal records would focus on students' use of spoken, written, and visual language.

INTEGRATING LANGUAGE ARTS ACROSS THE CURRICULUM

To maintain a "bear" theme and integrate math-related calendar concepts, you may read *How Do You Say It Today, Jesse Bear?* by Nancy Carlstrom. You may have students brainstorm the kinds of things that are fun to do in each of the months, while you document the monthly activities on chart paper. Each student chooses a favorite month and activity. In small groups, children take turns standing in front of the group and repeating, "In (name of month) I like to. . . ." Rather than finishing the sentence, the student dramatizes the activity. The other students in the group must guess what the activity is. The students take turns until all have had an opportunity to dramatize their favorite activity. Other Jesse Bear books that would be appropriate for creative dramatics include *Let's Count It Out, Jesse Bear* and *It's About Time, Jesse Bear: And Other Rhymes.*

HOME-SCHOOL CONNECTION

You can pack a literacy bag with *We're Going on a Bear Hunt,* the word cards, the poster board drawings, and the *We're Going on a Bear Hunt* Journal sheet (Exhibit 3.1.A). Students can take turns taking the bag home to share with family members. Parents, guardians, and siblings can read the book, learn the repetitive verse, and role-play the story. A family member can write a few sentences on the *We're Going on a Bear Hunt* Journal sheet to document the family's reactions to the book and activities. A note to family members (Exhibit 3.1.B) can be included in the literacy bag.

EXHIBIT **3.1.A**

We're Going on a Bear Hunt *Journal*

Name of child and family members:

Date of experience:

How did you use the *We're Going on a Bear Hunt* book and activities?

What did you and your child enjoy most about the experience?

Comments and/or questions:

EXHIBIT **3.1.B**

Dear Family Members,

Our class has been reading and enjoying *We're Going on a Bear Hunt*, by Michael Rosen. Enclosed you will find the book, word cards for the repetitive verse in the story, character drawings on poster board hangers, and the *We're Going on a Bear Hunt* Journal. You and/or your child will enjoy reading the story aloud. Family members can assist in writing out the repetitive verse with the word cards and reciting it during the reading of the story. Wearing the character drawings and role-playing the story can also be great fun. After your family has enjoyed the book and activities, please write a few sentences in the *We're Going on a Bear Hunt* Journal to describe your experiences. Please return the journal page to school, along with the other materials.

Thank you for helping your child experience the love of reading.

Sincerely,

CHILDREN'S LITERATURE

Carlstrom, N. (1990). *It's about time, Jesse Bear: And other rhymes.* Macmillan.

Carlstrom, N. (1992). *How do you say it today, Jesse Bear?* Scholastic.

Carlstrom, N. (2001). *Let's count it out, Jesse Bear.* Scholastic.

Rosen, M. (1989). *We're going on a bear hunt.* New York: Aladdin.

RESOURCES FOR CREATIVE DRAMATICS

Bissinger, K., & Renfro, N. (1990). *Leap into learning: Teaching K–7 curriculum through creative dramatics and dance.* Kristen Bissinger.

Heald, C. (2002). *Role-play activities (Early years activity chest).* Scholastic.

Lombardo, M. (2004). *Rhymes, writing, and role-play: Quick and easy lessons for beginning readers.* Linworth.

Strong, D., & Goldstein, R. (1998). *Once upon a stage: Story-based creative dramatics with young children.* Living the Good News, Inc.

INTERNET RESOURCES

KMR Scripts. (1998). Creative dramatics: General guidelines (Grades 1–5). Retrieved August 20, 2006, from www.kmrscripts.com/cdguide.html#CREATIVE%20DRAMATICS.

Lamb, A., & Johnson, L. (2002). Skits, plays and scripts. Retrieved August 20, 2006, from www.42explore.com/skits&plays.htm.

Pro Teacher (1998–2005). Drama. Retrieved August 20, 2006, from www.proteacher.com/080010.shtml.

ACTIVITY 3.2

Bugs for Lunch

(Insectos para el almuerzo)

GRADE LEVEL: **1–2**

OBJECTIVES

- To develop an understanding of and respect for diversity in language
- To use spoken language ~~to count to 10 in Spanish~~

MATERIALS

- One copy of *Bugs for Lunch (Insectos para el almuerzo)* by Margery Facklam (2002, Berkeley, CA: Ten Speed Press) (For suggestions of bilingual versions of other children's books, see the "Bilingual and Multilingual Versions of Children's Picture Books" section at the end of Activity 7.3 in Chapter 7.)
- Chart paper divided into three columns with the numerals 1 through 10 printed down the first column, the corresponding English number words in the middle column, and the corresponding Spanish number words in the third column

NCTE/IRA STANDARDS

9 Students develop an understanding of and respect for diversity in language use, patterns, and dialects across cultures, ethnic groups, geographic regions, and social roles.

10 Students whose first language is not English make use of their first language to develop competency in the English language arts and to develop understanding of content across the curriculum.

PROCEDURES

1. If you do not speak Spanish, invite a Spanish-speaking student or guest to help with the reading of the book. Persons to consider are English language learners in the class or the language support teacher.
2. Introduce the book *Bugs for Lunch (Insectos para el almuerzo)* by reading the title in English and Spanish. Discuss the book as a bilingual edition by showing the children that each page has both English and Spanish text.
3. Read the book, if necessary alternating with the person who is reading the Spanish parts. Track the words of the text as it is read aloud.
4. Following the reading of the book and discussion of the book's content, draw students' attention to the English–Spanish number word chart. Have the children count from 1 to 10 in English as you point to each numeral.
5. Draw students' attention to the corresponding English number words and have them say the words aloud together.
6. Point to each Spanish number word and have students repeat them after you. Practice saying the words together several times.
7. As a review, say either an English number word or a Spanish number word and have a volunteer find the word on the chart and say it aloud.

8. For additional practice with the Spanish number words, students can count aloud a certain number of items, such as pencils or magnets, using the Spanish words.

ASSESSMENT

You may observe students throughout the activity and record anecdotal notes related to student performance. Note which students participated and which did not. Consider pairing a Spanish-speaking student with an English-speaking student for additional practice counting in both languages.

INTEGRATING LANGUAGE ARTS ACROSS THE CURRICULUM

Label objects in the classroom, such as the door, chalkboard, bookcase, and so forth with both the English and Spanish words. Encourage use of the Spanish word by English-speaking students and use of the English word by Spanish-speaking students. As the class encounters words from other cultures in their stories, draw attention to these words.

HOME-SCHOOL CONNECTION

Have children bring in small objects from home, such as paper clips, pencils, magnets, and crayons, to share with the class. Each child may bring up to 10 of the same object. English-speaking students share their items and count them in Spanish, while Spanish-speaking students count in English. Provide support as needed.

REFERENCES

ALA Bilingual Books for Children Book List. Retrieved October 7, 2005. from www.ala.org/ala/alsc/alscresources/booklists/bilingualbooks.htm.

Facklam, M. (2002). *Bugs for lunch/Insectos para el almuerzo.* Berkeley, CA: Ten Speed Press.

Flannel Board Scenes

Combining Oral Language with Artistic Expression

GRADE LEVEL: **2–3**

OBJECTIVE

- To retell a scene accurately from a picture book, using a personal flannel board and characters

MATERIALS

- Sheets of flannel in a variety of colors
- Heavy-weight interfacing
- Flannel board
- Scissors (one pair per student)
- Colored pencils or markers
- Two-pocket folders (one per student or per small group)
- A selection of picture books (For a list of picture books suitable for flannel board retelling, see the list at the end of the activity.)
- Checklist for Flannel Board Retelling (one per student)

NCTE/IRA STANDARDS

10 Students whose first language is not English make use of their first language to develop competency in the English language arts and to develop understanding of content across the curriculum.

12 Students use spoken, written, and visual language to accomplish their own purposes (e.g., for learning, enjoyment, persuasion, and the exchange of information).

PROCEDURES

1. Choose a picture book suitable for retelling and make flannel board characters out of flannel or interfacing. Read the book aloud to students. Show students the flannel board characters and choose volunteers to place the characters on the flannel board as you retell the story.
2. Place students in groups of three or four. Have them choose and read a picture book. Picture books with few characters and simple plots work best for story retellings. Ask students to choose either a scene or the entire book for retelling. Students draw the characters and props on felt or trace them by placing the interfacing on the book illustrations. Once the characters and props are drawn, students cut them out using scissors. For more information on creating flannel boards, see the Flannel Board Resources and Internet Resources sections at the end of this activity.
3. Demonstrate to students how to make a personal flannel board by gluing a sheet of felt to the outside of a two-pocket folder. The flannel board characters and props can be stored in the folder's inside pockets. Each student can make his or her own personal flannel board, or students can create one per group.
4. Students then choose who will play each of the parts. Give them an opportunity to rehearse the retelling of the scene so that speaking parts

are fluent and students can decide how to move characters and props to and from the flannel board.

5. Have each group present their flannel board retelling to the class.
6. Placing students in mixed-ability groups for this activity assures that all students will find success with some aspect of the project (reading, writing, drawing and cutting, or retelling). English language learners can retell their parts in their first language.

ASSESSMENT

You may use the Checklist for Flannel Board Retelling (Exhibit 3.3.A) to assess students' oral language skills during the retellings. The checklist can become part of the child's language arts portfolio.

INTEGRATING LANGUAGE ARTS ACROSS THE CURRICULUM

You may use biographies for flannel board retellings in the social studies classroom to help children learn about famous people in history. Picture books about notable people include

- *Chico* (O'Connor, 2005), the story of the young life of Sandra Day O'Connor, the first female United States Supreme Court Justice
- *John, Paul, George, & Ben* (Smith, 2006), the story of America's Founding Fathers
- *They Called Her Molly Pitcher* (Rockwell, 2002), the tale of a woman who fetched water for soldiers in battle
- *A Picture Book of George Washington* (Adler, 1989), about America's first president

HOME-SCHOOL CONNECTION

Students can take turns taking a picture book home to read to family members. After the reading, students can use the flannel board characters to retell the story using their personal flannel board. Family members can take turns playing the parts of the characters. Extra felt could be made available to students who wish to make their own set of flannel board figures for this book or another book of their choice.

CHILDREN'S LITERATURE SUITABLE FOR FLANNEL BOARD RETELLING

Adler, D. (1989). *A picture book of George Washington.* Scholastic.

Barrett, J. (1982). *Cloudy with a chance of meatballs.* Aladdin.

Brown, A. (1997). *Alice Ramsey's grand adventure.* Houghton Mifflin.

Carle, E. (1994). *The very hungry caterpillar.* Scholastic.

Carle, E. (2004). *Mister seahorse.* Philomel.

Guarino, D. (1997). *Is your mama a llama?* Scholastic.

Keats, E. (1999). *Over in the meadow.* Puffin.

Lionni, L. (1995). *A busy year.* David McKay.

Littledale, F. (1989). *The magic fish.* Scholastic.

Lobel, A. (1979). *Frog and Toad are friends.* HarperCollins.

O'Connor, S. (2005). *Chico.* New York: Dutton.

Piper, W. (1978). *The little engine that could.* Grosset and Dunlap.
Numeroff, L. (1996). *If you give a mouse a cookie.* HarperCollins.
Rockwell, A. (2002). *They called her Molly Pitcher.* Random House.
Smith, L. (2006). *John, Paul, George, & Ben.* New York: Hyperion.
Trivizas, E. (1997). *The three little wolves and the big bad pig.* Aladdin.

FLANNEL BOARD RESOURCES

Bay, J. (1995). *Treasury of flannelboard stories.* Upstart Library Promotionals.
Hicks, D., & Mahaffey, S. (1996). *Flannelboard classic tales.* American Library Association Editions.
Krepelin, E., & Smith, B. (1995). *Ready-to-use flannel board stories, figures, and activities for ESL children.* Center for Applied Research in Education.
Sierra, J. (1997). *The flannelboard storytelling book.* H. W. Wilson.
Spann, M. (1987). *Alpha stories: Learning the alphabet through flannelboard stories.* First Teacher Books.
Wilmes, D., & Wilmes, L. (1994). *Felt board fun.* Gryphon House.

INTERNET RESOURCES

About, Inc. (2006). How to make a flannel board. Retrieved August 19, 2006, from http://babyparenting.about.com/od/activitiesandplay/a/flannelboard.htm.
Pratt, B. (2000–2003). Flannel board stories & instructions, songs and rhymes for children. Retrieved August 19, 2006, from www.fastq.com/%7Ejbpratt/education/mypages/flannelstories.html.
Rose, A. (2000). What is a flannel board? Retrieved August 19, 2006, from http://education.wlsc.edu/courses/rose/385/visualdesign/w3s7.html.
Storytime Felts. Feltboardstories.com. Retrieved August 19, 2006, from www.feltboardstories.com/index.html.
The Three Bears. Retrieved on August 19, 2006, from www.hubbardscupboard.org/the_three_bears.html.
Wisconsin Literacy Education and Reading Network Source. Retrieved on August 19, 2006, from http://wilearns.state.wi.us/apps/Default.asp?cid=608.

EXHIBIT **3.3.A**

Checklist for Flannel Board Retelling

Name ______________________________ Date ______________

1.	Student speaks clearly and loudly.	YES	NO
2.	Student speaks with expression.	YES	NO
3.	Student demonstrates an understanding of taking turns during a retelling.	YES	NO
4.	Student coordinates speaking with the placement of flannel board pieces.	YES	NO
5.	Student's flannel board pieces adequately depict details in the retelling.	YES	NO
6.	Student retells the story in the correct sequence and includes the important elements.	YES	NO

Teacher comments: ______________________________

ACTIVITY 3.4

Exploring Choral Speaking

The Hamster's on Vacation

GRADE LEVEL: **3–4**

OBJECTIVE

- To utilize varied choral speaking arrangements to communicate effectively (speaking expressively, clearly, and at the right volume and pace)

MATERIALS

- "The Hamster's on Vacation" handout (one per student) (For additional books of children's poetry, see the list at the end of the activity.)
- Choral Speaking Self-Evaluation Checklist (one per student)

NCTE/IRA STANDARD

4 Students adjust their use of spoken, written, and visual language (e.g., conventions, style, vocabulary) to communicate effectively with a variety of audiences and for different purposes.

PROCEDURES

1. Duplicate the poem "The Hamster's on Vacation" (Exhibit 3.4.A) and distribute to students.
2. Read the poem aloud and have students silently follow along as you read.
3. Divide the class into pairs and have them practice reading the poem to each other.
4. After sufficient practice, reassemble the students as a class and read the poem using different choral speaking arrangements. The arrangements are as follows:
   - Antiphonal arrangement: divide the class into two groups, such as boys and girls or high voices and low voices, and alternate the reading of stanzas by group.
   - Echo arrangement: a leader reads each line and the group echoes it back.
   - Line-a-child arrangement: each student reads a separate line.
   - Cumulative arrangement: one child begins by reading a line, a second reader joins in to read the next line, then a third reader joins in to read the next line, and so on.
   - Unison arrangement: the whole class reads the poem together at the same time.
   - Choral singing arrangement: sing the poem to the tune of "Row, Row, Row Your Boat."

   For more information on choral speaking, see the Internet Resources section at the end of this activity.
5. Have students discuss which arrangement works best for reading the poem. Ask each student to tell which is his/her favorite arrangement and why.

6. Ask students to bring in their favorite poems for the class to perform. Include the choral reading of a poem as part of the class's morning opening activities each day.
7. Older students might enjoy writing original poems about the class pet or their own pet for the class to perform. Small groups of students could perform the poems for another class. Less capable students might practice repeated readings of the poem with a more capable buddy reader. Struggling readers and English language learners would benefit from listening to an audio recording of the poem by an experienced, fluent reader as they practice reading the lines.

ASSESSMENT

Self-evaluation is an essential part of the assessment process. Audiotape students performing the poem using the six choral speaking arrangements and have them critically listen to it to assess the effectiveness of their communication skills. Ask students to evaluate themselves using the Choral Speaking Self-Evaluation Checklist (Exhibit 3.4.B), and then provide students with your own feedback.

INTEGRATING LANGUAGE ARTS ACROSS THE CURRICULUM

Students can practice the choral speaking arrangements in content areas by using them while reading aloud in class. Students can also be encouraged to create and perform found poems (poetry created from another text source). Found poetry is easy to write, because it has no rhythm or rhyme. Students may use their content area textbooks or related text, such as children's literature or newspaper and magazine articles, to locate material for found poems.

HOME–SCHOOL CONNECTION

Students may share the poem at home. Encourage them to try varied choral speaking arrangements with the members of their family. Each family member could draw a picture of the family pet on vacation in a different location. Students could bring the family pictures to school and tell the class about the pictures their family members drew.

CHILDREN'S POETRY

Bagert, B. (2000). *Elephant games: And other playful poems to perform.* Boyds Mills Press.

Bagert, B. (2002). *Giant children.* Dial Books for Young Readers.

Bagert, B. (2004). *The gooch machine: Poems for young people to perform.* Boyds Mills Press.

Bates, K. (2003). *America the beautiful.* G. P. Putnam's Sons.

Dotlich, R. (2001). *When riddles come rumbling: Poems to ponder.* Boyds Mills Press.

Fleischman, P. (1992). *Joyful noise: Poems for two voices.* HarperCollins Juvenile Books.

Florian, D. (1998). *Beast feast: Poems.* Voyager Books.

Frost, R. (1994). *A swinger of birches: Poems of Robert Frost for young people.* Stemmer House Publishing.

Hall, D. (2001). *The Oxford illustrated book of American children's poems.* Oxford University Press.

Holbrook, S. (2002). *Wham! It's a poetry jam: Discovering performance poetry.* Boyds Mills Press.

Kiesler, K. (2001). *Toasting marshmallows: Camping poems.* Clarion Books.

Lansky, B. (2004). *Mary had a little jam and other silly rhymes.* Meadowbrook.

Lear, E. (1997). *The owl and the pussycat.* Philomel Books.

Lee, D. (2001). *Alligator pie.* Key Porter Books.

Mitchell, S. (2003). *The wishing bone and other poems.* Candlewick Press.

Paolilli, P. (2001). *Silver seeds: A book of nature poems.* Viking Children's Press.

Prelutsky, J. (1984). *The new kid on the block.* Greenwillow.

Prelutsky, J. (1990). *Something big has been here.* William Morrow.

Prelutsky, J. (1993). *The dragons are singing tonight.* Greenwillow.

Prelutsky, J. (1999). *The gargoyle on the roof.* Greenwillow.

Prelutsky, J. (2000). *It's raining pigs and noodles.* Greenwillow.

Prelutsky, J. (2001). *Ogre's awful day.* Greenwillow.

Prelutsky, J. (2002). *The frog wore red suspenders.* Greenwillow.

Prelutsky, J., & Lobel, A. (2000). *The Random House book of poetry.* Random House Books for Young Readers.

Schiller, P. (2002). *The complete book of rhymes, songs, poems, fingerplays, and chants: Over 700 selections.* Gryphon House.

Silverstein, S. (1974). *Where the sidewalk ends.* Harper & Row.

Silverstein, S. (1981). *A light in the attic.* Harper & Row.

Silverstein, S. (1996). *Falling up.* HarperCollins.

Stevenson, R. (1999). *A child's garden of verses.* Simon & Schuster.

Yolen, J. (2003). *Color me a rhyme: Nature poems for young people.* Boyds Mills Press.

INTERNET RESOURCES

Choral speaking for children. Retrieved August 17, 2006, from http://falcon.jmu.edu/~ramseyil/choralpage.htm.

International Reading Association. (1992). Reading and young children: A practical guide for childcare providers. Retrieved August 17, 2006, from www.reading.org/publications/bbv/videos/v373/.

Walker, H., & Walker, L. Choral speaking script for young and older levels. Retrieved August 17, 2006, from www.scriptsforschools.com/29.html.

REFERENCES

Cazden, C. (1988). *Classroom discourse: The language of teaching and learning.* Portsmouth, NH: Heinemann.

Heath, S. (1983). Research currents: A lot of talk about nothing. *Language Arts,* 60, 999–1007.

National Standards for the English Language Arts. Retrieved May 16, 2004, from www.reading.org/advocacy/elastandards/standards.

Norton, D. (2004). *The effective teaching of language arts* (6th ed.). Upper Saddle River, NJ: Merrill/Prentice Hall.

Tompkins, G. (2002). *Language arts: Content and teaching strategies* (5th ed.). Upper Saddle River, NJ: Merrill/Prentice Hall.

Wells, G., & Chang-Wells, G. (1992). *Constructing knowledge together: Classrooms as centers of inquiry and literacy.* Portsmouth, NH: Heinemann.

The Hamster's on Vacation

The hamster's on vacation.
He's not been seen all day.
The hamster's on vacation.
Perhaps he's gone to stay.

He could be on an ocean cruise,
aboard a sailing ship.
Lying right beside the pool
before he takes a dip.

He could be hiking in the hills,
Climbing mountains high,
Or parasailing overhead
Across the pale blue sky.

He could have gone to Disneyland.
He could have traveled west.
After riding all the rides
He'll surely need a rest!

Perhaps he's swimming coral reefs
Dressed in furry scuba gear
among the brightly colored fish.
Oh, we wish that he were here!

The hamster's on vacation.
The whole class sobbed and cried,
until I opened my lunch bag
and found him there inside!

EXHIBIT **3.4.B**

Choral Speaking Self-Evaluation Checklist

Name ______________________________ Date ______________

Directions: Evaluate yourself honestly using the checklist below.

1. Did I cooperate with my partner while practicing?	YES	NO
2. Did I read with expression?	YES	NO
3. Did I vary the volume of my voice?	YES	NO
4. Did I pause and stop at the right places?	YES	NO
5. Did I keep pace with the other readers?	YES	NO
6. Did I speak clearly, so my words could be understood?	YES	NO
7. Did I try at least two different choral speaking arrangements?	YES	NO

8. I do a good job on

____

____

____

____

____

____

____

9. I need to work on

____

____

____

____

____

____

____

Story Pyramid Retellings

GRADE LEVEL: **3–4**

OBJECTIVE

- To retell a story using the story pyramid as a prompt to demonstrate understanding of story elements, using a good voice quality and making eye contact with the audience

MATERIALS

- A selection of picture books and chapter books
- One copy of *My Great Aunt Arizona*, by Gloria Houston (The Children's Literature section lists another suggested title for this activity.)
- Sample Story Pyramid for *My Great Aunt Arizona* (one per student)
- Story Pyramid handout (one per student)
- Story Pyramid Evaluation Rubric (one per student)

NCTE/IRA STANDARD

12 Students use spoken, written, and visual language to accomplish their own purposes (e.g., for learning, enjoyment, persuasion, and the exchange of information).

PROCEDURES

1. Ask students each to choose a picture book or chapter book he/she would like to read.
2. Review story elements such as character, setting, problem, main events, and solution.
3. Read *My Great Aunt Arizona* and provide each student with the Sample Story Pyramid for the book (Exhibit 3.5.A). For additional ideas for story retellings, see the Internet Resources section at the end of this activity. Discuss the descriptions of each of the story elements included in the story pyramid.
4. Have each student read the book he/she chose and complete a story pyramid for the book by recording information on the Story Pyramid handout (Exhibit 3.5.B), including:
   - Naming the main character
   - Describing the character in two words
   - Describing the setting in three words
   - Stating the problem in four words
   - Describing a significant event in five words
   - Naming a second significant event in six words
   - Describing a third significant event in seven words
   - Presenting the solution in eight words
5. In small groups, ask students to take turns retelling their stories, using their story pyramids as prompts.

6. Struggling readers may self-select a picture book appropriate for their reading level, or you or a classmate might read a book aloud to them. Students who have difficulty with writing or spelling may dictate their story pyramid entries for a classmate or teacher to transcribe. These students may also need additional cues in order to create story pyramid entries. Struggling readers and English language learners may wish to add picture clues to their story pyramid as additional prompts for story retelling. Extra rehearsals of the retelling may help these students gain confidence before they retell their story to a small group.

ASSESSMENT

You may use the Story Pyramid Evaluation Rubric (Exhibit 3.5.C) to guide the assessment process for the story pyramids. Inclusion of story elements and the quality of the retelling are aspects of the assessment.

INTEGRATING LANGUAGE ARTS ACROSS THE CURRICULUM

You may encourage students to choose biographies or nonfiction books that emphasize significant problems and events in social studies or science. For example, *Fireboat: The Heroic Adventures of the John J. Harvey*, by Maira Kalman, is the story of a 1930s fireboat that was called back into service to fight fires during the September 11, 2001, tragedy. Students can use this piece of literature for their story pyramid, including the main character, setting, problem, and main events of that day. Current literature makes for interesting retellings for several reasons. Most students in the class will be unfamiliar with newer publications such as this, and although they will certainly know about the events of September 11, they may not be knowledgeable about these kinds of human interest stories.

HOME–SCHOOL CONNECTION

Students can practice their retelling at home before performing it at school. If students are given an extra copy of the rubric to take home, family members could assist them in evaluating their performance before they present it at school.

CHILDREN'S LITERATURE

Houston, G. (1992). *My great Aunt Arizona.* HarperCollins.

Kalman, M. (2002). *Fireboat: The heroic adventures of the John J. Harvey.* G. P. Putnam's Sons.

INTERNET RESOURCES

ArtsEdge. (2006). Every picture tells a story. Retrieved August 20, 2006, from http://artsedge.kennedy-center.org/content/2471/.

ArtsEdge. (2006). Creating a wall story. Retrieved August 20, 2006, from http://artsedge.kennedy-center.org/content/2286/.

Haynes, J. (1998–2004). Who's inside the mitten? Retrieved August 20, 2006, from www.everythingesl.net/lessons/janbrett_mitten.php.

Northwest Regional Educational Laboratories. (2001). Retelling stories boosts kids' understanding. Retrieved August 20, 2006, from www.nwrel.org/comm/monthly/retelling.html.

Northwest Regional Educational Laboratories. (2003). The power of story retellings. Retrieved August 20, 2006, from www.nwrel.org/learns/tutor/spr2003/spr2003.html.

Story Arts. (2000). Storytelling in the classroom: Retelling folktales. Retrieved August 20, 2006, from www.storyarts.org/classroom/retelling/index.html.

Thirteen Ed Online. (2006). Cinderella stories. Retrieved August 20, 2006, from www.thirteen.org/edonline/lessons/cinderella/b.html.

Literature review: Story retelling. (2003). Retrieved August 20, 2006, from www.bridgew.edu/Library/CAGS_Projects/TPALINGO/web%20page/srlitrev.htm.

Sample Story Pyramid for My Great Aunt Arizona

by Gloria Houston

My Great Aunt Arizona

(title of story)

Arizona

(name of main character)

determined imaginative

(two words describing the main character)

Blue Ridge Mountains

(three words describing the setting)

dreamed of faraway places

(four words stating the problem)

papa got a new wife

(five words describing one main event)

Arizona taught in a one-room school

(six words describing a second main event)

Arizona got married and had a baby

(seven words describing a third main event)

Arizona loved teaching and dreamed of faraway places

(eight words presenting the solution to the problem)

EXHIBIT **3.5.B**

Story Pyramid

Name ______________________________ Date ____________

____

(title of story)

____

(name of main character)

______ ______

(two words describing the main character)

______ ______ ______

(three words describing the setting)

______ ______ ______ ______

(four words stating the problem)

______ ______ ______ ______ ______

(five words describing one main event)

______ ______ ______ ______ ______ ______

(six words describing a second main event)

______ ______ ______ ______ ______ ______ ______

(seven words describing a third main event)

______ ______ ______ ______ ______ ______ ______ ______

(eight words presenting the solution to the problem)

Story Pyramid Evaluation Rubric

Record Sheet

Name ______________________________ Date ______________

CRITERIA	5 POINTS	3 POINTS	1 POINT	SCORE
ACCURACY OF STORY ELEMENTS	All story pyramid entries accurately reflect the character, setting, events, problem, and solution in the book.	Some of the story pyramid entries accurately reflect the character, setting, events, problem, and solution in the book.	The story pyramid entries do not reflect the character, setting, events, problem, and solution in the book.	☐
LEVEL OF PREPARATION	Student was well prepared for retelling and maintained the attention of the audience.	Student was somewhat well prepared for retelling and maintained the attention of the audience through most of the retelling.	Student was not well prepared for retelling and failed to maintain the attention of the audience.	☐
RETELLING SKILLS	Student used good voice quality and made eye contact with the audience.	Student's voice quality varied throughout the retelling and student made little eye contact with the audience.	Student's voice quality was poor and no eye contact was made with the audience.	☐
			TOTAL POINTS	☐ / 15

ACTIVITY 3.6

Exploring Reader's Theater

Mr. Popper's Penguins

GRADE LEVEL: **3–4**

OBJECTIVE

- To participate in a reader's theater performance in order to use spoken language for learning and enjoyment (aesthetic talk)

MATERIALS

- A selection of books appropriate for reader's theater
- Reader's Theater Script for *Mr. Popper's Penguins* (one per student) (For additional scripts or ideas for scripts, see the Reader's Theater Resources and Internet Resources sections at the end of the activity.)
- One copy (minimum) of *Mr. Popper's Penguins*, by Richard and Florence Atwater

NCTE/IRA STANDARD

12 Students use spoken, written, and visual language to accomplish their own purposes (e.g., for learning, enjoyment, persuasion, and the exchange of information).

PROCEDURES

1. Ask students how many of them have pets at home. Discuss the variety of pets and ask students if they know of people who have unusual pets.
2. Ask students to read *Mr. Popper's Penguins*. The reading can be done as a large group read-aloud, with buddy readers, or independently.
3. Foster discussion of the story, using the following questions as a guide:
   - How would you describe Mr. Popper?
   - What words would you use to describe Mrs. Popper?
   - Why do you think that Mr. Popper wanted penguins?
   - What was life like for the Poppers as they adjusted to living with penguins?
   - What were some of the humorous events that took place with penguins in the house?
   - Did the story end the way you thought it should?
   - Would you like to have penguins as pets? Why or why not?
4. Ask for volunteers for the six parts in the script and have students perform the Reader's Theater Script for *Mr. Popper's Penguins* (Exhibit 3.6.A). To make the performance a little more dramatic, students can sit on stools facing away from the audience and turn around to face the class only when it is their turn to speak.
5. New volunteers can be chosen for each of the six parts and the readers' theater script can be performed again for a new audience.

6. In small groups, have students choose another chapter from *Mr. Popper's Penguins* or a scene from another book of their choice. Students can write both narrator and characters' parts, using the *Mr. Popper's Penguins* script as a model. Any book that contains considerable dialogue can make a good reader's theater script. Have each small group perform their script for the class.
7. Struggling readers can choose below-grade-level books for their reader's theater scripts, work in a mixed-ability group so that they receive assistance, or get help from a peer or teacher to modify the vocabulary in the book. English language learners might create scripts for wordless picture books in their first language. Repeated rehearsals of the script prior to the class performance might also give English language learners and struggling readers more confidence.

ASSESSMENT

Informal feedback from peers is a good way for students to evaluate their performance and identify ways to make improvements. For this activity, the students in the audience can provide verbal feedback to the cast by answering the following questions:

- Was the cast well prepared for the performance? Could you tell they had rehearsed?
- Did the cast speak fluently and with expression?
- Did the cast speak loudly enough for the audience to hear?
- What were the strengths of this performance?

An optional assessment activity would be for the cast to do a small group self-assessment after receiving feedback from peers. The group might choose to make changes based on peer and self-assessments and do an additional performance for another audience.

INTEGRATING LANGUAGE ARTS ACROSS THE CURRICULUM

With a book like *Mr. Popper's Penguins*, students can research related social studies, science, or health concepts. For example, students might investigate Admiral Drake (the South Pole explorer), the Antarctic, or penguins through books, newspaper articles, or Internet sources. In small groups, students could conduct a panel discussion, sharing the information they discovered. Teachers and students might discuss the ways that authors conduct and use their own research in the writing process.

HOME–SCHOOL CONNECTION

Students could bring reader's theater scripts home prior to the in-class performance to practice with family members. In-class performances could be videotaped and students could take turns taking the videotape home to share with parents.

CHILDREN'S LITERATURE

Atwater, R., & Atwater, F. (1938). *Mr. Popper's penguins.* Scholastic.

READER'S THEATER RESOURCES

Barchers, S. (1993). *Reader's theatre for beginning readers.* Teacher Ideas Press.

Barchers, S. (1997). *Fifty fabulous fables: Beginning reader's theatre.* Teacher Ideas Press.

Barchers, S. (2000). *Multicultural folktales: Reader's theatre for elementary students.* Teacher Ideas Press.

Blau, L. (1997). *Super science: Reader's theatre scripts and extended activities.* One from the Heart.

Ellermeyer, D., & Rowell, J. (2004). *Ancient civilizations reader's theater.* Creative Teaching Press.

Evan-Moor Publishers. (2003). *Reader's theater (grades 1–5).*

Fredericks, A. (1993). *Frantic frogs and other frankly fractured folktales for reader's theatre.* Teacher Ideas Press.

Fredericks, A. (2000). *Silly salamanders and other slightly stupid stuff for reader's theatre.* Teacher Ideas Press.

Latrobe, K., & Laughlin, M. (1989). *Reader's theatre for young adults: Scripts and script development.* Teacher Ideas Press.

Laughlin, M., Black, P., & Loberg, M. (1991). *Social studies reader's theatre for children: Scripts and script development.* Teacher Ideas Press.

Shepard, A. (2003). *Folktales on stage: Children's plays for reader's theater.* Shepard Publications.

Sierra, J. (1996). *Multicultural folktales for the feltboard and reader's theater.* Greenwood.

Sloyer, S. (2003). *From the page to the stage: The educator's complete guide to reader's theater.* Greenwood.

INTERNET RESOURCES

Aaron, S. (1996). Aaron Shepard's RT page. Retrieved August 19, 2006, from www.aaronshep.com/rt/index.html.

Bridges, L. Readers theater for bilingual/ESL students. Retrieved August 19, 2006, from http://litsite.alaska.edu/uaa/workbooks/readtheater.html.

InCollaboration, Inc. (2006). Teaching and learning: The power of reader's theater. Retrieved August 19, 2006, from www.readers.org/readerstheater.htm.

LiteracyConnections. (2001–2006). Readers' theater. Retrieved August 19, 2006, from http://literacyconnections.com/ReadersTheater.html.

Pearson Scott Foresman. Readers' theater bulletin. Retrieved August 19, 2006, from www.scottforesman.com/reading/readerstheater/index.cfm.

Reader's theater links. Retrieved August 19, 2006, from www.gardenofpraise.com/tlink10.htm.

Reader's theatre. Retrieved August 19, 2006, from www.vtaide.com/png/theatre.htm.

Teaching is a work of heart. (2001). Reader's theater scripts and plays. Retrieved August 19, 2006, from www.teachingheart.net/readerstheater.htm.

Reader's Theater Script

Mr. Popper's Penguins

Chapter 8: ***Penguin's Promenade***

Characters

Narrator	Mr. Popper
Captain Cook	First Man
Mrs. Callahan	Second Man

Narrator: Mr. Popper knew that it was not easy to take a penguin for a stroll. Captain Cook didn't like being on a leash, but Mr. Popper insisted. He tied one end of the clothesline to the penguin's fat throat and the other end to his own wrist.

Captain Cook: Ork!

Narrator: Mr. Popper put on his best Sunday derby and opened the front door with Captain Cook waddling graciously beside him.

Captain Cook: Gaw. Gook!

Narrator: Captain Cook raised his flippers, leaned forward, and bravely tobogganed down the steps on his stomach. Mr. Popper followed and they headed for the street ahead. They came upon a neighbor, Mrs. Callahan, with her arms full of groceries.

Mrs. Callahan: Heavens have mercy on us! It isn't an owl and it isn't a goose.

Mr. Popper: It isn't. It's an Antarctic penguin, Mrs. Callahan.

Mrs. Callahan: Get away from me. An anteater, is it?

Mr. Popper: Not anteater! Antarctic! It was sent to me from the South Pole.

Mrs. Callahan: Take your South Pole goose away from me at once.

Narrator: Mr. Popper pulled on the clothesline, while Captain Cook took a parting peck at Mrs. Callahan's striped stockings.

Mrs. Callahan: Heaven preserve us! I must stop in and see Mrs. Popper at once. I would never have believed it. I will be going now.

Mr. Popper: So will I.

Narrator: Captain Cook dragged Mr. Popper down the street and they stopped at the drugstore. Suddenly a car wheeled to the nearby curb with a shriek of its brakes, and two young men sprang out, one of them bearing a camera.

First Man: This must be it.

(continued)

EXHIBIT **3.6.A**

Reader's Theater Script, continued

Second Man:	It's them, all right.
Narrator:	The cameraman set up his tripod on the sidewalk. A small crowd gathered around.
Second Man:	You're Mr. Popper of 432 Proudfoot Avenue, aren't you?
Mr. Popper:	Yes.
First Man:	Hey, pelican, turn around and see the pretty birdie.
Second Man:	That's no pelican. Pelicans have a pouch in their bills.
First Man:	I'd think it was a dodo, only dodos are extinct. This will make an elegant picture, if I can ever get her to turn around.
Mr. Popper:	It's a penguin. Its name is Captain Cook.
Captain Cook:	Gook!
Narrator:	Captain Cook walked over and examined the camera tripod.
First Man:	Probably thinks it's a three-legged stork.
Second Man:	This bird of yours, is it a he or a she? The public will want to know.
Mr. Popper:	Well, I call it Captain Cook.
Second Man:	That makes it a he.
Narrator:	Captain Cook walked around and around the tripod until the clothesline, the penguin, Mr. Popper, and the tripod were all tangled up. One of the bystanders finally straightened them out by having Mr. Popper walk around the tripod three times in the opposite direction. Captain Cook stood beside Mr. Popper, and the cameraman snapped a picture.
Second Man:	One last question. Where did you get your strange pet?
Mr. Popper:	From Admiral Drake, the South Pole explorer. He sent him to me for a present.
Narrator:	The two young men jumped in their car. Mr. Popper and Captain Cook continued their walk, with quite a crowd following and asking questions. The crowd was getting so thick that, in order to escape, Mr. Popper led Captain Cook into a barbershop. The man who kept the barbershop had, up to this time, been a very good friend of Mr. Popper's.

ACTIVITY 3.7

Creating Radio Commercials

Inventions Then and Now

GRADE LEVEL: **4–6**

OBJECTIVES

- To allow students whose first language is not English to make use of their first language to develop competency in the English language arts
- To use spoken, written, and visual language to foster learning

MATERIALS

- One copy of *Marvelous Mattie: How Margaret E. Knight Became an Inventor*, by Emily Arnold McCully (See the Children's Literature section at the end of this activity for additional titles.)
- Library and Internet resources

NCTE/IRA STANDARDS

10 Students whose first language is not English make use of their first language to develop competency in the English language arts and to develop understanding of content across the curriculum.

12 Students use spoken, written, and visual language to accomplish their own purposes (e.g., for learning, enjoyment, persuasion, and the exchange of information).

PROCEDURES

1. Read *Marvelous Mattie* aloud and discuss Margaret Knight's many inventions.
2. Have students create radio commercials for famous inventions throughout the ages. Begin by dividing the class into groups of three to five students. Have each group choose an invention (see suggestions below). Groups will begin by thoroughly researching the invention and then creating a radio commercial for it. Commercials can be audiotaped and shared with the whole class. Students can visit the websites in the Internet Resources section at the end of this activity for more information on inventions. They can also read other books on inventions.

INVENTIONS THROUGHOUT THE AGES

automobile	airplane	dynamite	lie detector
telephone	ballpoint pen	drinking straw	matches
wheel	bicycle	elastic	miniature golf
telegraph	bifocals	computer	Morse code
printing press	blue jeans	French fries	paint roller
answering machine	bubble gum	graham crackers	penicillin
microwave oven	camera	jet ski	potato chips
television	compass	kaleidoscope	roller coaster
light bulb	diapers	kitty litter	safety pin
cotton gin	dishwasher	laser	teddy bear

3. Small group projects allow students to use their talents in a variety of ways. In this activity, students will need to research an invention, write a commercial, perform the commercial, and operate the audio equipment. Students can determine within their groups how each person's talents might best be used. This allows all students to experience success. English language learners may wish to audiotape their commercial in their first language and in English. During the class performance, these students could play their radio commercial in their first language before playing it in English. This will give the students who do not speak that language an opportunity to listen closely and guess the product being advertised.

ASSESSMENT

You may use the Radio Commercial Assessment Checklist (Exhibit 3.7.A) to assess the performance of each small group. The checklist can be given to students at the beginning of the activity so they can plan their best possible performances.

INTEGRATING LANGUAGE ARTS ACROSS THE CURRICULUM

This activity can be adapted for the mathematics classroom by having students research inventions created to further mathematical knowledge and use. For example, students can research and create commercials for computers, calculators, adding machines, protractors, tape measures, slide rules, and the abacus, to name a few.

HOME-SCHOOL CONNECTION

Students can take turns taking their audiotaped commercials home to share with family members. Family members might also enjoy creating and taping a radio commercial advertising their favorite vacation spot, restaurant, or board game.

CHILDREN'S LITERATURE

Flatow, I. (1993). *They all laughed . . . From light bulbs to lasers: The fascinating stories behind the great inventions that have changed our lives.* Harper.

McCully, E. (2006). *Marvelous Mattie: How Margaret E. Knight became an inventor.* Farrar Straus Giroux.

Thimmesh, C. (2000). *Girls think of everything: Stories of ingenious inventions by women.* Houghton Mifflin.

Wulffson, D. (1999). *The kid who invented the Popsicle: And other surprising stories about inventions.* Puffin.

Wulffson, D. (2001). *The kid who invented the trampoline: More surprising stories about inventions.* Dutton.

INTERNET RESOURCES

Educational Technology Center—KSU. (2005). Inventors/inventions. Retrieved August 20, 2006, from http://edtech.kennesaw.edu/web/inventor.html.

Inventors Assistance League. (1999–2005). African-American inventors: African women inventors. Retrieved August 20, 2006, from www.inventions.org/culture/african/africanwomen.html.

Smithsonian. American inventors and inventions. Retrieved August 20, 2006, from www.150.si.edu/150trav/remember/amerinv.htm.

REFERENCES

Famous Inventions: A to Z. Retrieved June 3, 2006, from http://inventors.about.com/library/bl/bl12.htm.

Radio Commercial Assessment Checklist

Group Members ______________________ Date ________

Invention ______________________

	YES (5)	SOMEWHAT (3)	NO (0)
1. Students thoroughly researched their invention.	____	____	____
2. Students demonstrated creativity in the writing of their commercial.	____	____	____
3. Students were well rehearsed.	____	____	____
4. Students' voices were clear and expressive.	____	____	____
Total points:	____ / 20		

Comments: ______________________

A Meeting of the Minds

Reaching Group Consensus

GRADE LEVEL: **4–6**

OBJECTIVES

- To use spoken and written language for persuasion and exchange of information
- To participate as knowledgeable, reflective, creative, and critical members of an academic literacy community

MATERIALS

- One copy of a children's book that contains a controversial topic, such as *Ebony Sea*, by Irene Smalls, or *Sweet Clara and the Freedom Quilt*, by Deborah Hopkinson (For other ideas, see the reference list at the end of the activity.)
- Reaching Group Consensus Activity Sheet (one per group)
- Pencils

NCTE/IRA STANDARDS

11 Students participate as knowledgeable, reflective, creative, and critical members of a variety of literacy communities.

12 Students use spoken, written, and visual language to accomplish their own purposes (e.g., for learning, enjoyment, persuasion, and the exchange of information).

PROCEDURES

1. Select and read a children's book that contains a controversial topic. As a class, discuss the theme of the book and create a controversial statement related to that theme.
2. Divide the class into groups of four to six students.
3. Give each group a copy of the Reaching Group Consensus Activity Sheet (Exhibit 3.8.A) and have a student from each group write the controversial statement related to the book at the top of the sheet. This student will serve as recorder for the group.
4. Instruct groups to brainstorm reasons why a person might support the statement and write these under the appropriate heading. English language learners may benefit from having a bilingual tutor available for translating their thoughts to the group.
5. Next, tell groups to brainstorm reasons why a person might oppose the statement and write these under the appropriate heading.
6. Once the small groups are finished discussing and recording their responses, combine two small groups to form groups of 8 to 12 students.
7. Have students discuss their combined responses and reach a consensus regarding how they generally feel about the controversial statement as a group.
8. Groups can share their conclusions with the entire class.

Examples of Books and Related Controversial Statements

Book	Controversial Statement
Ebony Sea	Dying for what you believe in is noble.
Sweet Clara and the Freedom Quilt	It is never right to be deceitful.
Charlotte's Web	Pets should be treated like humans.
Hansel and Gretel	Folktales are too violent to share with children.
Pink and Say	Citizens should have the right to vote on whether their country should go to war or not.

9. The teacher may require fewer arguments (reasons) per group if students are having difficulty thinking of pro and con statements. Higher-ability students might be encouraged to research the topic further through the use of the Internet or related reference books before brainstorming and discussing pro and con arguments.

ASSESSMENT

You may observe students' ability to work within groups and contribute to the group discussion by circulating as students work and observing individual participation. You should informally observe students' exchange of information and use of persuasive statements. To further evaluate students' use of persuasion, you may also collect group worksheets at the end of the period.

INTEGRATING LANGUAGE ARTS ACROSS THE CURRICULUM

Use other quality children's books to explore and discuss controversial social studies issues. Suggested titles include: *Follow the Drinking Gourd* (Winter, 1998), *The Vietnam War: 20th Century Perspectives* (Willoughby, 2001), *Faithful Elephants: A True Story of Animals, People and War* (Tsuchiya, 1988), *So Far from the Sea* (Bunting, 1998), *Coming to America: The Story of Immigration* (Maestro, 1996), and *Through My Eyes* (Bridges, 1999).

HOME–SCHOOL CONNECTION

Ask students to find newspaper or magazine articles containing controversial issues and to discuss the articles at home with family members. Invite students to bring their articles to school and share them with the class. Articles can be displayed on a classroom bulletin board entitled, "In the News . . ."

CHILDREN'S/YOUNG ADULT LITERATURE

Bridges, R. (1999). *Through my eyes.* Scholastic.

Bunting, E. (1998). *So far from the sea.* Scholastic.

Hopkinson, D. (1993). *Sweet Clara and the freedom quilt.* Alfred A. Knopf.

Maestro, B. (1996). *Coming to America: The story of immigration.* Scholastic.

Polacco, P. (1994). *Pink and Say.* Scholastic.

Smalls, I. (1995). *Ebony sea.* Longmeadow Press.

Tsuchiya, Y. (1988). *Faithful elephants: A true story of animals, people and war.* Houghton Mifflin.

White, E. B. (1974). *Charlotte's web.* HarperTrophy.

Willoughby, D. (2001). *The Vietnam War: 20th century perspectives.* Heinemann Library.

Winter, J. (1998). *Follow the drinking gourd.* Trumpet.

Zelinsky, P. (1984). *Hansel and Gretel.* G. P. Putnam's Sons.

INTERNET RESOURCES

Consensus: How to and why. Retrieved August 20, 2006, from www.msu.edu/%7Ecorcora5/org/consensus.html.

Consensus Building. Retrieved August 20, 2006, from www.siue.edu/MLTE/Demonstration%20Lessons%20DONE/Demonstration%20lessons%20website/consensus_building.htm.

Consensus Works! (2006). Basics of consensus. Retrieved August 20, 2006, from www.ic.org/nica/Process/Consensusbasics.htm.

Reaching Group Consensus Activity Sheet

Small Group Members

______________________ ______________________ ______________________
______________________ ______________________ ______________________

Book Title

____

Controversial Statement

____
____

Arguments in Support of Statement (1 point each)

1. ____
2. ____
3. ____
4. ____
5. ____

Arguments Against Statement (1 point each)

1. ____
2. ____
3. ____
4. ____
5. ____

Group Consensus Statement (2 points)

____
____
____
____
____

ACTIVITY 3.9

Interviewing to Learn About the Past

GRADE LEVEL: **5–6**

OBJECTIVES

- To generate questions and gather, evaluate, and synthesize information from people through interviewing
- To use spoken and written language for learning, data gathering, and exchange of information

MATERIALS

- Video clip of a televised interview
- Television set
- VCR/DVD player
- Learning About the Past Interview Form (one per student)
- Interview Scoring Rubric (one per student)

NCTE/IRA STANDARDS

7 Students conduct research on issues and interests by generating ideas and questions, and by posing problems. They gather, evaluate, and synthesize data from a variety of sources (e.g., print and non-print texts, artifacts, people) to communicate their discoveries in ways that suit their purpose and audience.

12 Students use spoken, written, and visual language to accomplish their own purposes (e.g., for learning, enjoyment, persuasion, and the exchange of information).

PROCEDURES

1. Show the class a video clip of a televised interview. Nickelodeon or age-appropriate 60 *Minutes* interviews might be a good source for interview video clips.
2. Discuss interviewing as a valuable technique for learning about others and their personal experiences.
3. Discuss components of a successful interview, such as prepared, thoughtful questions; attentive and reflective listening skills; effective follow-up questions; careful and precise note-taking skills; respect for the speaker; and the ability to summarize interview information. See the Internet Resource section at the end of this activity for additional tips on interviewing. Relate each area back to the televised interview.
4. To practice interviewing skills, decide on a school staff member, teacher, or administrator to be interviewed in class. Brainstorm interview questions, including effective follow-up questions, and schedule the interview. Allow students to take turns asking questions, while all class members take notes. After the interview, have students discuss and write a group summary of the interview information. Analyze the strengths and weaknesses of the interview and changes in interviewing techniques that might have made the interview more effective.
5. Tell students they will be interviewing a grandparent or another senior citizen within the community to learn more about the person and the time period in which he/she grew up. Students can use the Learning

About the Past Interview Form (Exhibit 3.9.A) and may be required to think of three additional questions of their own to ask.

6. After conducting the interview, students will orally share the interview information in class and summarize the results. Allow questions from the audience.
7. Some students may benefit from using an audiotape recorder during the interview to record responses. An audio recorder might be used during the practice interview in class so that students can become comfortable with the operation of the equipment. Other students may benefit from referring to note cards during the class presentation. English language learners can be encouraged to conduct the interview in their first language.

ASSESSMENT

You may use the Interview Scoring Rubric (Exhibit 3.9.B) to assess students' spoken and written language and ability to synthesize interview information.

INTEGRATING LANGUAGE ARTS ACROSS THE CURRICULUM

Extend language arts into social studies and science by having students conduct mock interviews of famous American men and women who have made significant contributions to society. Begin by pairing students up and having them choose or randomly draw the name of a famous American. (See the Children's Literature section below for suggested titles.) After students read the suggested book or another suitable related book, have them create questions for the famous American to be interviewed based on information from the book. One student can assume the role of the famous person, while the other assumes the role of interviewer. After sufficient practice, pairs can present their interview to the entire class or videotape it.

HOME-SCHOOL CONNECTION

Have students use the interview questions to interview a parent or other adult relative about the same age. Have them reflect on similarities and differences between the two generations interviewed.

CHILDREN'S LITERATURE

Adler, D. (1982). *A picture book of Harriet Tubman.* Scholastic.

Adler, D. (1990). *A picture book of Helen Keller.* Trumpet Club.

Adler, D. (1990). *A picture book of Benjamin Franklin.* Trumpet Club.

Adler, D. (1991). *A picture book of Christopher Columbus.* Trumpet Club.

Adler, D. (1999). *A picture book of George Washington Carver.* Holiday House.

Atkins, J. (1999). *Mary Anning and the Sea Dragon.* Farrar Straus Giroux.

Bains, R. (1982). *Clara Barton: Angel of the battlefield.* Troll.

Bains, R. (1986). *James Monroe: Young patriot.* Troll.

Bradby, M. (1995). *More than anything else.* Orchard.

Brant, K. (1986). *Lou Gehrig: Pride of the Yankees.* Troll.

Bridges, R. (1999). *Through my eyes.* Scholastic.

Brown, D. (1997). *Alice Ramsey's grand adventure.* Houghton Mifflin.

Cooney, B. (1996). *Eleanor.* Puffin.

Corey, S. (2000). *You forgot your skirt, Amelia Bloomer.* Scholastic.

Frady, M. (1996). *Jesse Jackson: A biography.* Random House.

King, S. (1994). *Maya Angelou: Greeting the morning.* Millbrook Press.

Lasky, K. (2000). *Vision of beauty: The story of Sarah Breedlove Walker.* Candlewick.

Mattern, J. (1992). *Young Martin Luther King, Jr.: I have a dream.* Troll.

McGovern, A. (1966). *If you grew up with Abraham Lincoln.* Scholastic.

McKissack, P. (1994). *Sojourner Truth: Ain't I a woman?* Scholastic.

MacLeod, E. (1999). *Alexander Graham Bell: An inventive life.* Scholastic.

Pinkney, A. (1998). *Duke Ellington.* Hyperion.

Pinkney, A. (1994). *Dear Benjamin Banneker.* Harcourt Brace.

INTERNET RESOURCE

Career Consulting Center. (2006). Interviewing tips: General tips to follow when interviewing. Retrieved August 19, 2006, from www.careercc.com/interv3.shtml.

Learning About the Past Interview Form

Name ______________________________ Date ____________

1. What is your name?
2. Where were you born?
3. When were you born?
4. With whom did you live when you were growing up?
5. Where did you go to elementary school?
6. What subjects did you study in school? What was your favorite subject? Tell why.
7. What kinds of games did you play as a child? In what other ways did children entertain themselves?
8. What were considered modern conveniences at that time?
9. What was the price of a loaf of bread? a gallon of milk? a postage stamp? a candy bar? a gallon of gasoline?
10. Who was president when you were born?
11. How did you help your parents around the house? Did you receive an allowance? If so, how much?
12. How is growing up today the same? How is it different?
13. ______________________________
14. ______________________________
15. ______________________________

EXHIBIT **3.9.B**

Interview Scoring Rubric

Name ______________________________ Date ______________

5 = Excellent 4 = Very Good 3 = Good 2 = Satisfactory 1 = Needs Improvement

1. Completed the interview form	5	4	3	2	1
2. Effectively conducted the interview	5	4	3	2	1
3. Asked follow-up questions	5	4	3	2	1
4. Demonstrated effective note taking	5	4	3	2	1
5. Created at least three additional questions	5	4	3	2	1
6. Effectively shared results with class	5	4	3	2	1
7. Demonstrated organization	5	4	3	2	1
8. Demonstrated effective speaking skills	5	4	3	2	1
9. Effectively summarized	5	4	3	2	1
10. Responded effectively to questions	5	4	3	2	1

Total Score _______ / 50

Comments: ______________________________

ACTIVITY 3.10

Involving Students in Research Discussions

GRADE LEVEL: **5–6**

OBJECTIVES

- To gather information that will provide an answer to a research discussion question
- To lead a small group research discussion by sharing information and involving peers in a discussion of a research question
- To encourage English language learners to use their first language, as well as English, to present research content

MATERIALS

- Library and Internet access
- Evaluation Rubric for Research Discussions (one per student)

NCTE/IRA STANDARDS

7 Students conduct research on issues and interests by generating ideas and questions, and by posing problems. They gather, evaluate, and synthesize data from a variety of sources (e.g., print and non-print texts, artifacts, people) to communicate their discoveries in ways that suit their purpose and audience.

8 Students use a variety of technological and information resources (e.g., libraries, databases, computer networks, video) to gather and synthesize information and to create and communicate knowledge.

10 Students whose first language is not English make use of their first language to develop competency in the English language arts and to develop understanding of content across the curriculum.

PROCEDURES

1. Provide students with a variety of research topics from which to choose. Provide enough topics so that there are four or five students for each topic. Topics might include bullying, careers, exercise, television, current events, or drugs and alcohol. After each student lists his/her top three choices, place each student in a group of four or five.
2. Have the students meet in their small group and provide them with research questions for their topics. Give the same number of questions as there are students in the group. For example, if a group of five were researching exercise, the students might be given the following questions:
   - How does exercise affect weight?
   - How does exercise affect general health?
   - How much exercise do people of varying ages need?
   - What kinds of exercise do people enjoy most?
   - How many calories are burned with various kinds of exercises?
3. Students gather information to answer their research question from books, magazines, newspapers, and encyclopedias. Students could also use the Internet or conduct personal interviews. Students take notes on the information they find to answer their research question.
4. On the day of the research discussions, students get in their small groups and determine the order of presentation. Each student gets 8 to 10 minutes

to lead a discussion of his/her research question. The discussion leader not only presents information on the research question, but also asks questions about the topic to foster group discussion. For example, on the topic of exercise, the discussion leader might ask group members what kinds of exercise they enjoy most or what health benefits they believe exercise offers them.

5. While all of the groups are holding their discussions simultaneously, monitor the time and stop the group after 8 to 10 minutes. Provide a discussion period of two to three minutes after each student's presentation for group members to offer feedback to the discussion leader. Assess each student's presentation before the next discussion begins. Circulate through the small groups during the presentations to hear a few minutes of each student's discussion.
6. For less capable students or struggling readers, provide research materials at their reading level and/or assign a research question for which personal interviews would be a major research source. Reluctant speakers and English language learners could benefit from practice sessions with more confident speakers prior to the research discussion day. Give English language learners the option to present their research discussions in their first language as well as in English.

ASSESSMENT

For the research discussion activity, the evaluation consists of self-assessment and feedback from peers using the Evaluation Rubric for Research Discussions (Exhibit 3.10.A). Each student will receive feedback on his/her presentation from peers in the small group. The discussion leader can document this feedback on the rubric and use the rubric to determine the point value for each criterion.

INTEGRATING LANGUAGE ARTS ACROSS THE CURRICULUM

Research discussions can be incorporated into subject areas such as science, social studies, and health. Good topics for research discussions often come from issues or subjects that students are interested in or curious about. For example, after reading their American history textbooks, students might begin to wonder why more women are not represented. They might choose women's history as their topic and research women inventors, women's rights, women in politics, and women in the Old West.

HOME-SCHOOL CONNECTION

Students could gather personal interview data from family members, as appropriate to their research question. Students could also rehearse the research discussion with family members the night before the presentation to help them gain confidence and become familiar with the topic.

INTERNET RESOURCES

Annenberg Media. (1997–2006). Whole group discussions. Retrieved August 20, 2006, from www.learner.org/channel/libraries/makingmeaning/makingmeaning/wholegroup/.

Arizona Board of Regents. (2003). Guidelines for constructive dialogue in the classroom. Retrieved August 20, 2006, from www.asu.edu/provost/intergroup/resources/class guidelines.html.

Reineke, M. In-class discussions. Retrieved August 20, 2006, from http://fp.uni.edu/reineke/guidelin.htm.

San Mateo County Office of Education. (1997). Student-led discussions. Retrieved August 20, 2006, from http://pblmm.k12.ca.us/PBLGuide/Activities/studentdiscussions.html.

Thorn, N. (2002). Effective classroom discussions. Retrieved August 20, 2006, from www.venture-learn.org/training/classroom_discussions.htm.

University of Washington. (2001–2004). Group work/Discussions. Retrieved August 20, 2006, from www.washington.edu/doit/Faculty/Strategies/Academic/Groupwork/.

EXHIBIT **3.10.A**

Evaluation Rubric for Research Discussions

Name ______________________________ Date ______________

3 = Strongly agree   2 = Agree   1 = Disagree

CRITERIA	PEER EVALUATION	SELF-EVALUATION
Speaker was well prepared.	3 2 1	3 2 1
	Comments:	
Speaker spoke clearly and could be easily heard.	3 2 1	3 2 1
	Comments:	
Speaker used good eye contact with group members.	3 2 1	3 2 1
	Comments:	
Speaker involved group members in the discussion.	3 2 1	3 2 1
	Comments:	
Speaker answered questions asked by group members.	3 2 1	3 2 1
	Comments:	

Total points ______ / 30

READING

Breaking the Code for Meaning and Understanding

INTRODUCTION

Reading is an essential skill that is central to understanding in every area of the curriculum. Literacy acquisition begins to develop, however, long before children even enter school. The world that surrounds them is saturated with print media—from the environmental print on street signs and billboards to the menus at restaurants. Youngsters soon discover that being able to read opens up a whole new world to them. Reading, clearly, is a survival skill for everyday existence in modern society.

By definition, reading is "a process in which we construct meaning from print" (Gunning, 2003). In essence, reading involves breaking the mysterious code of written communication in order to gain meaning and understanding. Teachers assist students in becoming competent readers by presenting them with a comprehensive reading program that "honor[s] children's rights to excellent instruction' (IRA, 2000). The International Reading Association (2000) asserts 10 rights to which all children are entitled as they learn to read:

- Early reading instruction that meets individual needs
- Reading instruction that builds skill and the desire to read increasingly complex materials
- Well-prepared teachers who keep their skills up to date
- A variety of books and other reading material in their classrooms and in school and community libraries
- Assessment that identifies strengths as well as needs and involves students in making decisions about their own learning
- Supplemental instruction from professionals specifically prepared to teach reading
- Instruction that involves parents and communities in students' academic life
- Instruction that makes meaningful use of first-language skills
- Equal access to instructional technology
- Classrooms that optimize learning opportunities

A comprehensive reading program equips students with a variety of essential skills that they need to become successful readers. Past reading debates, which asserted that one reading approach was more effective than another, have been replaced with the awareness that teachers need to use a variety of approaches to meet the needs of all their students. This is referred to as the *comprehensive approach* to reading instruction, and it includes instruction in phonemic awareness, phonics, fluency, vocabulary development, and comprehension strategies.

The activities that follow are designed to engage students in meaningful and engaging literacy activities that complement a comprehensive reading approach. These activities are easily adaptable to meet the needs of diverse learners.

Classroom Vignette

Students in Ms. Tillman's class look forward with anticipation each day to reading workshop. Ms. Tillman begins the period by distributing student folders and stating her expectations for each student. When she concludes, every student clearly knows what should be accomplished during the next 55 minutes. Throughout the class period, the room is abuzz with a variety of activities designed to create lifelong readers. Stacey makes herself comfortable in the reading corner and quickly begins reading the next chapter in her book. Min records information in her reading log. A small group of students assembles to listen as Tony presents a timeline that accurately depicts the important events within the novel he recently finished reading. Ms. Tillman conducts a reading conference with Brandy and records her observations in the form of detailed anecdotal records. When the conference concludes, a small group gathers with the teacher and completes an exercise on finding the main idea and supporting details. At the end of the period, the students return their materials to their reading folders and move to Mrs. Wilson's classroom to begin math.

DISCUSSION QUESTIONS

1. How is reading workshop similar to and different from the way you learned to read?
2. Would you feel comfortable facilitating reading workshop in your classroom? Explain why or why not.
3. Describe the activities in which students engage during reading workshop.
4. What are the advantages and disadvantages of reading workshop?
5. Is reading workshop a comprehensive approach to teaching reading? Explain why or why not.

References

Gunning, T. (2003). *Creating literacy instruction for all children* (4th ed.). Boston: Allyn & Bacon.

International Reading Association. (2000). *Honoring children's rights to excellent reading instruction.* Newark, DE: Author.

ACTIVITY 4.1

Pick a Stick

Working with Onsets and Rimes

GRADE LEVEL: **K–1**

OBJECTIVE

- To apply the skill of blending to create words from onsets and rimes

MATERIALS

- 60 large craft sticks
- Two empty soup cans
- Decorative adhesive paper for covering soup cans
- One red marker
- One black marker

NCTE/IRA STANDARD

3 Students apply a wide range of strategies to comprehend, interpret, evaluate, and appreciate texts. They draw on their prior experience, their interactions with other readers and writers, their knowledge of word meaning and of other texts, their word identification strategies, and their understanding of textual features (e.g., sound–letter correspondence, sentence structure, context, graphics).

PROCEDURES

1. Begin by covering the two empty soup cans with decorative adhesive paper. Label one can *Onsets* in red marker and the other *Rimes* in black marker. See Exhibit 4.1.A for a list of onsets and rimes.
2. Divide the large craft sticks into two equal piles. In red marker, print common onsets on one set of sticks. In black marker, print common rimes on the other set of sticks.
3. Place each set of sticks into the appropriately labeled can.
4. Demonstrate how to create new words by drawing a stick from each can and blending the onset and rime together. Identify the word as either a real word or a nonsense word. Return the sticks to the appropriate cans and do several more examples. Make sure that English language learners are able to see your mouth as you pronounce the onsets and rimes. Repeat each one several times, and ask English language learners to pronounce the sounds with you.
5. Call on student volunteers to do the same. After pronouncing the word, the student should tell whether the word is a real word or a nonsense word. English language learners should be encouraged to write the newly formed words as well as say them aloud several times. Place the activity in a classroom center for student use.

ASSESSMENT

You may informally assess students' abilities to blend onsets and rimes correctly by listening to them. Individual assistance may be provided to those students experiencing difficulty.

INTEGRATING LANGUAGE ARTS ACROSS THE CURRICULUM

Call students' attention to common rimes as they are encountered in reading materials across content areas. A classroom word wall can be constructed to display common rimes. Use the wall daily by randomly choosing a rime and having students brainstorm words that contain that rime.

HOME–SCHOOL CONNECTION

On a weekly basis, assign students a rime and ask them to brainstorm, with their families, as many real words as they can that contain the rime. Record answers on paper during morning meeting and have students share how many words they were able to create for the selected rime.

INTERNET RESOURCES

Author House. (2006). Phonics, rhythms and rhymes. Retrieved August 19, 2006, from www.phonicsrhythmsrhymes.com/index.html.

Houghton Mifflin Company. (1998). The role of phonics in the teaching of reading: A Houghton Mifflin Position Paper by Dr. John J. Pikulski. Retrieved August 19, 2006, from www.eduplace.com/lds/article/phonics.html.

Jordan School District. Phonemic awareness and phonics. Retrieved August 19, 2006, from http://t4.jordan.k12.ut.us/Balanced_Literacy/Reading/phonics_and_decoding.htm.

LD Online. (2006). Phonological awareness: Instructional and assessment guidelines. Retrieved August 19, 2006, from www.ldonline.org/article/6254.

Read. Activities to teach phonological awareness, phonemic awareness, phonics and fluency. Retrieved August 19, 2006, from http://ecc.eeisd.org/~sabedra/Reading.htm.

Reading Rockets. (2006). How now brown cow: Phonemic awareness activities. Retrieved August 19, 2006, from www.readingrockets.org/articles/388.

Teaching Resource Center. (2002–2004). Word work: Word families. Retrieved August 19, 2006, from www.ldonline.org/article/6254.

Word Way. Word family database. Retrieved August 19, 2006, from http://teachers.santee.k12.ca.us/carl/word_way.htm.

EXHIBIT **4.1.A**

Common Rimes and Onsets

Common Rimes

-ack	-all	-ain	-ake	-ale	-ame	-an	-ank	-ap	-ash
-at	-ate	-aw	-ay	-eat	-ell	-est	-ice	-ick	-ide
-ight	-ill	-in	-ine	-ing	-ink	-ip	-ir	-ock	-oke
-op	-or	-ore	-uck	-ug	-ump	-unk			

Common Onsets

b-	br-	bl-	c-	cr-	cl-	d-	dr-	f-	fr-
fl-	g-	gr-	gl-	h-	j-	k-	l-	m-	n-
p-	pr-	pl-	r-	s-	sc-	sh-	sk-	sl-	sm-
sn-	sp-	st-	sw-	scr-	spl-	spr-	t-	tr-	thr-
w-	y-								

ACTIVITY 4.2

Enhancing Vocabulary Development

through Antonym Word Sorts

GRADE LEVEL: **1–2**

OBJECTIVE

- To increase knowledge of word meanings of opposites in order to improve comprehension skills

MATERIALS

- Picture books on opposites, such as *Exactly the Opposite*, by Tana Hoban (See the Children's Literature section at the end of this activity for additional titles.)
- Butcher paper
- Antonym Word Cards (one set)
- Stickers (optional)

NCTE/IRA STANDARD

3 Students apply a wide range of strategies to comprehend, interpret, evaluate, and appreciate texts. They draw on their prior experience, their interactions with other readers and writers, their knowledge of word meaning and of other texts, their word identification strategies, and their understanding of textual features (e.g., sound–letter correspondence, sentence structure, context, graphics).

PROCEDURES

1. Share and discuss books on opposites. The Internet Resources section at the end of this activity includes additional sources of information on opposites. After a book is read, ask students to name the opposites in the book and write them on butcher paper. When appropriate, ask students to pantomime the words to assist English language learners in understanding the meanings of the opposites. Introduce and explain the word *antonym*.
2. Cut Antonym Word Cards (Exhibit 4.2.A) apart. Consider placing clip art that illustrates each antonym beside the words on the cards for struggling readers and English language learners. English language learners would also benefit from the inclusion of the words in their first language on the word cards for additional support.
3. Place like symbols or stickers on the back of each pair so that the word sort activity is self-checking. Laminate the word cards for increased durability. Place the word cards in a pocket folder. Explain to students that they are to match the word pairs that are opposites or antonyms. This activity can be available to students during center time.
4. Since the activity is self-checking, students with less well developed word identification or vocabulary skills will have built-in clues. The more challenging opposites, such as *clean* and *dirty* and *solid* and *liquid*, make this activity appropriate for students who are already well-developed readers. You might create similar word sorts for emergent readers, with each word card paired with a picture card.

ASSESSMENT

Since the activity is self-checking, students can evaluate their own performance. During center time or individual conference time, observe to ensure that students have learned to match the opposites without using the self-checking clues.

INTEGRATING LANGUAGE ARTS ACROSS THE CURRICULUM

The opposites written on butcher paper can be used in a variety of writing activities. In addition, many of the word sort cards, such as wet/dry, high/low, solid/liquid, and cold/hot, contain science vocabulary and could easily be incorporated into science activities and lessons.

HOME-SCHOOL CONNECTION

The word sort learning center can be sent home with students for extra practice. Family members can be encouraged to assist the child in matching the opposites, discussing the word meanings, and using the cards to label objects in their home.

CHILDREN'S LITERATURE

Hoban, T. (1997). *Exactly the opposite.* HarperTrophy.

Pittau, F., & Gervais, B. (2001). *Elephant elephant: A book of opposites.* Harry N. Abrams.

Seuss, Dr. (1996). *The foot book: Dr. Seuss's wacky book of opposites.* Random House.

INTERNET RESOURCES

Alphabet Soup. (2006). Opposites. Teacher tools: Opposites. Retrieved August 19, 2006, from www.alphabet-soup.net/ttools/opposites.html.

Dositey Corporation. (1998–2005). Antonyms. Retrieved August 19, 2006, from www.dositey.com/language/grammar/synonyms_antonyms/antonyms1.htm.

Enchanted Learning.com. (2003–2006). Opposites at Enchanted Learning. Retrieved August 19, 2006, from www.enchantedlearning.com/themes/opposites.shtml.

Kids' Lab. Antonym page. Retrieved August 19, 2006, from www.manatee.k12.fl.us/sites/elementary/palmasola/antonyms.htm.

REFERENCES

Bear, D. R., Invernizzi, M., Templeton, S., & Johnston, F. (1996). *Words their way: Word study for phonics, vocabulary, and spelling instruction.* Upper Saddle River, NJ: Merrill/Prentice Hall.

Schlagal, R. C., & Schlagal, J. H. (1992). The integral character of spelling: Teaching strategies for multiple purposes. *Language Arts, 69,* 418–424.

EXHIBIT **4.2.A**

Antonym Word Cards

big	little
sad	happy
good	bad
clean	dirty
fast	slow

Antonym Word Cards, continued

day	night
high	low
solid	liquid
tall	short
old	young

EXHIBIT **4.2.A**

Antonym Word Cards, continued

cold	hot
wet	dry
outside	inside
yes	no
to	from

ACTIVITY 4.3

Using a Word Wall

to Enhance Word Recognition and Comprehension

GRADE LEVEL: **2**

OBJECTIVES

- To read texts that help students understand cultures of the United States and the world
- To apply strategies in word identification and word meaning to comprehend and appreciate texts
- To develop an understanding of and respect for diversity in language use across cultures and ethnic groups

MATERIALS

- A selection of picture books with language characteristic of diverse cultures, such as *Mice and Beans,* by Pam Muñoz Ryan (See the Children's Literature section at the end of this activity for additional titles.)
- Butcher paper and markers
- Family letter (one per student)
- Word cards

NCTE/IRA STANDARDS

1 Students read a wide range of print and non-print texts to build an understanding of texts, of themselves, and of the cultures of the United States and the world; to acquire new information; to respond to the needs and demands of society and the workplace; and for personal fulfillment. Among these texts are fiction and nonfiction, classic and contemporary works.

3 Students apply a wide range of strategies to comprehend, interpret, evaluate, and appreciate texts. They draw on their prior experience, their interactions with other readers and writers, their knowledge of word meaning and of other texts, their word identification strategies, and their understanding of textual features (e.g., sound–letter correspondence, sentence structure, context, graphics).

9 Students develop an understanding of and respect for diversity in language use, patterns, and dialects across cultures, ethnic groups, geographic regions, and social roles.

PROCEDURES

1. Introduce the book, for example, *Mice and Beans,* by Pam Munoz Ryan, and ask students to listen closely for the Spanish words in the story. Read the book aloud, pausing to ask the following questions:
   - Where was the party to take place? (Answer: Rosa Maria's house)
   - What was on the menu? (Answer: enchiladas, rice and beans, birthday cake, lemonade, and a piñata filled with candy)
   - Where did Rosa Maria get the birthday cake? (Answer: at the *pasteleria*)
   - What did Rosa Maria fill with candy? (Answer: the piñata)
   - How did Rosa Maria say happy birthday to Catalina? (Answer: *feliz cumpleanos*)
   - What did Rosa Maria not want in her house? (Answer: mice)
2. As students answer the questions, write their answers on butcher paper to make a word wall. (See the Internet Resources section at the end of this activity.) Add any other Spanish words that students are able to identify in the story. Discuss the meaning of each word and refer back to the story, as necessary, so students are able to hear each word in context.
3. To improve word identification skills, have students match word cards (Exhibit 4.3.A) with either a translation card or a picture card. The match-

ing can be done either with a pocket chart or in a learning center activity. Laminate the word cards for increased durability.

4. Encourage Spanish-speaking students to assist with the pronunciation of words on the word wall. Some students may need assistance, additional time, or more repetitions with the matching activity. The book should always be made available so students can refer to text and illustrations for assistance.

ASSESSMENT

Observe students as they answer questions, recommend words for the word wall, and participate in word card matching activities. Make anecdotal records to be placed on file or in a student's literacy portfolio. For students with less well developed word identification skills, schedule individual conference time to assist with and observe word card matching.

INTEGRATING LANGUAGE ARTS ACROSS THE CURRICULUM

The author includes a recipe for rice and beans on the back cover. Students could volunteer to bring ingredients for this recipe and for enchiladas in order to make and sample diverse foods. Encourage students to measure ingredients and monitor cooking times to incorporate math skills.

HOME-SCHOOL CONNECTION

Make a literacy bag with the book and the word cards. Encourage family members to read the book aloud and assist with the word card matching activity. A letter to family members (Exhibit 4.3.B) could be included in the literacy bag.

CHILDREN'S LITERATURE

Emberly, R. (2000). *My day/mi dia: A book in two languages/un libro en dos lenguas.* Little Brown.

Emberly, R. (2000). *Let's go/vamos: A book in two languages/un libro en dos lenguas.* Little Brown.

Munoz Ryan, P. (2001). *Mice and beans.* Scholastic.

Rosa-Casanova, S. (1997). *Mama Provi and the pot of rice.* Atheneum.

Rosa-Mendoza, G., & Cifuentes, C. (2001). *The weather/el tempo: Bilingual* (English–Spanish Foundations Series, vol. 6). Me + Mi Publishing.

WORD WALL INTERNET RESOURCES

ABC Teach. (2001–2006). Word walls! Retrieved August 19, 2006, from www.abcteach.com/directory/teaching_extras/word_walls/.

EdHelper.com. Word walls. Retrieved August 19, 2006, from www.edhelper.com/word_walls.htm.

LEADERS: University of Pittsburgh. (2001). Word walls in a nut shell. Retrieved August 19, 2006, from www.education.pitt.edu/leaders/FAQ/wordwallnutshell.htm.

Minneapolis Public Schools. (2006). Word walls. Retrieved August 19, 2006, from http://tis.mpls.k12.mn.us/word_walls.html.

Teaching First. (2006). Word wall activities. Retrieved August 19, 2006, from www.teaching-first.net/wordwallact.htm.

REFERENCE

Tompkins, G. E. (2005). *Literacy for the twenty-first century: A balanced approach* (4th ed.). Upper Saddle River, NJ: Merrill/Prentice Hall.

Word Cards

bolsa	casita
dulces	enchiladas
feliz cumpleaños	fiesta
fijate	frijoles

EXHIBIT **4.3.A**

Word Cards, continued

no importa	pasteleria
piñata	que boba soy
ratones	tortillas

Translation/Picture Cards

bag

house

candy

enchiladas

happy birthday

party

imagine that

beans

EXHIBIT **4.3.A**

Translation/Picture Cards, continued

it doesn't matter	pastry shop
piñata 	silly me
mice 	tortillas 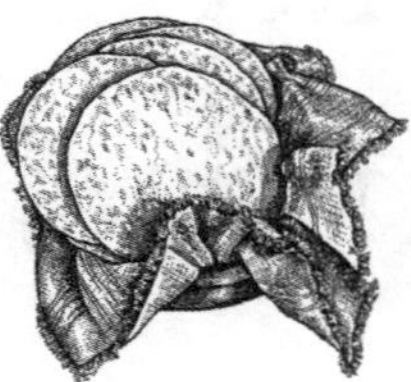

EXHIBIT **4.3.B**

Dear Family Members,

Our class has been reading and enjoying *Mice and Beans*, by Pam Munoz Ryan. In the bag you will find the book and a word card matching activity. You and your child will enjoy reading the story aloud. Pronunciations for the Spanish words can be found at the end of the story, but your child should be able to help you! After reading the book, encourage your child to match the Spanish words with either a picture card or a translation card. You might even want to try the recipe for rice and beans on the back cover. Thank you for sharing the love of reading with your child.

Sincerely,

ACTIVITY 4.4

Developing Sequencing Skills

GRADE LEVEL: **3**

OBJECTIVES

- To read nonfiction texts to acquire new information and for personal fulfillment
- To apply strategies to comprehend and interpret texts

MATERIALS

- Nonfiction picture books, such as *Snowflake Bentley*, by Jacqueline Briggs Martin (See the Children's Literature section at the end of this activity for additional titles.)
- *Snowflake Bentley* Sequencing Activity handout (one per student)
- Scissors (one pair per student)

NCTE/IRA STANDARDS

1 Students read a wide range of print and non-print texts to build an understanding of texts, of themselves, and of the cultures of the United States and the world; to acquire new information; to respond to the needs and demands of society and the workplace; and for personal fulfillment. Among these texts are fiction and nonfiction, classic and contemporary works.

3 Students apply a wide range of strategies to comprehend, interpret, evaluate, and appreciate texts. They draw on their prior experience, their interactions with other readers and writers, their knowledge of word meaning and of other texts, their word identification strategies, and their understanding of textual features (e.g., sound–letter correspondence, sentence structure, context, graphics).

PROCEDURES

1. Choose a nonfiction picture book to read aloud. *Snowflake Bentley*, by Jacqueline Briggs Martin, will be used for this sample activity.
2. Read the book aloud, asking students to listen closely for what happens first, second, third, and so on in the story. Have students consider questions such as:
   - What did Willie Bentley love as a boy? (Answer: He loved snow more than anything else.)
   - How do you think the area of the country where he grew up affected his life? (Answer: He grew up in Jericho, Vermont, which is considered the "heart of the snow belt.")
   - How did Willie's parents support his interests? (Answer: His mother bought him a microscope that he used to examine snowflakes.)
   - What did he discover about snowflakes? (Answer: Willie discovered that snowflakes are ice crystals, and they almost always have six branches.)
   - What did Willie do with his snowflake photographs? (Answer: He gave copies away, sold some, made pictures as gifts for birthdays, and published them in magazines.)
   - How did his community remember him after his death? (Answer: It built a monument dedicated to Willie in the center of town.)
3. Give each student a *Snowflake Bentley* Sequencing Activity handout (Exhibit 4.4.A). Have them cut apart the sentences and put them in the order in which they happened in the story. The picture cues will aid struggling readers and English language learners.

4. Allow students to pair up with a buddy and compare the sequence of their sentences. If they cannot reach consensus, they can refer to the book to check their work and make necessary changes. Discuss the sequence as a class and allow students to make corrections.
5. Students who might have difficulty reading the sentence strips can be paired with a partner for the sequencing activity. Those students with short-term memory impairments could benefit from repeated readings of the story.

ASSESSMENT

The sequence of the sentence strips should be as follows:

1. Willie Bentley was born in 1865 in the snow country of Vermont.
2. Willie loved the snow and enjoyed reading about science.
3. Willie's mother gave him a microscope and he began looking at snowflakes and ice crystals.
4. Willie began drawing pictures of snowflakes and learned that most of them have six branches.
5. His parents used their savings to buy him a camera with a microscope.
6. Willie began photographing snowflakes.
7. He learned how moisture, cold, and wind affect the development of snowflakes.
8. Mr. Bentley really enjoyed the big snowstorm of 1928.
9. Mr. Bentley began selling photographs of snowflakes and publishing photographs in magazines.
10. Mr. Bentley died after taking a walk in a snowstorm.

INTEGRATING THE LANGUAGE ARTS ACROSS THE CURRICULUM

Biographies of people of color can be used to enhance a multicultural social studies curriculum. Examples include *Duke Ellington* by Andrea Pinkney, *Martin's Book Words: The Life of Dr. Martin Luther King, Jr.*, by Doreen Rappaport, *Tallchief: America's Prima Ballerina,* by Maria Tallchief and Rosemary Wells, and *More Than Anything Else* by Marie Bradby.

HOME–SCHOOL CONNECTION

Students can put their sentence strips into an envelope or plastic baggy and take them home. They can put the sentences in order and retell the story to family members.

CHILDREN'S LITERATURE

Atkins, J. (1999). *Mary Anning and the sea dragon.* Farrar Straus Giroux.

Bradby, M. (1995). *More than anything else.* Orchard Books.

Martin, J. B. (1998). *Snowflake Bentley.* Houghton Mifflin.

Pinkney, A. (1998). *Duke Ellington.* Hyperion.

Rappaport, D. (2001). *Martin's big words: The life of Dr. Martin Luther King, Jr.* Scholastic.

Tallchief, M., & Wells, R. (1999). *Tallchief: America's prima ballerina.* Penguin Putnam.

INTERNET RESOURCES

Best Web Search. (2003–2006). 20 sequencing activities. Retrieved August 19, 2006, from www.best-web-search.net/search?said=78&q=sequencing%20activities.

DLTK's Printable Crafts for Kids. The very hungry caterpillar: Story sequencing cards. Retrieved August 19, 2006, from www.dltk-teach.com/books/hungrycaterpillar/sequencing.htm.

EXHIBIT **4.4.A**

Snowflake Bentley Sequencing Activity

Directions: Cut apart the sentence strips. Put the sentences in the order in which they happened in the story.

Mr. Bentley began selling photographs of snowflakes and publishing photographs in magazines.

Willie Bentley was born in 1865 in the snow country of Vermont.

His parents used their savings to buy him a camera with a microscope.

Willie loved the snow and enjoyed reading about science.

Mr. Bentley died after taking a walk in a snowstorm.

Willie's mother gave him a microscope and he began looking at snowflakes and ice crystals.

Mr. Bentley really enjoyed the big snowstorm of 1928.

Willie began drawing pictures of snowflakes and learned that most of them have 6 branches.

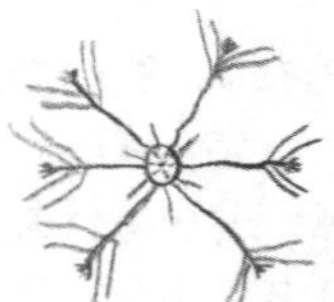

He learned how moisture, cold, and wind affect the development of snowflakes.

Willie began photographing snowflakes.

Semantic Character Analysis

GRADE LEVEL: **3**

OBJECTIVES

- To read classic and contemporary versions of a text to learn information and for personal fulfillment
- To apply strategies to comprehend, interpret, and appreciate texts

MATERIALS

- One copy of *The Fourth Little Pig,* by Teresa Celsi
- One copy of *The Three Little Wolves and the Big Bad Pig,* by Eugene Trivizas
- One copy of *The Three Pigs,* by David Wiesner
- One copy of *The True Story of the 3 Little Pigs!* by Jon Scieszka
- Copies of above folktales in the first languages of English language learners
- Character Analysis—The Three Little Pigs handout (one per student)

NCTE/IRA STANDARDS

1 Students read a wide range of print and non-print texts to build an understanding of texts, of themselves, and of the cultures of the United States and the world; to acquire new information; to respond to the needs and demands of society and the workplace; and for personal fulfillment. Among these texts are fiction and nonfiction, classic and contemporary works.

3 Students apply a wide range of strategies to comprehend, interpret, evaluate, and appreciate texts. They draw on their prior experience, their interactions with other readers and writers, their knowledge of word meaning and of other texts, their word identification strategies, and their understanding of textual features (e.g., sound–letter correspondence, sentence structure, context, graphics).

Activity adapted from Rasinski, T., & Padak, N., 2000.

PROCEDURES

1. Read aloud the four versions of The Three Little Pigs. The stories can be read on the same day or over a period of two to three days. As you are reading, ask students to listen closely for information about the characters and how they are different in each version of the story. English language learners can be given copies of the tales in their first language or have a bilingual tutor translate the tales read by the teacher.
2. Give each student a Character Analysis—The Three Little Pigs handout (Exhibit 4.5.A). Have them compare the characters in each version of the story. Have students make a plus (+) to represent yes, a minus (–) to represent no, or a (+/–) to represent sometimes in the blocks for each book. English language learners can be paired with a partner or work with the bilingual tutor in completing the activity. For more information on character analysis, see the Internet Resources section at the end of this activity.
3. Have students discuss each version of the book and its characters, while comparing responses from the Character Analysis handout. If questions arise, refer back to the books to clarify. Some character traits, such as "creative," are open to interpretation, and so make for good discussion.

4. The books should be made available as students are completing the Character Analysis handout. Some students may need additional time to reread the stories if they are unable to remember details of each version. Students with less well developed memory or comprehension skills may benefit from literature circles for small-group discussion and completion of the handout.

ASSESSMENT

You can collect the Character Analysis handouts (Exhibit 4.5.A) for assessment purposes. However, it is important to give students an opportunity to explain their responses, since character traits such as "creative" are open to interpretation.

INTEGRATING LANGUAGE ARTS ACROSS THE CURRICULUM

Books with a social studies theme could be used for character analysis. For example, using the stories *Sybil's Night Ride*, by Karen Winnick, and *And Then What Happened, Paul Revere*, by J. Fritz, students could compare Sybil Ludington and Paul Revere and their rides to warn of a British invasion.

HOME-SCHOOL CONNECTION

The four books can be packed in a literacy bag with blank Character Analysis handouts. Students may take turns taking the bag home to share the books and activity with their family members. Many parents may not be aware that there are so many versions of this story.

CHILDREN'S LITERATURE

Celsi, T. (1992). *The fourth little pig.* Raintree Steck-Vaughn.

Fritz, J. (1996). *And then what happened, Paul Revere?* Putnam Juvenile.

Scieszka, J. (1989). *The true story of the 3 little pigs!* Scholastic.

Trivizas, E. (1993). *The three little wolves and the big bad pig.* Aladdin.

Wiesner, D. (2001). *The three pigs.* Scholastic.

Winnick, K. (2000). *Sybil's night ride.* Boyds Mills Press.

INTERNET RESOURCES

IRA/NCTE. (2002–2006). Charting characters for a more complete understanding of the story. Retrieved August 20, 2006, from www.readwritethink.org/lessons/lesson_view.asp?id=267.

IRA/NCTE. (2002–2006). Using picture books to teach characterization in writing workshop. Retrieved August 20, 2006, from www.readwritethink.org/lessons/lesson_view.asp?id=101.

Scholastic, Inc. (1996–2006). Books for teaching character analysis. Retrieved August 20, 2006, from http://cc.msnscache.com/cache.aspx?q=3919627492027&lang=en-US&mkt=en-US&FORM=CVRE4.

REFERENCE

Rasinski, T., & Padak, N. (2000). *Effective reading strategies* (2nd ed.). Upper Saddle River, NJ: Prentice Hall.

Character Analysis: The Three Little Pigs

Name ____ Date ______________

Directions: For each book, make a + for yes, a – for no, or a +/– for sometimes.

	Three pigs in story	Pigs made houses of straw, twigs, and brick	Wolf is the bad guy	Dragon in the story	Three pigs tell the story	Female pig in the story	Pigs are creative
The Three Pigs							
The True Story of the 3 Little Pigs!							
The Three Little Wolves and the Big Bad Pig							
The Fourth Little Pig							

ACTIVITY 4.6

Read It Again

GRADE LEVEL: **4–5**

OBJECTIVES

- To improve fluency through repeated readings
- To adjust spoken language to communicate effectively

MATERIALS

- Two shoeboxes
- Passages for Repeated Readings handout (one copy)
- Character Voices handout (one copy)
- Repeated Readings Fluency Checklist (one copy)

NCTE/IRA STANDARD

4 Students adjust their use of spoken, written, and visual language (e.g., conventions, style, vocabulary) to communicate effectively with a variety of audiences and for different purposes.

PROCEDURES

1. Duplicate the Passages for Repeated Readings handout (Exhibit 4.6.A) and the Character Voices handout (Exhibit 4.6.B). Cut apart, fold, and place the passages in one shoebox and the character voices in another. Label one shoebox *Passages* and the other *Characters.*
2. Tell students that they are going to become different characters and practice using their voices to portray a variety of moods and emotions.
3. Write the following on the chalkboard and ask a student volunteer to read it aloud:

   "I can't help you! You need to take control and help yourself. You don't need to be afraid. I know that you can do it."

4. Next, ask another volunteer to repeat the same quote, but this time, they are to read it in a discouraged voice.
5. Have volunteers read the same quote using a variety of voices, such as an angry voice, a happy voice, a shy voice, and so on.
6. Divide the class into small groups of four or five students. Have each child randomly select a passage and a character voice from the shoeboxes prepared earlier.
7. Each student should practice reading his/her passage in the designated voice for five minutes. After five minutes, have students present their passages within their groups.
8. After each student has presented, have them exchange character voices with another student within the small group. Students then practice the same passage in the new character voice for five minutes. At the end of five minutes, students present within the small group.

9. Repeat step 8 until each student in the group has gotten a chance to present each character voice. English language learners can be encouraged to read the passage in their first language, as well as the language of the passage.
10. Collect the passages and character voices and return them to the appropriate shoeboxes. Repeat the activity on subsequent days.

ASSESSMENT

You can use informal teacher observation and the Repeated Readings Fluency Checklist (Exhibit 4.6.C) to assess student participation in the activity.

INTEGRATING LANGUAGE ARTS ACROSS THE CURRICULUM

Students can be encouraged to use the repeated readings strategy with readers' theater scripts they write in other content areas, such as social studies and science. They can practice and read a variety of parts within the same script.

HOME-SCHOOL CONNECTION

Encourage students to practice repeated readings with character voices at home with family members. Any written material can serve as the basis of repeated readings: newspaper articles, favorite poems, cereal boxes, advertisements, and so on.

INTERNET RESOURCES

Best Web Search. (2003–2006). Reading fluency activities. Retrieved August 19, 2006, from www.best-websearch.net/search?said=81&q=reading%20fluency%20activities.

Busy Teacher's Café. Improving reading fluency in young readers. Retrieved August 19, 2006, from www.busyteacherscafe.com/units/fluency.htm.

Kuck, P. (2002). Fluency links. Retrieved August 19, 2006, from www.readingrailroad.net/readingrailroad/literacy+tips/fluency.asp.

LD Online. (2001). Reading fluency. Retrieved August 19, 2006, from www.ldonline.org/article/6354.

National Institute for Literacy. (2006). Put reading first: Fluency instruction. Retrieved August 19, 2006, from www.nifl.gov/partnershipforreading/publications/reading_first1fluency.html.

Reading Consortium. Fluency links. Retrieved August 19, 2006, from http://msit.gsu.edu/readingconsortium/SBRR/html/suggested_resources2.html.

Reading Rockets. (2006). Fluency. Retrieved August 19, 2006, from www.readingrockets.org/article/c59/.

EXHIBIT **4.6.A**

Passages for Repeated Readings

"It's the perfect day for a picnic. Let's pack some sandwiches and sodas and head down to the beach. Remember to bring your sun-screen."	"This is horrible news! I can't believe that I left my homework on the kitchen counter again. Mr. Blair will never believe this!"
"Kittens make the best pets. You don't have to bathe them or take them for walks. They are playful and curl up in the most unusual places."	"How could you do this to me? What were you thinking? Were you thinking at all? I can't believe that you would be so thoughtless and inconsiderate."
"Blah, blah, blah! All he ever does is talk. From morning until night, his mouth never stops! Why, he even talks in his sleep all night long!"	"The cafeteria menu for today includes sloppy Joes, canned corn, and chocolate brownies for dessert. Peanut butter sandwiches are also available."
"Look at the new baby, Harry. Have you ever seen anything cuter? Her fingers are so tiny. Her skin is so very soft. She looks exactly like her mother."	"I've lost my keys! I've looked every-where imaginable, and they just can't be found. Perhaps they're in my coat pocket. Look! Here they are!"
"The paperboy always throws my newspaper in the grass. When it rains, the paper's a soggy mess. On windy days, it ends up on the Harris' porch."	"To get to Third Street, go east for three blocks. When you get to the stop sign, turn left. Go straight through two traffic lights, and then turn right at the market."
"The ad read: For sale. One boy's bicycle. Red with whitewall tires. Slight dent in the front fender. Call 555-1234 after 5:00 p.m. if interested."	"I won the lottery? Are you joking? I've never played before. I bought that ticket with my last dollar. I never thought that I would win!"

Passages for Repeated Readings, continued

"The sun set ever so slowly and disappeared behind the large oak trees that stood silently in a single row. The bright blue sky dimmed to a deep violet."	"Tomorrow will be mostly sunny with a 50 percent chance of an evening thunderstorm. The high temperature will be 78 degrees with an overnight low of 65 degrees."
"There are no words to describe how you feel when you lose your best friend. Why do parents take jobs in other states? Why can't things just stay the same?"	"I can't wait for summer break—no more getting up early in the morning, no more homework, and no more cafeteria food! I think I'll sleep until noon every day."
"The librarian snapped and told us to be quiet. Even after we quit talking, she just kept staring at us. Her cold glares seemed to cut right through me."	"Lost—a female golden retriever in the vicinity of Harvard Boulevard. Wearing a red collar with silver tags. Very friendly and answers to the name Buffy."
"Spaghetti again? I think we have spaghetti every Thursday for dinner. I like it, but not every week! Can't we go out for dinner tonight?"	"Do you remember when we first met? I'll never forget that day for as long as I live. It was at the Ridgeway Mall. Or was it the theater? Or the stadium?"
Create your own.	Create your own.
Create your own.	Create your own.

EXHIBIT **4.6.B**

Character Voices

Read it in a frightened voice.	Read it in a slow, deliberate voice.
Read it in a shy voice.	Read it in a sharp voice.
Read it in an excited voice.	Read it in an uncertain voice.
Read it in a nervous voice.	Read it in a monotone voice.
Read it in a sleepy voice.	Read it in a whispering voice.
Read it in a surprised voice.	Read it in a loud voice.
Read it in a demanding voice.	Read it in a calm voice.
Read it in a confident voice.	Read it in a matter-of-fact voice.
Read it in an angry voice.	Read it in a pleasant voice.
Read it in a frustrated voice.	Read it in a dull voice.

Repeated Readings Fluency Checklist

(4) Excellent = Reads with excellent expression, ease, fluency, and voice.

(3) Good = Reads with good expression, ease, fluency, and voice.

(2) Fair = Reads with fair expression, ease, fluency, and voice.

(1) Poor = Reads with poor expression, ease, fluency, and voice.

STUDENTS' NAMES	(4) EXCELLENT	(3) GOOD	(2) FAIR	(1) POOR

ACTIVITY 4.7

Literature Graffiti

GRADE LEVEL: **4–6**

OBJECTIVES

- To read fiction (or nonfiction) texts to acquire new information and for personal fulfillment
- To apply strategies to comprehend, interpret, evaluate, and appreciate texts

MATERIALS

- A selected chapter book appropriate for grades 4–6 (See the Children's Literature section at the end of this activity for possible titles.)
- Chart paper
- Markers

NCTE/IRA STANDARDS

1 Students read a wide range of print and non-print texts to build an understanding of texts, of themselves, and of the cultures of the United States and the world; to acquire new information; to respond to the needs and demands of society and the workplace; and for personal fulfillment. Among these texts are fiction and nonfiction, classic and contemporary works.

3 Students apply a wide range of strategies to comprehend, interpret, evaluate, and appreciate texts. They draw on their prior experience, their interactions with other readers and writers, their knowledge of word meaning and of other texts, their word identification strategies, and their understanding of textual features (e.g., sound–letter correspondence, sentence structure, context, graphics).

Activity adapted from Rose-Colley, Bechtel, & Cinelli, 1994.

PROCEDURES

1. Choose a chapter book that is appropriate for grades 4–6. Either fiction or nonfiction will work for this activity. As an example, *Stargirl*, by Jerry Spinelli, will be highlighted.
2. Read the book aloud to the class over several days, or have students read it independently or with a buddy if class copies are available. If possible, obtain copies of the book in the languages of English language learners (e.g., Spinelli, J., *Stargirl*, Spanish-language edition).
3. Create sentence stems and write each one on a large piece of chart paper. Sentence stems for *Stargirl* could include:
   - I would describe Stargirl as . . .
   - Stargirl cared for other people by . . .
   - Stargirl is unique because . . .
   - I think Stargirl kept changing her name because . . .
   - I would consider Stargirl a strong female character because . . .
4. Tape or attach the chart paper at various locations throughout the classroom. Divide students into the same number of groups as there are sentence stems. Have each group move to one of the sentence stems. Give the groups one minute to write their responses to the sentence stem. All group members must write at the same time, so that no one has time to read or think about someone else's response.

5. At the end of one minute, have the groups rotate around the room to the next sentence stem. The process continues until all groups have responded to all sentence stems.
6. Have the groups rotate through the sentence stems one more time, giving students one minute at each sentence stem to read each other's responses.
7. To process the activity, assign each group a sentence stem. Give the groups four or five minutes to summarize the responses for that stem in one or two sentences. Have each group write its summary at the bottom of the chart paper or on a new sheet. Ask each group to select a spokesperson to share its summary with the class. Discuss each summary statement and allow students to share reactions and comments.
8. For several reasons, this is a good activity for students with learning problems. The book can be read aloud to them, they can react in words or phrases, and spelling doesn't count. English language learners can write in English or in their first language. If they choose to write in their first language, they can interpret their writing orally, and another member of their group can write the response in English.

ASSESSMENT

Literature graffiti affords you the opportunity to observe students and make anecdotal records. During the activity, observe students in the areas of participation, cooperation, and leadership. When students are processing responses, assess their ability to comprehend, evaluate, and interpret the text.

INTEGRATING LANGUAGE ARTS ACROSS THE CURRICULUM

Chapter books with themes in social studies, science, or health can be selected for the literature graffiti activity. Social studies examples might include *Kira-Kira*, by Cynthia Kadobata; *Number the Stars*, by Lois Lowry; and *Fever 1793*, by Laurie Halse Anderson.

HOME–SCHOOL CONNECTION

Anecdotal records, such as those taken during this activity, can be shared with parents. Observations of a child's participation, cooperation, and leadership skills give parents a clearer view of school experiences and performance than grades provide. If students are participating in the conference, encourage them to share the literature graffiti activity with their parents, showing their responses and summary statements as examples.

CHILDREN'S LITERATURE

Anderson, L. H. (2002). *Fever 1793*. Aladdin.

Kadobata, C. (2004). *Kira-Kira*. Atheneum.

Lowry, L. (1998). *Number the stars*. Laurel Leaf.

Spinelli, J. (2000). *Stargirl*. Scholastic.

Spinelli, J. (2004). *Stargirl*. (Spanish-language edition). Santillana USA.

REFERENCE

Rose-Colley, M., Bechtel, L., & Cinelli, B. (1994). Using graffiti to uncover values. *The Health Educator, 26*(1), 29–31.

ACTIVITY 4.8

Newspaper Scavenger Hunt

GRADE LEVEL: **5–6**

OBJECTIVE

- To use skimming and scanning techniques to locate information quickly in print media

MATERIALS

- Old newspapers
- Scissors (one pair per group)
- Newspaper Scavenger Hunt Record Sheet (one per group)
- Highlighters (one marker per group)

NCTE/IRA STANDARD

8 Students use a variety of technological and information resources (e.g., libraries, databases, computer networks, video) to gather and synthesize information and to create and communicate knowledge.

PROCEDURES

1. Discuss the purpose of newspapers. Talk about the 5 W's that are addressed in most newspaper articles: who, what, where, when, and why. Discuss the fact that newspaper articles typically tell who (the person or group) the article is about, what they did or are going to do, where the activity took place, when it occurred, and why it happened.
2. Ask a student volunteer to read a selected brief newspaper article, and have the remaining students identify the 5 W's.
3. Tell students they are going on a newspaper scavenger hunt. Distribute the Newspaper Scavenger Hunt Record Sheet (Exhibit 4.8.A).
4. Discuss skimming and scanning techniques. *Skimming* involves reading through a text quickly to locate information. When skimming, a reader does not read every single word. For example, a reader might only read the first and last paragraph of an article, or only read the title of the article and the first sentence of each paragraph to get the general idea of the article. *Scanning* involves moving your eyes quickly down the page seeking specific words and phrases. When scanning, readers often look for the author's use of organizers such as numbers, letters, steps, or the words *first*, *second*, or *next*. Words that are boldfaced, italicized, or in a different font size, style, or color can also be helpful when scanning a text. Tell students that they will use skimming and scanning techniques during the scavenger hunt.
5. Divide students into groups of five, and give each group five newspapers, a pair of scissors, and a highlighter marker.
6. Tell students they will have 15 minutes to find all 10 items listed on the Newspaper Scavenger Hunt Record Sheet. Once they locate an article, the group should cut it out and highlight the requested information. English language learners should work closely with a partner in the group.

7. Groups may trade newspapers with other groups. If a group finds all 10 items before time is called, have them signal to end the scavenger hunt.
8. At the end of 15 minutes, or whenever a group finds all 10 items listed on the Newspaper Scavenger Hunt Record Sheet, call the search to a halt. Have groups share the contents of the articles they found.

ASSESSMENT

Use informal teacher observation to assess students' ability to locate information quickly through the use of skimming and scanning.

INTEGRATING LANGUAGE ARTS ACROSS THE CURRICULUM

Trade books and textbooks can be used in scavenger hunts. Students can locate parts of the books, such as the title page, copyright, publisher, place of the publishing house, table of contents, index, glossary, and so forth and record the page number on which each is found.

HOME-SCHOOL CONNECTION

Encourage students to read newspapers at home with their families and discuss current events together. Students can have newspaper scavenger hunts with family members.

INTERNET RESOURCES

Capital Newspapers. (2006). Newspapers in education. Retrieved August 19, 2006, from www.capitalnewspapers.com/readers/nie_prog.php.

Education World. (1996–2006). Read all about it: Ten terrific newspaper lessons! Retrieved August 19, 2006, from www.education-world.com/a_lesson/lesson205.shtml.

Forum Communications Company. (2005). Newspapers in education. Retrieved August 19, 2006, from www.in-forum.com/specials/nie/.

Newspapers in Education. 100 ways to use the newspaper. Retrieved August 19, 2006, from http://web.redding.com/community/nie/index_lessons.shtml.

The Seattle Times Company. (2005). Curriculum guides for elementary school. Retrieved August 19, 2006, from http://services.nwsource.com/nie/times/educators/guides Elementary.asp.

EXHIBIT **4.8.A**

Newspaper Scavenger Hunt Record Sheet

Directions: Locate newspaper articles that include each of the items below. Select one article and identify the 5 W's in the article.

1. An article about an unusual animal

   ____

   ____

2. An article that contains the name *James*

   ____

   ____

3. An article that is exactly five paragraphs long

   ____

   ____

4. An article that mentions a date

   ____

   ____

5. An article that mentions a western state

   ____

   ____

6. A humorous article

   ____

   ____

7. An article about a politician

   ____

   ____

8. An article about a well-known woman

   ____

   ____

9. An article with a direct quote

   ____

   ____

10. An article that mentions a holiday

    ____

    ____

You'll Take to This Like a Duck Takes to Water

Exploring Figurative Language

GRADE: **5–6**

OBJECTIVE

- To apply a wide range of strategies to comprehend, interpret, and appreciate texts

MATERIALS

- *There's a Frog in My Throat*, by Loreen Leedy and Pat Street (See the Children's Literature section at the end of this activity for additional titles.)
- 8 $^1/_2$" x 11" paper (one sheet per student)
- Figurative Language Evaluation Rubric (one per student)

NCTE/IRA STANDARDS

3 Students apply a wide range of strategies to comprehend, interpret, evaluate, and appreciate texts. They draw on their prior experience, their interactions with other readers and writers, their knowledge of word meaning and of other texts, their word identification strategies, and their understanding of textual features (e.g., sound–letter correspondence, sentence structure, context, graphics).

6 Students apply knowledge of language structure, language conventions (e.g., spelling and punctuation), media techniques, figurative language, and genre to create, critique, and discuss print and non-print texts.

PROCEDURES

1. Read some of the figurative animal sayings in *There's a Frog in My Throat* and ask students to explain what they mean. Discuss the meaning of simile, metaphor, idiom, and proverb as outlined in the letter from the authors found in the beginning of the book. For more information about teaching figurative language, see the Internet Resources section at the end of the activity.
2. Ask students to think of another example of figurative language. Give each student a sheet of plain paper. On one side have them write their saying and draw a picture to represent the literal, humorous meaning of the saying. On the other side of the paper, ask students to write and illustrate the common meaning of their saying. For example, the saying, "He went to the head of the line" could be illustrated figuratively by showing a child going to the beginning of a line of students, while a literal interpretation might include a comical drawing of a child going to a large head that is "sitting" at a desk in the classroom. If students have difficulty thinking of a saying to visually represent, books such as *Duke Ellington*, by Andrea Pinkney, and *The King Who Rained* and *A Chocolate Moose*, by Fred Gwynne, contain numerous examples of figurative language. The humorous side of the drawings can be posted in the hallway so students in other classes can guess their meaning.
3. Students can share their figurative language selections by playing charades. Volunteers can come to the front of the room and silently act out the literal, humorous meaning of their saying. The student who correctly guesses the saying should be prepared to explain its common meaning.

4. Young children, English language learners, and children with hearing impairment often have particular difficulty with figurative language. They may need special guidance to choose and interpret a saying. Students with limited reading ability or cognitive skills may choose to select a saying directly from *There's a Frog in My Throat.* Those students who benefit from extra challenge could attempt to label each example of figurative language as either a simile, metaphor, idiom, or proverb.

ASSESSMENT

The objective of this lesson is for students to comprehend both the literal, humorous meaning and the common meaning of their saying. You can use the Figurative Language Evaluation Rubric (Exhibit 4.9.A) to assess comprehension of figurative language as students illustrate their sayings.

INTEGRATING LANGUAGE ARTS ACROSS THE CURRICULUM

It is fun for teachers and students to try to incorporate figurative language into their spoken and written language. Challenge students to see how many figurative expressions they can use in a single school day as they interact with peers and teachers. Then ask students to write a funny one-page story using as many figurative sayings as they can. The more humorous, the better!

HOME-SCHOOL CONNECTION

Challenge students to see how many figurative expressions they can use in conversation during an evening at home. Ask them to monitor how long it takes their families to catch on to what they are doing.

CHILDREN'S LITERATURE

Gwynne, F. (1970). *The king who rained.* Aladdin.

Gwynne, F. (1976). *A chocolate moose.* Trumpet.

Leedy, L., & Street, P. (2003). *There's a frog in my throat! 440 animal sayings a little bird told me.* Scholastic.

Parish, P. (2003). *Amelia Bedelia 40th anniversary collection.* HarperTrophy.

Pinkney, A. (1998). *Duke Ellington.* Hyperion.

Taylor, M. (1976). *Roll of thunder, hear my cry.* Scholastic.

INTERNET RESOURCES

Figurative language. Retrieved August 19, 2006, from http://volweb.utk.edu/Schools/bedford/harrisms/1poe.htm.

IRA/NCTE. (2002–2006). Figurative language: Teaching idioms. Retrieved August 19, 2006, from http://orgwww.readwritethink.org/lessons/lesson_view.asp?id=254.

Teacher Created Resources. Figuratively speaking. Retrieved August 19, 2006, from www.teachercreated.com/lessons/020621il.shtml.

RESOURCES

Rosen, M. (1995). *Walking the bridge of your nose: Wordplay poems and rhymes.* Kingfisher.

Terban, M. (1993). *It figures! Fun figures of speech.* Scholastic.

Terban, M. (1998). *Scholastic dictionary of idioms, phrases, sayings, and expressions.* Scholastic.

Figurative Language Evaluation Rubric

Name ______________________________ Date ______________

CRITERIA	POINT VALUE
Student chose an appropriate example of figurative language for illustration.	☐ / 5
Student demonstrated comprehension of the literal, humorous meaning of the saying.	☐ / 10
Student demonstrated comprehension of the common meaning of the saying.	☐ / 10
TOTAL POINTS	☐ / 25

ACTIVITY 4.10

Vocabulary Cubes

Building Word Meaning and Spelling Skills

GRADE LEVEL: **5–6**

OBJECTIVES

- To spell and define vocabulary words
- To demonstrate understanding of vocabulary words by identifying corresponding parts of speech, synonyms, and antonyms

MATERIALS

- Cube Pattern (one per group)
- Scissors (one per group)
- Transparent tape (one roll per group)
- Paper
- Pencils

NCTE/IRA STANDARDS

3 Students apply a wide range of strategies to comprehend, interpret, evaluate, and appreciate texts. They draw on their prior experience, their interactions with other readers and writers, their knowledge of word meaning and of other texts, their word identification strategies, and their understanding of textual features (e.g., sound–letter correspondence, sentence structure, context, graphics).

4 Students adjust their use of spoken, written, and visual language (e.g., conventions, style, vocabulary) to communicate effectively with a variety of audiences and for different purposes.

PROCEDURES

1. Duplicate the Cube Pattern (Exhibit 4.10.A), one per group of students.
2. Divide the class into small groups of five or six students, and have each group assemble a cube and tape it along the seams.
3. Each group should then write their weekly vocabulary words on small pieces of paper. Fold the slips of paper to hide the words, and place them at the center of the group.
4. The group chooses a student to begin the activity. The student to the right of the first player chooses a vocabulary word. The first player then rolls the cube and does whatever the cube directs. The student will spell the vocabulary word, define it, use the word correctly in a sentence, identify the part of speech, identify a synonym of the word, or identify an antonym of the word. The student to the left of the first player will decide if the player is correct.
5. The vocabulary word returns to the center of the table, and play continues with the next student.

ASSESSMENT

Use informal teacher observation to assess students' participation in the vocabulary practice activity. You can use a written vocabulary assessment to assess students' understanding of the words. The test might be a match test where students match words with definitions, or a fill-in-the-blank format where students fill in the correct vocabulary word using the context of the provided sentence.

INTEGRATING LANGUAGE ARTS ACROSS THE CURRICULUM

A similar activity can be used to review key concepts and terms in other content areas. Simply duplicate the cube pattern and assemble so that the words are hidden inside the cube. Print other appropriate directions on each face of the cube and key concepts and terms on the slips of paper.

HOME–SCHOOL CONNECTION

For additional weekly practice of vocabulary words, each student can be given a cube to assemble and use at home.

INTERNET RESOURCES

Education World. (1996–2006). Vocabulary fun. Retrieved August 19, 2006, from www.educationworld.com/a_special/vocabulary.

English Club.com. (1996). ESL Activities and Games. Retrieved August 19, 2006, from www.englishclub.com/esl-lesson-plans/activities-games.htm.

Instructor Web. (2002–2004). Language arts: Vocabulary. Retrieved August 19, 2006, from www.instructorweb.com/resources/vocabulary.asp.

Oxford University Press. (2006). Vocabulary. Retrieved August 19, 2006, from www.oup.com/elt/global/products/englishfile/elementary/b_vocabulary/.

Pro Lingua Associates. ESL vocabulary materials. Retrieved August 19, 2006, from www.prolinguaassociates.com/Pages/vocabulary.html.

Vocabulary Games. Retrieved August 19, 2006, from www.gamequarium.com/evocabulary.html.

Vocabulary University. (2006). Vocabulary. Retrieved August 19, 2006, from www.vocabulary.com/.

EXHIBIT **4.10.A**

Cube Pattern

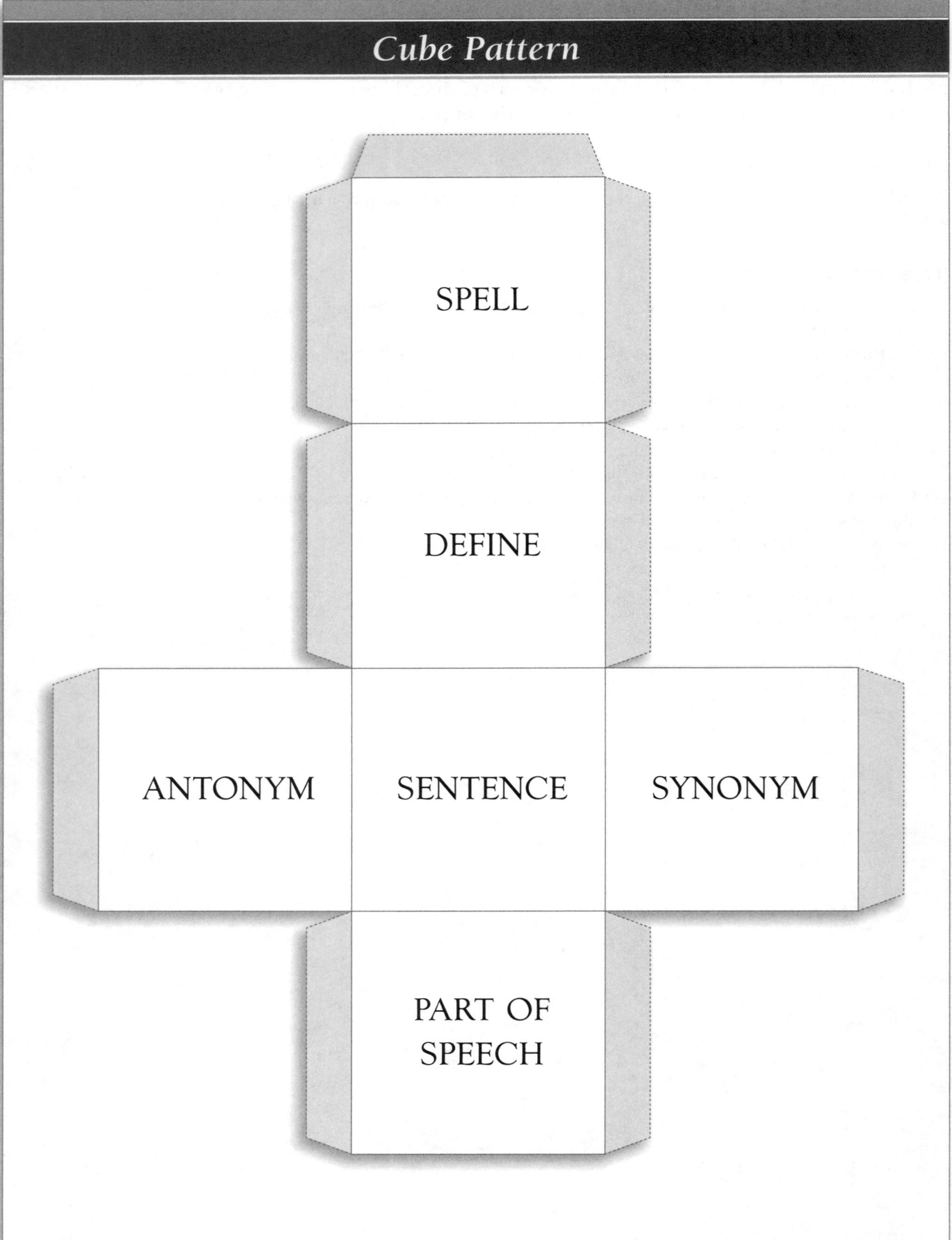

CHAPTER 5 WRITING

Teaching Students to Become Authors

INTRODUCTION

"Children want to write" (Graves, Tuyay, & Green, 2004, p. 88). Donald Graves wrote those words more than 20 years ago, and he continues to believe them today. He acknowledges, however, that teaching and schools have changed. Teachers are accountable for a greatly expanded curriculum, and much of language arts time is spent exclusively on reading. When writing is addressed, schools often treat the writing process as a set of steps "set in stone." In these classrooms, students can be so caught up in brainstorming, drafting, revising, and publishing, that the flexibility necessary to be a true writer is often lost (Graves, Tuyay, & Green, 2004).

Educators understand that astute methods of teaching children to write make a vast difference in writing outcomes and students' attitudes about writing. Students need opportunities to choose their own topics, because they can only write best about what they know and have experienced. They benefit from discussing how writers get their ideas, how writers use everyday experiences as possibilities for narrative, and how to share writing with others who love the same things. Thus, children need to be treated as writers (Graves, Tuyay, & Green, 2004; Ray, 2004).

Writing takes time, effort, and perseverance. Tompkins (2005) suggests that teachers schedule 60- to 90-minute periods each day for writing workshop. Throughout this time period, teachers teach mini-lessons related to writing workshop procedures, literary concepts, and writing skills and strategies (Portalupi & Fletcher, 2001). In addition to participating in mini-lessons, students engage in the writing process by choosing their own topics, writing multiple drafts, conferencing with classmates, revising, editing, and sharing their writing with others (Calkins, 1994). Students should be encouraged to be good decision makers. They can independently determine what piece to work on and when to move on to something new. Decisions on genre and the publication and display of their work should always involve the writer (Graves, Tuyay, & Green, 2004; Ray, 2004).

Above all, students need to see the purpose for writing. If the teaching of writing is broken down into basic skills such as mechanics and penmanship, students often miss the purpose, and writing becomes merely an exercise (Roe & Ross, 2006). Calkins (1994) affirms that we must teach writers, not writing. In doing so, teachers must themselves be readers and writers, and plan according to what interests people who are writers (Ray, 2004).

Classroom Vignette

Ms. Spencer announces to her students that it is now time to begin daily writing workshop. After students retrieve their folders from the writing center, Ms. Spencer asks Tommy if he'd like to share his finished story about his trip to Mexico with the class. He eagerly agrees and takes his place on the special sharing chair before beginning to read to his peers. After his reading, classmates congratulate Tommy on a job well done. Next, the teacher reminds each student about what he/she should be working on throughout the period. She tells Tyler, Jaime, Venita, Jimmy, and Josh that they need to peer conference with at least two classmates before conferencing with her today on their finished pieces of writing. Jose, Phil, Terry, and LaTonya are reminded that they need to choose a new topic from their Personal Writing Topics list and begin their first drafts today. Jennifer, Ryan, Cari, and Austin are asked to finish word processing their completed pieces, which will be displayed on the class bulletin board before being added to the class book, housed in the classroom library. Remaining students are called to a corner of the classroom for a 15-minute mini-lesson that Ms. Spencer will teach on paragraphing. After answering several student questions, the children in Room 2-B assume their roles as authors and begin their work.

DISCUSSION QUESTIONS

1. Name at least three tasks that students are asked to perform throughout writing workshop and relate them to the stages of the writing process.
2. How does Ms. Spencer support her students throughout writing workshop?
3. Should student writers be required to share their writing with others? Justify your response.
4. Besides serving as a tool for word processing, how can technology support writers?
5. Compare your own experiences with writing during the elementary years. How are your experiences similar? How are your experiences different?

References

Calkins, L. (1994). *The art of teaching writing.* Portsmouth, NH: Heinemann.

Graves, D., Tuyay, S., & Green, J. (2004). What I've learned from teachers of writing. *Language Arts, 82*(2), 88–95.

Portalupi, J., & Fletcher, R. (2001). *Nonfiction craft lessons: Teaching information writing K–8.* Portland, ME: Stenhouse.

Ray, K. W. (2004). Why Cauley writes well: A close look at what a difference good teaching can make. *Language Arts, 82*(2), 100–110.

Roe, B., & Ross, E. (2006). *Integrating language arts through literature & thematic units.* New York: Pearson.

Tompkins, G. (2005). *Literacy for the 21st century: A balanced approach* (4th ed.). Upper Saddle River, NJ: Merrill/Prentice Hall.

ACTIVITY 5.1

All About Me Journals

GRADE LEVEL: **K–1**

OBJECTIVES

- To complete writing prompts using experimental spellings
- To demonstrate awareness of concepts of print and that writing is a form of communication

MATERIALS

- Teacher-created writing journals (one per student)
- All About Me Writing Prompts (one copy)
- All About Me Writing Checklist (one per student)
- Pencils
- Crayons or markers

NCTE/IRA STANDARD

3 Students apply a wide range of strategies to comprehend, interpret, evaluate, and appreciate texts. They draw on their prior experience, their interactions with other readers and writers, their knowledge of word meaning and of other texts, their word identification strategies, and their understanding of textual features (e.g., sound–letter correspondence, sentence structure, context, graphics).

PROCEDURES

1. Using the provided All About Me Writing Prompts (Exhibit 5.1.A), create journals for students. Begin by either printing or word processing one writing prompt per page. Prompts for English language learners can be written in their first language, along with the standard English version. Duplicate journal pages, add a cover sheet for each student's name, and staple together.
2. Establish a daily time for journal writing. Five to 10 minutes per day is sufficient for younger students. Have students respond to one writing prompt each day.
3. Read the daily prompt aloud. Students should be encouraged to finish the prompt using experimental spellings. Remind students to place a period at the end of each sentence.
4. After responding to the prompt, students may illustrate their response using crayons or markers.
5. Have each student read his/her response, and transcribe what the student intended to write below the writing.
6. Responses can be used to assess the child's phonological awareness and concepts of print.

ASSESSMENT

The All About Me Writing Checklist (Exhibit 5.1.B) can be used to assess students' writing.

INTEGRATING LANGUAGE ARTS ACROSS THE CURRICULUM

Young children should become aware that writing is a way to communicate with others and that written communication can take many different forms, including stories, poems, letters, recipes, lists, invitations, and directions. Providing children with a variety of stimulating writing materials and opportunities to write is essential.

HOME–SCHOOL CONNECTION

Students can be encouraged to write at home through the use of Family Literacy Backpacks. To create these, simply fill several small, durable backpacks with materials that encourage reading and writing at home. Materials could include story starters, trade books, different-colored paper, pencils, markers or crayons, alphabet stencils, envelopes, and so forth. Students can take turns taking the backpacks home to share with family members.

EXHIBIT **5.1.A**

All About Me Writing Prompts

1. My name is ________________________________
2. I like to ________________________________
3. I can ________________________________
4. I like to eat ________________________________
5. I play ________________________________
6. I read ________________________________
7. I am happy when I ________________________________
8. My hair is ________________________________
9. My eyes are ________________________________
10. Today, I will ________________________________
11. I want to ________________________________
12. I run ________________________________
13. My friends ________________________________
14. I have ________________________________
15. Once, I ________________________________
16. I found ________________________________
17. I lost ________________________________
18. I think ________________________________
19. I saw ________________________________
20. I feel ________________________________

All About Me Writing Checklist

Name ______________________ Date __________ Writing Prompt # __________

The student:	YES	NO
1. displayed a knowledge of left to right directionality.	☐	☐
2. responded appropriately to the prompt.	☐	☐
3. evidenced some knowledge of letter–sound relationships.	☐	☐
4. was able to repeat the sentence after the teacher.	☐	☐
5. attempted to use punctuation.	☐	☐
6. completed the writing prompt within the time provided.	☐	☐
7. displayed a positive attitude toward writing.	☐	☐
8. evidenced knowledge that writing communicates.	☐	☐
9. drew a picture that illustrated the completed prompt.	☐	☐

ACTIVITY 5.2

Organizing for Writing

GRADE LEVEL: **K–1**

OBJECTIVE

- To distinguish between the beginning, middle, and end of a story

MATERIALS

- Popular and well-known traditional folktales from books or websites (See bibliography at the end of this activity for suggested titles.)
- 8 $^{1}/_{2}$" x 11" white drawing paper (one per student)
- Crayons or colored markers

NCTE/IRA STANDARDS

3 Students apply a wide range of strategies to comprehend, interpret, evaluate, and appreciate texts. They draw on their prior experience, their interactions with other readers and writers, their knowledge of word meaning and of other texts, their word identification strategies, and their understanding of textual features (e.g., sound–letter correspondence, sentence structure, context, graphics).

6 Students apply knowledge of language structure, language conventions (e.g., spelling and punctuation), media techniques, figurative language, and genre to create, critique, and discuss print and non-print texts.

PROCEDURES

1. Begin by discussing the terms *beginning, middle,* and *end.* Have students give examples of things they do at the beginning of the day (for example, wake up, get dressed, eat breakfast, brush teeth), during the middle of the day (for example, eat lunch, take a nap, play with toys), and at the end of the day (for example, eat dinner, get ready for bed, listen to a story).
2. Call students to the reading corner of the classroom and read a traditional folktale, such as *Goldilocks and the Three Bears, The Three Little Pigs,* or *The Three Billy Goats Gruff.* Numerous websites, such as www.americanfolklore.net and www.pitara.com/talespin/folktales.asp, contain both American and international folktales. Tell students to listen carefully to hear what happens at the beginning of the story, during the middle, and at the end.
3. Draw three large squares on the chalkboard. Label the first square "B" for beginning, the second square "M" for middle, and the third square "E" for end.
4. Have students discuss what happened at the beginning of the story and draw a simple sketch of it in the "B" square on the chalkboard. Below the sketch, print a simple sentence that summarizes the beginning of the story. For example, if the original version of *The Three Little Pigs* was shared, the teacher could print beneath the picture: "The three little pigs built their homes in the forest." Point out the capital letter at the beginning of the sentence and the period at the end. Repeat the process for the other two squares to summarize the story's middle and end.
5. Throughout the week, explore other folktales and have student volunteers draw the sketches on the board and compose the summary sentences.

6. Once students seem to understand the beginning–middle–end concept, read another folktale to them and have them complete the activity independently by giving each child a sheet of drawing paper that has been folded into thirds lengthwise. English language learners can be paired with native speakers. Have them label the three columns "B," "M," and "E." Tell them to draw what happened in each section of the story and write a sentence below. Remind them to use a capital letter at the beginning of each sentence and a period at the end.
7. When complete, students can share their beginning–middle–end graphic organizers with each other.

ASSESSMENT

Informal teacher observation of the pictures and corresponding sentences should be used to assess students' understanding of story parts, capitalization, and end punctuation.

INTEGRATING LANGUAGE ARTS ACROSS THE CURRICULUM

Students can be asked to identify the beginning, middle, and ending of other stories that they read. Encourage them to use simple sequence words like *first*, *then*, and *next*. Use these words when giving students oral directions for other classroom activities.

HOME-SCHOOL CONNECTION

Invite parents to continue practicing this skill at home by asking their children to identify the beginnings, middles, and endings of stories shared at home. Share this idea with parents at a scheduled parent–teacher conference.

A BIBLIOGRAPHY OF WELL-KNOWN FOLKTALES

Andersen, H. (1999). *The princess and the pea.* Abbeville Kids.

Brett, J. (1996). *Goldilocks and the three bears.* Putnam Juvenile Books.

Galdone, P. (1985). *The little red hen.* Clarion Books.

Galdone, P. (1984). *The three little pigs.* Clarion Books.

Galdone, P. (1981). *The three billy goats gruff.* Clarion Books.

Grimm, J. (1986). *Rumpelstiltskin.* Dutton Juvenile.

Jaiman, A. (2006). *Pitara Kids Network.* Available at www.pitara.com/talespin/folktales.asp.

Kellogg, S. (1997). *Jack and the beanstalk.* Harper Trophy.

Kellogg, S. (1987). *Chicken little.* Harper Trophy.

Marshall, J. (1993). *Hansel and Gretel.* Puffin.

Schlosser, S. (2006). *American folklore.* Available at www.americanfolklore.net/.

Wattenberg, J. (2000). *Henny-Penny.* Scholastic Press.

Zelinsky, P. (1997). *Rapunzel.* Dutton Books.

A C T I V I T Y 5.3

Creating Colorful Word Pictures

Similes

GRADE LEVEL: **2–3**

OBJECTIVES

- To identify similes in writing
- To write and illustrate original similes

MATERIALS

- One copy of *I'm as Quick as a Cricket*, by Audrey Wood (1990, Child's Play International)
- Websites such as library.thinkquest.org/J0112392/simile.html
- White drawing paper (one per student)
- Crayons or colored markers

NCTE/IRA STANDARD

6 Students apply knowledge of language structure, language conventions (e.g., spelling and punctuation), media techniques, figurative language, and genre to create, critique, and discuss print and non-print texts.

PROCEDURES

1. Introduce similes to students by writing the following on the chalkboard:

   Tommy was *as* hungry as a bear.

   The train moved *like* a lightning bolt.

2. Have students close their eyes as you read the first sentence. Ask: "What did you imagine as I read the sentence to you?" After students share, ask them to identify what is being compared in the first example. Underline the words *Tommy* and *bear*. Focus students' attention on the word *as*, used to compare the two. Repeat the process with the second example, underlining the words *train* and *lightning bolt*, and calling attention to the comparison word, *like*.
3. Introduce the term *simile:* A simile is a comparison of two unlike things, using the word *like* or *as*. Tell students that writers use similes to help readers form colorful mental images about what they are reading.
4. Create several similes together, and then ask students if they know any other similes. Ask volunteers to write their similes on the board and identify the two things being compared and the word that is used in the comparison (*like* or *as*).
5. Read the book *I'm as Quick as a Cricket*, by Audrey Wood. Pause after each simile and ask students to identify what is being compared and the word used in helping to make the comparison. To give students more practice in identifying similes, read some of the poems at library.thinkquest.org/J0112392/simile.html.
6. After reading and discussing the book and poems, tell students they are going to create original similes of their own. Assign each student a different simile starter from the list below, and ask them to complete it. English

language learners may be paired with other students. Remind them to be creative and to use capital letters and punctuation correctly. When they are finished writing, have them peer conference with a classmate to revise and edit as needed.

7. Once similes are complete, students may illustrate them and share them with the class. For example, a student might write: *She is as fast as a cheetah.* An accompanying illustration might depict a cheetah-like creature with the head of a female, running through a forest.

LIST OF SIMILE STARTERS

as fast as	as big as	as goofy as
slow like	tiny like	disappointed like
as angry as	as mean as	as surprised as
smart like	tired like	dry like
as cute as	as jumpy as	as soft as
heavy like	green like	early like
as hot as	as shy as	as straight as
cold like	loud like	twisted like
as happy as	as tasty as	as secret as
funny like	warm like	hidden like

ASSESSMENT

Collect student papers and assess as follows:

+1 point if the student supplied two unlike objects for comparison

+1 point if the comparison made sense to the reader

+1 point if the illustration corresponded to the simile

+1 point for correct use of punctuation

+1 point for correct use of capital letters

INTEGRATING LANGUAGE ARTS ACROSS THE CURRICULUM

Call students' attention to similes as they are encountered in other written materials in other areas of the curriculum.

HOME-SCHOOL CONNECTION

Ask students to record any similes that they hear or see at home for the rest of the week. For example, similes may be heard in people's spoken description of events, in radio commercials, or in television programs. Similes can be seen in books students are reading at home and in magazines or on the Internet. Create a Simile Wall in the classroom by having students record their similes on sentence strips and attach them to a classroom wall. The class can use this display as a reference source during writing workshop.

REFERENCE

Lummis Elementary School. (2006). *ThinkQuest: Similes.* Available at library.thinkquest.org/J0112392/simile.html.

ACTIVITY 5.4

What Am I?

Writing Five-Sense Riddles

GRADE LEVEL: **2–3**

OBJECTIVES

- To write accurate and vivid descriptions of familiar objects in riddle format
- To identify common objects based on accurate written descriptions

MATERIALS

- A collection of familiar objects such as a piece of fruit, a pencil, a cotton ball, a slice of bread, a shoe, a stick of chewing gum, a baseball, a football, a jump rope, a piece of composition paper, a child's lunchbox, a mitten, a can of soda, a toothbrush
- What Am I? handout (one per student)
- What Am I? Descriptive Riddle Writing Rubric (one copy)

NCTE/IRA STANDARDS

4 Students adjust their use of spoken, written, and visual language (e.g., conventions, style, vocabulary) to communicate effectively with a variety of audiences and for different purposes.

5 Students employ a wide range of strategies as they write and use different writing process elements appropriately to communicate with different audiences for a variety of purposes.

12 Students use spoken, written, and visual language to accomplish their own purposes (e.g., for learning, enjoyment, persuasion, and the exchange of information).

PROCEDURES

1. Write the following riddle on the chalkboard and ask a student volunteer to read it aloud:

   I **look** shiny and round, and can be red or green.

   I **smell** like a freshly baked pie or a cup of fruit juice.

   I **sound** like "plop" when I fall from the tree.

   I **taste** sweet when I'm red and sour when I'm green.

   I **feel** smooth to the touch.

   What am I? *(Answer: an apple)*

2. After students solve the riddle, draw their attention to the boldfaced words and discuss how the five senses help us learn about things in our environment. On the chalkboard, draw five columns with the headers *Looks like . . .*, *Smells like . . .*, *Sounds like . . .*, *Tastes like . . .*, and *Feels like . . . .* Ask students to brainstorm possible words that can used to describe how something
   - Looks (size, color, shape, etc.)
   - Smells (yummy, unpleasant, fruity, sweet, etc.)
   - Sounds (soft, loud, etc.)
   - Tastes (sweet, sour, bitter, etc.)
   - Feels (smooth, rough, soft, hard, etc.)

3. Distribute the What Am I? handout (Exhibit 5.4.A) and direct students' attention to a collection of familiar objects.
4. Tell students that each of them should mentally choose one of the familiar objects and write a riddle that accurately describes it. Students will record answers on the handout.
5. After riddles are complete, have individuals share them with the class. Classmates can guess which objects are being described.

ASSESSMENT

You can assess students' written descriptions by using the What Am I? Descriptive Riddle Writing Rubric (Exhibit 5.4.B) provided.

INTEGRATING LANGUAGE ARTS ACROSS THE CURRICULUM

Students can practice descriptive riddle writing in other content areas. In math, students can write riddles for geometric solids, using math terms. For example, riddles can disclose the number of edges or corners, whether the shape rolls or slides, and objects in nature that resemble the geometric figure. Students can also write descriptive riddles for literary characters and people and places that are explored in social studies.

HOME–SCHOOL CONNECTION

At home, ask students to draw a picture, or find one in a magazine or clip art collection, of a familiar object and write a corresponding descriptive riddle. Pictures and riddles can be used to create an interactive classroom bulletin board entitled "Riddling Pictures." Begin by mounting pictures and descriptions on separate pieces of poster board or construction paper. Attach pictures in one column and descriptions in another column onto the bulletin board with magnetic strips or push pins. Shuffle riddles and instruct students to match the pictures and riddles by aligning them side by side.

EXHIBIT **5.4.A**

What Am I?

Name ______________________________ Date ______________

Directions: Use the sentence starters below to describe one of the objects. Think about how the object looks, smells, tastes, sounds, and feels.

I look ______________________________

____

I smell ______________________________

____

I taste ______________________________

____

I sound ______________________________

____

I feel ______________________________

____

What am I?

Answer: ______________________________

____

What Am I?: Descriptive Riddle Writing Rubric

Name ______________________________ Date ____________

Student's Name	Object Described	*3* Riddle is highly descriptive, accurate, and includes all 5 senses	*2* Riddle is somewhat descriptive, accurate, and includes 3–4 senses	*1* Riddle lacks adequate description and accuracy. Includes fewer than 3 senses

ACTIVITY 5.5

Creative Coffee Can Tales

GRADE LEVEL: **3**

OBJECTIVE

- To apply knowledge of written language structure and conventions to compose a creative story

MATERIALS

- Three large, empty coffee cans
- Decorative self-adhesive shelf paper or colored construction paper
- Coffee Can Characters (one copy)
- Coffee Can Settings (one copy)
- Coffee Can Conflicts (one copy)
- Coffee Can Tales Assignment Rubric (one per student)
- Scissors (one pair)
- Composition paper
- Pencils
- Crayons, markers, or colored pencils

NCTE/IRA STANDARD

6 Students apply knowledge of language structure, language conventions (e.g., spelling and punctuation), media techniques, figurative language, and genre to create, critique, and discuss print and non-print texts.

PROCEDURES

1. Cover three large, empty coffee cans with decorative self-adhesive shelf paper or colored construction paper. Label one can *Characters*, one can *Settings*, and the third can *Conflicts*.
2. Duplicate and cut apart the Coffee Can Characters (Exhibit 5.5.A), Coffee Can Settings (Exhibit 5.5.B), and Coffee Can Conflicts (Exhibit 5.5.C). Place each set in the corresponding can.
3. Begin by reviewing basic story elements with students, including characters, setting, conflict, and resolution.
4. Draw students' attention to the three coffee can labels: Characters, Settings, and Conflicts. Randomly draw a few slips of paper from each can and read them aloud. Model the creation of a story from the slips that were selected.
5. Tell students that each of them will randomly draw a character, setting, and conflict from the cans, and then write a creative story using them. Students should create an appropriate resolution for their stories.
6. Discuss the concept of gender stereotyping with students and provide examples, such as doctors are always male, females are emotional, males are strong and aggressive. Caution them to avoid the use of gender stereotyping in their stories.

7. Distribute the Coffee Can Tales Assignment Rubric (Exhibit 5.5.D) and discuss assignment expectations.
8. Provide sufficient time for drafting over several writing periods. English language learners can be paired with native English speakers.
9. Encourage peer conferencing and editing before conferencing with individual students.
10. Once final drafts are completed, have volunteers share their stories in class. Compositions may be collected and made into a class book of short stories or displayed on a bulletin board.

ASSESSMENT

You may use the Coffee Can Tales Assignment Rubric (Exhibit 5.5.D) to assess students' writing. Discuss assignment expectations in clear and understandable terms with students before they begin writing. Allow ample opportunities for peer conferencing, editing, and revision before evaluating story work.

INTEGRATING LANGUAGE ARTS ACROSS THE CURRICULUM

Writing across the curriculum is essential. Students need to understand that writing is a lifelong skill that helps us to communicate in a variety of contexts. Students can write creative and imaginative stories about historical figures and events that incorporate factual details. Likewise, groups of students can write creative readers' theater scripts about people who have made significant contributions in the area of science.

HOME-SCHOOL CONNECTION

Writers often write about what they know best—people in their lives, places they have visited, personal struggles and experiences, favorite hobbies and activities, family pets, and so forth. Tell students to brainstorm a list of possible writing topics that come from their own lives. Encourage students to talk with family members about experiences they have shared. The list of possible topics can be placed in students' writing folders for future use.

EXHIBIT **5.5.A**

Coffee Can Characters

two girls	the confused math teacher
a circus clown	my mother
a boy	my dad
three playful kittens	my new puppy
the librarian	my Uncle Todd
a lonely old lady	a clumsy acrobat
the kind zookeeper	a goofy farmer
the loud bus driver	my best friend
a shy newspaper reporter	a beautiful movie star
the weird next-door neighbor	a large football player
a brave fireman	a helpful police officer
a sick doctor	a sad dentist
three mischievous farm animals	the Cub Scout leader
my Grandpa Joe	a talented ballet dancer
a funny baby	an angry parrot

Coffee Can Settings

the schoolyard	a bank
during science class	a dark forest
the bus	a cave
a mountain top	on the stage
the cafeteria	a scary jungle
the principal's office	post office
a farm	busy city
my backyard	my living room
the park	the zoo
a small town	my best friend's house
the parking lot	in a car
doctor's office	the circus
the grocery store	the auditorium
the beach	on a train
on a boat	in an airplane

EXHIBIT **5.5.C**

Coffee Can Conflicts

someone tells a secret	something gets lost
a disagreement occurs	someone gets lost
something gets broken	someone tells a lie
a wallet filled with money is found	a snowstorm changes plans
a party is cancelled	someone cheats
someone gets sick	something is stolen
something is hidden	an accident happens
someone gets grounded	a house catches on fire
a lunchbox is missing	an important letter gets lost
a huge tree falls	a key is lost
the traffic light breaks	the dog eats an important paper
music is too loud	a water pipe bursts
the lights go out	the concert is cancelled
someone gets fired at work	the weather forecaster is wrong
someone leaves early	the winning raffle ticket disappears

Coffee Can Tales Assignment Rubric

Name ______________________________ Date ______________

	3	2	1
Title	Title is very creative, interesting, and appropriate.	Title is somewhat creative, interesting, and appropriate	Title lacks creativity, fails to stimulate interest, or is inappropriate.
Characters	Characters are highly believable and very interesting. Gender stereotyping is completely avoided.	Characters are somewhat believable and interesting. Gender stereotyping is somewhat avoided.	Characters are not believable or interesting. Gender stereotyping is used throughout.
Setting	Setting is very well described.	Setting is somewhat described.	Setting is not adequately described.
Conflict	Conflict is highly developed.	Conflict is adequately developed.	Conflict is not adequately developed.
Resolution	The ending of the story is very clear and logical.	The ending of the story is somewhat clear and logical.	The ending of the story is neither clear nor logical.
Organization	Story has a very clear beginning, middle, and ending.	Story has a somewhat clear beginning, middle, and ending.	Story lacks overall organization.
Word choice	Highly descriptive language is used throughout the story.	Somewhat descriptive language is used throughout the story.	Little to no descriptive language is used throughout the story.
Sentence structure and fluency	Sentences are varied and highly fluent.	Sentences are somewhat varied and fluent.	Little to no sentence variety and fluency are evident.
Writing conventions	0–3 errors noted in spelling, capitalization, and punctuation.	4–6 errors noted in spelling, capitalization, and punctuation.	7 or more errors noted in spelling, capitalization, and punctuation.
Neatness	Final draft is very neat and attractive.	Final draft is somewhat neat and attractive.	Final draft is neither neat nor attractive.

Score ________ / 30

Comments: ______________________________

Quickwrites

A Technique to Activate Prior Knowledge

GRADE LEVEL: **4**

OBJECTIVE

- To use writing to activate and assess prior knowledge prior to reading

MATERIALS

- A selected chapter book (See the Children's Literature section at the end of this activity for suggested titles.)
- Chart paper

NCTE/IRA STANDARDS

10 Students whose first language is not English make use of their first language to develop competency in the English language arts and to develop understanding of content across the curriculum.

12 Students use spoken, written, and visual language to accomplish their own purposes (e.g., for learning, enjoyment, persuasion, and the exchange of information).

PROCEDURES

1. Select a chapter book for students to read.
2. Select the topic you want students to write about. The topic of the quick-write should relate to the main events, main ideas, or characters in the story. For example, if students were to read *Out of the Dust* (Hesse, 1997), you might ask students to write on what they know about the Oklahoma Dust Bowl during the Great Depression. If they were preparing to read *Dog Jack* (Biros, 1981), students might write about what they know about the Civil War.
3. Have students write on the chosen topic for three to five minutes. Inform students that their writing will not be graded.
4. Divide students into groups of four or five. Allow them to share what they know about the topic and pool their information. Have one student in each group act as recorder.
5. Ask the students in each group to share what they know about the topic with the whole class. One student from each of the groups can act as spokesperson, and the ideas can be shared and recorded on chart paper.
6. Have students read the chapter book individually or with a buddy. Students should check the accuracy of their prior knowledge against the facts in the book. Comparisons can be discussed in literature circles or in the large group.
7. Students with less well developed writing skills should have success with quickwrites because mechanics are not evaluated and the writing is not graded. However, students with more serious disabilities may opt to do a quickdraw, in which students draw instead of write. English language learners can do their quickwrite in their first language or in English.

ASSESSMENT

Quickwrites are not evaluated or graded. Observe students during the writing and small group discussion process to note skills such as participation, small group interaction, and leadership, as well as the extent of their prior knowledge on the topic.

INTEGRATING LANGUAGE ARTS ACROSS THE CURRICULUM

Quickwrites can be implemented in numerous ways. They may be used to activate and assess prior knowledge of any subject, including topics in math, health, science, and social studies. They may also be used during instruction or as a follow-up activity to assess what students have learned. During value-based discussions, quickwrites allow students to write what they believe about issues such as bullying or report cards.

HOME-SCHOOL CONNECTION

Students can select a book to take home and share with family members. Before reading the book, both students and family members could do a quickwrite describing what they already know about the topic of the book, or what they believe the book might be about. They can compare their quickwrites and then read the book to see if their predictions and knowledge of the topic were correct.

CHILDREN'S LITERATURE

Biros, F. (1981). *Dog Jack.* Sonrise Publications.

Hesse, K. (1997). *Out of the dust.* Scholastic.

REFERENCE

Elbow, P. (1973). *Writing without teachers.* London: Oxford University Press.

ACTIVITY 5.7

Choices in Poetry Writing

Poetry Contracts

GRADE LEVEL: **5**

OBJECTIVES

- To use written and visual language to communicate effectively through poetry
- To use written and visual language for learning and enjoyment

MATERIALS

- A selection of poetry books (See the Children's Literature section at the end of this activity for suggested titles.)
- A selection of poetry websites
- Poetry Forms Sample handout (one per student)
- Poetry Evaluation Rubric (one per student)
- Poetry Contract (one per student)

NCTE/IRA STANDARDS

4 Students adjust their use of spoken, written, and visual language (e.g., conventions, style, vocabulary) to communicate effectively with a variety of audiences and for different purposes.

10 Students whose first language is not English make use of their first language to develop competency in the English language arts and to develop understanding of content across the curriculum.

12 Students use spoken, written, and visual language to accomplish their own purposes (e.g., for learning, enjoyment, persuasion, and the exchange of information).

PROCEDURES

1. Introduce students to various types of poetry by reading aloud selections from books such as *I'm Still Here in the Bathtub: Brand New Silly Dilly Songs* (Katz, 2004). Also introduce students to poetry from the children's poetry websites found in the Internet Resources section at the end of this activity.
2. Share and discuss the Poetry Form Samples handout (Exhibit 5.7.A), which describes different types of poetry, including
   - Acrostic
   - Diamante
   - Haiku
   - Limerick

   Discuss directions for writing each type of poem.
3. To give students practice in poetry writing, have them participate in the writing of class collaboration poems, using each of the types of poetry.
4. Give students a Poetry Contract (Exhibit 5.7.B) and have them choose three of the options to complete. The choices give students the freedom to explore poetry in their own way. Some choices allow students to illustrate poems or share their poems with younger students. You might choose to approve contracts in advance.
5. Compile poems into a class collaboration poetry book. Make a bound copy for each student.
6. Encourage English language learners to write poems in their first language and/or in English. Students who have difficulty with writing tasks may

need cues or prompts, extra modeling of poetry forms, or dictation. If several students need assistance, you might help them create small-group collaboration poems. Students who are artistic may want to volunteer to illustrate the class collaboration book and its cover.

ASSESSMENT

You may assess this activity by using the Poetry Evaluation Rubric (Exhibit 5.7.C). Provide the rubric to students along with the poetry contract so they can use it to guide their work and performance.

INTEGRATING LANGUAGE ARTS ACROSS THE CURRICULUM

Books such as *Lives: Poems About Famous Americans* (Hopkins, 1999), *All By Herself: 14 Girls Who Made a Difference* (Paul, 1999), and *This Place I Know: Poems of Comfort* (Heard, 2002), which was compiled after the September 11, 2001 tragedy, are useful for incorporating poetry into the teaching of history and social studies. Students may also be encouraged to select a famous person from history and write a biographical poem about that person.

HOME-SCHOOL CONNECTION

Students can share their Poetry Contract (Exhibit 5.7.B) with family members so parents are informed of the requirements for this project. Parents may also enjoy reading or hearing their child's poems and others from the class collaboration poetry book.

CHILDREN'S LITERATURE

Heard, G. (2002). *This place I know: Poems of comfort.* Candlewick Press.

Hopkins, L. (1999). *Lives: Poems about famous Americans.* HarperCollins.

Katz, A. (2003). *I'm still here in the bathtub: Brand new silly dilly songs.* Scholastic.

Paul, A. W. (1999). *All by herself: 14 girls who made a difference.* Harcourt.

Prelutsky, J. (1982). *The baby uggs are hatching.* Mulberry.

Prelutsky, J. (1983). *Zoo doings.* Trumpet.

Prelutsky, J. (1993). *The dragons are singing tonight.* Scholastic.

RELATED POETRY

Adoff, A. (1997). *I am the darker brother: An anthology of modern poems by African Americans.* Pocket Books.

Alexander, R. (1990). *Poetry place anthology.* Scholastic.

Hopkins, L. (1994). *Hand in hand: An American history through poetry.* Simon & Schuster.

Little, L. (2000). *Children of long ago.* Lee & Low.

INTERNET RESOURCES

Heaney, S. (2006). *The poetry archive.* Available at www.poetryarchive.org/childrensarchive/home/do.

Nesbitt, K. (2006). *Giggle poetry.* Available at www.gigglepoetry.com/index.aspx.

Nesbitt, K. (2006). *Children's poetry playground: Poetry4Kids.com.* Available at www.poetry4kids.com/index.php.

EXHIBIT **5.7.A**

Poetry Forms Sample

Name ______________________________ Date __________

ACROSTIC POEMS

Relax	**B**arreling down a hill
Enjoy	**I**n the sunshine
Anticipate	**C**an make
Delight	**Y**ou happy and take your
	Cares away
	Laughing and loving
	Every moment

DIAMANTE POEMS

Form

Noun
Adjective Adjective
Participle Participle Participle
Noun Noun Noun Noun
Participle Participle Participle
Adjective Adjective
Noun

Example

Ice Cream
Cold Sweet
Melting Dripping Freezing
Dessert Treat Meat Ketchup
Grilling Sizzling Burning
Tasty Spicy
Hot Dog

HAIKU POEMS

Form

Line 1: 5 syllables
Line 2: 7 syllables
Line 3: 5 syllables

Example

A trip to the beach,
take in the waves, sand, seagulls,
and enjoy the sun.

LIMERICKS

Form

Five line verse
Lines one, two, and five rhyme
Lines three and four rhyme

Example

There was a giant baboon,
Who played an amazing bassoon,
When he sounded each note,
Of the song he just wrote,
His friends thought it a wonderful tune.

Poetry Contract

Name ______________________________ Date ______________

Directions: Choose three options in the poetry contract and make an X in each of those boxes. Have your contract approved before you begin writing.

OPTION #1	OPTION #2	OPTION #3
Write an acrostic poem about your favorite hobby, food, or sport.	Write a diamante about two things that are very different.	Write a haiku about nature, the seasons, or the environment.
OPTION #4	**OPTION #5**	**OPTION #6**
Write a limerick with or without a partner.	Use the Internet to research concrete or visual poems and write one. Be artistic!	Illustrate one of your poems.
OPTION #7	**OPTION #8**	**OPTION #9**
Read your poems to a student in a lower grade.	Your choice! I will ______________ ______________	Your choice! I will ______________ ______________

Student signature: ______________________________

Teacher signature: ______________________________

Date contract is to be completed: ______________________________

EXHIBIT **5.7.C**

Poetry Evaluation Rubric

Name ______________________________ Date ____________

5 = Strongly agree   3 = Agree   1 = Disagree

CRITERIA	QUALITY POINTS
Student follows the form based on the samples for the types of poetry chosen and completes poetry contract as scheduled.	5 3 1 *Comments:* ______________
Student's poems have defined themes, and the writing is clearly expressed and interesting to readers.	5 3 1 *Comments:* ______________
Student makes appropriate word choices such as powerful, energetic verbs and adjectives that paint memorable pictures.	5 3 1 *Comments:* ______________

Total points ______ / 15

Students as Reporters

Creating a Classroom Newspaper

GRADE LEVEL: **5–6**

OBJECTIVES

- To use written language to communicate effectively through the writing of newspaper articles
- To apply knowledge of language structure and conventions to create newspaper articles
- To conduct research by gathering, evaluating, and synthesizing information from sources such as print texts and people

MATERIALS

- Chart paper
- Access to research sources such as newspapers, Internet resources, and people
- Access to word processing capability
- Newspaper Story Format handout (one per student)
- Reporter's Notes handout (one per student)
- Newspaper Article Evaluation Rubric (one per student)

NCTE/IRA STANDARDS

4 Students adjust their use of spoken, written, and visual language (e.g., conventions, style, vocabulary) to communicate effectively with a variety of audiences and for different purposes.

6 Students apply knowledge of language structure, language conventions (e.g., spelling and punctuation), media techniques, figurative language, and genre to create, critique, and discuss print and non-print texts.

7 Students conduct research on issues and interests by generating ideas and questions, and by posing problems. They gather, evaluate, and synthesize data from a variety of sources (e.g., print and non-print texts, artifacts, people) to communicate their discoveries in ways that suit their purpose and audience.

PROCEDURES

1. Share current newspaper articles from local, national, and school newspapers. Students can also read school newspapers online at the website of the National Elementary Schools Press Association (NESPA) at www.nespa.org. Discuss with students the "5 W's" in a good article: who, what, where, when, and why. Encourage students to share reasons why the 5 W's are important and what information would be lacking from the articles that were shared if one of the W's were missing. Give each student a Newspaper Story Format handout (Exhibit 5.8.A) and allow students to discuss the purpose and organization of the headline, 5 W's, and details. As a class, have students use the newspaper story format to analyze an article and identify the headline, 5 W's, and details. See the Resources section at the end of the activity for additional guidance for writing newspaper articles.
2. Have students brainstorm topics that might be appropriate for school newspaper articles. Encourage them to consider topics at the school, local, and national level. Document ideas on chart paper. English language learners and other interested students might incorporate topics that would add diversity and contribute to multicultural understanding.

3. Ask students to choose a topic that they will investigate for an article to be printed in a class newspaper. Hold two-minute pre-writing conferences with each student to approve the topic and provide guidance and support. Share research options such as interviewing and researching other newspapers and Internet sites. Stress the importance of accuracy of facts to be reported.
4. Give each student a Reporter's Notes handout (Exhibit 5.8.B), which they can use to take notes as they are interviewing people and investigating their story topic. Discuss the necessity for documentation of people interviewed, dates of interviews, and research sources. Interviewing and researching can be done both at school and during after-school hours. Give students opportunities to discuss their progress, ask questions, and report concerns. Explain the Newspaper Article Evaluation Rubric (Exhibit 5.8.C) to students and encourage them to consider the evaluation components as they complete their research and rough drafts.
5. Have students write a rough draft of their newspaper article using the Newspaper Story Format as their guide. In pairs, have students read each other's drafts and identify the headline, 5 W's, and details. Allow time for revision, and conduct writing conferences with students to discuss their progress and give feedback. Students who wish to word process their second draft should be encouraged to do so.
6. Have students return to their partner to share second drafts. For this second reading, partners should not only focus on article content and organization, but also on language conventions such as spelling and punctuation. Students can use feedback from partners and/or the teacher to revise and edit their final draft.
7. Newspaper articles may be compiled into a class newspaper. See the Resources section at the end of the activity for information about creating a class newspaper. Assistance from parent volunteers or older students with computer experience may be an asset to this process.
8. Students who have difficulty writing will need assistance throughout this activity. Interviews might be tape recorded for students who are unable to take notes. Articles could also be written in pairs or teams so that writing opportunities are shared. Some students might benefit from alternative assignments such as cartoon design, photography, or newspaper compilation.

ASSESSMENT

You may use the Newspaper Article Evaluation Rubric (Exhibit 5.8.C) to assess this assignment. Any accommodations or modifications made for particular students may be documented on the rubric.

INTEGRATING LANGUAGE ARTS ACROSS THE CURRICULUM

Students could write school newspaper articles in the areas of health, science, current events, and mathematics. Have students brainstorm topics in these subject areas that will affect them in their lifetime. For example, students may want to write articles on subjects such as global warming, obesity, or risks involved in tanning.

HOME-SCHOOL CONNECTION

Depending on the topic, family members might serve as interview subjects. Family volunteers could be very helpful in compiling and printing the class newspaper. Students can take their personal copy of the newspaper home to share with parents and siblings.

RESOURCES

Carroll, D. (1993). *Good news: How sharing the newspaper with your children can enhance their performance in school.* Penguin.

National Elementary Schools Press Association. (n.d.). *Helping elementary and middle school students publish since 1994.* Available at www.nespa.org.

Gorges, J. (1995). How to make a newspaper. *Children's Digest*, 45(6), 28–30.

Bedfordshire Libraries. (n.d.). *How to write a newspaper article.* Available at www.galaxy.bedfordshire.gov.uk/webingress/bedfordshire/vlib/0.children_teenagers/vhc_how_newspaper.htm.

EXHIBIT **5.8.A**

Newspaper Story Format

Name ______________________________ Date ______________

HEADLINE

____

____

5 W's

Who? ______________________________

____

What? ______________________________

____

Where? ______________________________

____

When? ______________________________

____

Why? ______________________________

____

DETAILS

Important details

1. ______________________________

2. ______________________________

3. ______________________________

Less important details

1. ______________________________

2. ______________________________

Reporter's Notes

Name ______________________________ Date ____________

Who? ______________________________

____

What? ______________________________

____

____

Where? ______________________________

____

When? ______________________________

____

Why? ______________________________

____

____

People Interviewed:

1. ______________________________ *Date* ____________

2. ______________________________ *Date* ____________

3. ______________________________ *Date* ____________

Research Sources:

1. ______________________________

2. ______________________________

3. ______________________________

EXHIBIT **5.8.C**

Newspaper Article Evaluation Rubric

Name ______________________________ Date ______________

QUALITY POINTS

Criteria	5	3	1
Interviewing and researching	A minimum of three interview and research sources	A minimum of two interview and research sources	Fewer than two interview and research sources
5 W's	All 5 W's included in article content	Three or four W's included in article content	Fewer than three W's included in article content
Supporting details	A minimum of three supporting details included in article content	A minimum of two supporting details included in article content	Fewer than two supporting details included in article content
Language conventions	Fewer than three errors in grammar, spelling, and punctuation	Fewer than five errors in grammar, spelling, and punctuation	Fewer than seven errors in grammar, spelling, and punctuation

Total points ______ / 20

Student accommodations and modifications:

ACTIVITY 5.9

All About Me

Writing Autobiographies

GRADE LEVEL: **6**

OBJECTIVES

- To use pre-writing strategies and writing process elements to communicate information about themselves
- To apply knowledge of language structure and language conventions such as spelling, grammar, and punctuation to create print text

MATERIALS

- A variety of autobiographies appropriate for the intermediate grades (See the Children's/ Young Adult Literature section at the end of this activity for suggested titles. For more examples, see *Using Literature in the Content Areas* (2007), by Sharon Kane.)
- Organized Cluster Autobiography handout (one per student)
- Autobiography Evaluation Rubric (one per student)

NCTE/IRA STANDARDS

5 Students employ a wide range of strategies as they write and use different writing process elements appropriately to communicate with different audiences for a variety of purposes.

6 Students apply knowledge of language structure, language conventions (e.g., spelling and punctuation), media techniques, figurative language, and genre to create, critique, and discuss print and non-print texts.

PROCEDURES

1. Provide a variety of autobiographies for reading aloud and for students' independent reading.
2. Discuss with students the essential elements of a well-written autobiography, including information about birth, family, important events, and education and future plans. Using one of the published autobiographies as an example, allow students to discuss ways the author shares information on these four elements.
3. Provide students with an Organized Cluster Autobiography handout (Exhibit 5.9.A) with the four essential elements. Have students brainstorm ideas related to these four elements that they might want to include in an autobiography. Have students use their Organized Cluster Autobiography handout to begin a rough draft of their autobiography. Two to four pages is a reasonable length for sixth grade students. Encourage students to include family traditions and stories that will keep readers interested. Explain the Autobiography Evaluation Rubric (Exhibit 5.9.B) for this assignment so students can use it to self-assess as they are writing.
4. When rough drafts are completed, divide students into groups of three and have them read their autobiographies out loud. Ask members of each group to give feedback to each writer on content, organization, and inter-

est level. Then have students exchange papers so each author can receive feedback on sentence structure, grammar, punctuation, and capitalization.

5. With feedback from peers, students can now begin a second draft. As students are writing, schedule individual conferences to gauge progress, answer questions, and provide assistance. After students have had their individual conferences, they can begin final drafts. Emphasize the importance of both revising and editing. Discuss rethinking and reflecting on what they have written, as well as making changes at the word and sentence level. When editing, students should pay attention to language conventions such as spelling, grammar, sentence structure, punctuation, and capitalization.
6. Ask students to use the Autobiography Evaluation Rubric (Exhibit 5.9.B) as a self-assessment tool before turning in their final draft. After they complete the rubric, they should be encouraged to make any changes they believe will improve their writing.
7. If students are to read published autobiographies independently, less skilled readers may need assistance in choosing an autobiography at their reading level. Students with more severely limited reading skills would benefit from a read-aloud. These same students will also require assistance in all stages of the writing process. They might be encouraged to form each of the organized cluster elements into a paragraph. Students with more serious disabilities may need to dictate their autobiography to you or to a peer tutor. Depending on students' needs, other accommodations that might be helpful include buddy readers, oral autobiographies, outline formats, and direct instruction in language conventions such as spelling and punctuation.

ASSESSMENT

You may use the Autobiography Evaluation Rubric (Exhibit 5.9.B) for evaluation purposes. Students should do a self-assessment and make any necessary changes before turning in their final draft. At the bottom of the rubric, document any modifications or accommodations made for students during the activity.

INTEGRATING LANGUAGE ARTS ACROSS THE CURRICULUM

Students may enjoy reading biographies of famous people in the areas of history, science, and mathematics. Examples include *Laura Ingalls Wilder: A Biography,* by William Anderson; *Helen Keller's Teacher,* by Margaret Davidson; *Benjamin Franklin,* by Wil Mara; *Albert Einstein,* by DK Publishing; *George Washington Carver,* by Lynea Bowdish; *Thomas Alva Edison,* by Wil Mara; *A to Z Women in Science and Math,* by Lisa Yount; and *Math and Mathematicians: The History of Math Discoveries around the World,* by Leonard Bruno. Also see *Using Literature in the Content Areas,* by Sharon Kane.

HOME-SCHOOL CONNECTION

As students are preparing to write their rough drafts, have them share their Organized Cluster Autobiography handouts with family members. Encourage students to seek feedback and information about their birth, early life, and family, so the details of their autobiography are accurate. Have students share their final drafts with parents before they are turned in.

CHILDREN'S/YOUNG ADULT LITERATURE

Anderson, W. (1995). *Laura Ingalls Wilder: A biography.* HarperTrophy.

Asgedom, M. (2003). *Of beetles and angels: A boy's remarkable journey from a refugee camp to Harvard.* Sagebrush.

Bowdish, L. (2004). *George Washington Carver.* Children's Press.

Bruno, L. (2002). *Math and mathematicians: The history of math discoveries around the world.* UXL.

Cohen, S. (2005). *Sasha Cohen: Fire on ice: Autobiography of a champion figure skater.* HarperCollins.

Cole, J., & Saul, W. (1996). *On the bus with Joanna Cole: A creative autobiography.* Heinemann.

Davidson, M. (1992). *Helen Keller's teacher.* Scholastic.

DK Publishing. (2005). *Albert Einstein.* Author.

Mara, W. (2004). *Thomas Alva Edison.* Children's Press.

Mara, W. (2006). *Benjamin Franklin.* Children's Press.

O'Ree, W., & McKinley, M. (2000). *The autobiography of Willie O'Ree: Hockey's black pioneer.* Sagebrush.

Peet, B. (1994). *Bill Peet: An autobiography.* Houghton Mifflin.

Spinelli, J. (1998). *Knots in my yo-yo string.* Knopf.

Yount, L. (1999). *A to Z women in science and math.* Facts on File.

REFERENCE

Kane, S. (2007). *Using literature in the content areas.* Scottsdale, AZ: Holcomb Hathaway.

EXHIBIT **5.9.A**

Organized Cluster Autobiography

Name ______________________________ Date ______________

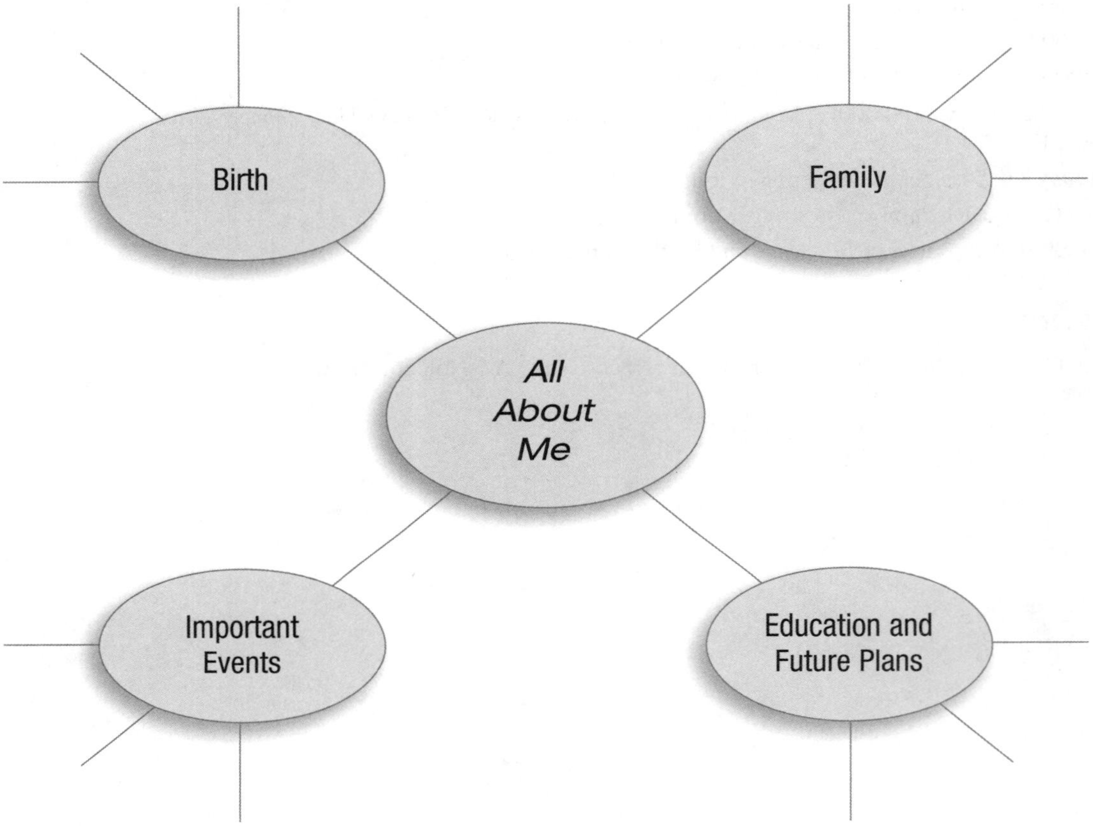

Autobiography Evaluation Rubric

Name ____ Date ______________

10 = Strongly agree   5 = Agree   1 = Disagree

CRITERIA	SELF-EVALUATION	TEACHER EVALUATION
Student created an organized cluster to brainstorm essential elements of an autobiography and used the cluster to complete a rough draft.	10 5 1 *Comments:*	10 5 1 *Comments:*
Student accepted feedback from peers and teacher on organization, content, sentence fluency, and conventions (spelling, punctuation, etc.) to complete a second draft.	10 5 1 *Comments:*	10 5 1 *Comments:*
Student varied sentence length and structure to ensure sentence fluency.	10 5 1 *Comments:*	10 5 1 *Comments:*
Student completed a self-assessment before turning in the following: organized cluster, rough draft, second draft, final draft.	10 5 1 *Comments:*	10 5 1 *Comments:*
Student included all four elements in his or her autobiography and applied knowledge of language conventions such as spelling, grammar, and punctuation.	10 5 1 *Comments:*	10 5 1 *Comments:*

Total points ______ / 100

Modifications or accommodations required for this student:

ACTIVITY 5.10

Back to Nature

Creating Travel Brochures for Our National Parks*

GRADE LEVEL: **6**

OBJECTIVES

- To use a variety of technological and information resources to gather and synthesize information and communicate knowledge
- To use written language to communicate effectively
- To apply knowledge of language conventions such as spelling and punctuation to create print texts
- To help students whose first language is not English to use their first language to develop competency in writing

MATERIALS

- Construction paper or other stiff paper (one sheet per student)
- Markers, crayons, glue, scissors, rulers
- Access to Internet resources on our national park system (See the Internet Resources section at the end of the activity.)
- Library books, magazines, and other resources (See the Resources section at the end of the activity.)
- Chart paper
- Sample travel brochures
- Travel Brochure Evaluation Rubric (one per student)

NCTE/IRA STANDARDS

4 Students adjust their use of spoken, written, and visual language (e.g., conventions, style, vocabulary) to communicate effectively with a variety of audiences and for different purposes.

6 Students apply knowledge of language structure, language conventions (e.g., spelling and punctuation), media techniques, figurative language, and genre to create, critique, and discuss print and non-print texts.

8 Students use a variety of technological and information resources (e.g., libraries, databases, computer networks, video) to gather and synthesize information and to create and communicate knowledge.

10 Students whose first language is not English make use of their first language to develop competency in the English language arts and to develop understanding of content across the curriculum.

PROCEDURES

1. On chart paper, complete a KWL chart with students on the national park system. Ask students to state what they already know about our national parks and what they would like to learn.
2. Have students imagine they work for a travel agency and are promoting the national park system. Have them research the parks using Internet and library resources.
3. After students have completed some preliminary research, return to the KWL chart and fill in the "L" column with new information they have learned.

*Note: A state park system may also be used.

4. Have students choose one of the 56 national parks to research in more depth. Encourage them to choose diverse national parks, so that each student is researching a different one. Explain that they will be designing a travel brochure for the park they choose, to encourage people to visit. Show sample travel brochures to give students ideas for format and design. Have students brainstorm the kinds of information that would be important to include on a travel brochure. Ideas can be recorded on chart paper.
5. Allow students to return to library and Internet resources to gather and synthesize information on the park they have chosen.
6. Give each student one piece of stiff paper for their brochure. Discuss the use of information and language that will entice visitors to their park. If a color printer is available, students can print pictures for their brochure, or they can cut them from magazines. Written information can be handwritten or word processed.
7. After the brochures are complete, they can be displayed on a "Visit Our National Parks" table in the classroom.
8. Some students, including those English language learners whose skills in reading English are not well developed, may need assistance with research activities. They may want to design their brochure in both their first language and in English, to attract bilingual readers to their parks.
9. To provide a technology component to the activity, students with well-developed computer skills can be encouraged to use those skills to design and create the written and visual components of their brochures.

ASSESSMENT

You may use the Travel Brochure Evaluation Rubric (Exhibit 5.10.A) to assess the brochures. Students can self-assess before you complete a final evaluation. The evaluation rubric should be explained to students at the beginning of the project so they can use it to guide their performance.

INTEGRATING LANGUAGE ARTS ACROSS THE CURRICULUM

After the travel brochures are completed, students can use math skills and research skills to estimate the following: miles from their home to the park of their choice, cost to drive or fly to their destination, costs for camping and/or lodging, costs for cooking at a campsite or for restaurant meals. Students who are interested in science may want to explore the wildlife and plant life in the park of their choice. They may also want to determine what the national parks are doing to maintain an environmentally friendly park system and to save those animals that live in the park that are on the endangered species list.

HOME–SCHOOL CONNECTION

Encourage students who have visited one or more of the national parks to bring in pictures, slides, or souvenirs of their visit. Family members could be invited to school to view the brochures and listen to mini travel presentations on our national parks.

RESOURCES

Brett, M. (2001). *The national parks of America.* Barron's Educational Books.

Domeniconi, D. (2003). *M is for majestic: A national parks alphabet.* Thomson Gale.

Fodor's. (2004). *Fodor's official guide to America's national parks* (12th ed.). Author.

National Geographic. (2003). *National Geographic guide to the national parks of the United States* (4th ed.). Author.

Peterson, D. (2001). *National parks (True books).* Children's Press.

INTERNET RESOURCES

National Parks Conservation Association (n.d.). Homepage. Retrieved May 17, 2005, from www.npca.org.

National Park Foundation. (n.d.). Homepage. Retrieved May 17, 2005, from www.nationalparks.org/Home.asp.

U. S. Department of the Interior. (n.d.). National Park Service Homepage. Retrieved May 17, 2005, from www.nps.gov.

Uhler, J. (1997). U. S. National Parks Net. Retrieved May 17, 2005, from www.us-nationalparks.net.

Travel Brochure Evaluation Rubric

Name ______________________________ Date ____________

5 = Strongly agree 3 = Agree 1 = Disagree

CRITERIA	SELF-EVALUATION	TEACHER EVALUATION
Student presented a well-defined national park theme and included accurate facts about that park. Student used a variety of technology and information resources.	5 3 1 *Comments:* ______________	5 3 1 *Comments:* ______________
Student used written language that was clearly expressed and interesting to readers. Student's words painted memorable pictures in readers' minds.	5 3 1 *Comments:* ______________	5 3 1 *Comments:* ______________
Student used correct language conventions in grammar, spelling, punctuation, and capitalization. Student used editing and proofreading skills to ensure accuracy.	5 3 1 *Comments:* ______________	5 3 1 *Comments:* ______________
Student presented a brochure that was neat and readable with appropriate illustrations.	5 3 1 *Comments:* ______________	5 3 1 *Comments:* ______________
Extra Credit Student used technology skills to create the visual and written components of the brochure.	5 3 1 *Comments:* ______________	5 3 1 *Comments:* ______________

Total points ______ / 40

Accommodations for students who demonstrate difficulty with research, reading, or writing:

____

Accommodations for English language learners:

____

CHAPTER 6

VIEWING

Teaching Students to Become Competent Critical Viewers

INTRODUCTION

For many years, four distinct language arts areas were identified and recognized: reading, writing, speaking, and listening. Two of these relate to oral language skills (speaking and listening), and two relate to written skills (reading and writing). It was assumed that all communication occurred in either spoken or written form. In recent years, however, the National Council of Teachers of English (NCTE), together with the International Reading Association (IRA), has acknowledged two additional language arts: viewing and visually representing. These two have been classified as *visual literacy*, or ways to communicate information through visual means.

Strickland, Galda, and Cullinan (2004) assert that viewing is an essential part of students' everyday language arts experience and that students need to be able to acquire and use information from a variety of visual and print media. Viewing occurs, for example, when students interact with videos, computer simulations, the World Wide Web, CD-ROMs, video games, book illustrations, graphs, charts, tables, diagrams, maps, and other print media (Yellin, Blake, & DeVries, 2004).

The importance of teaching students to become competent and critical viewers has intensified in recent years, largely because the Internet has become such a popular source of information for students. Additionally, high-tech, computerized video games have replaced other forms of recreation for many students and adults alike.

Although reading and writing remain high-priority areas in schools, teachers are now recognizing the importance of providing students with opportunities to develop visual literacy skills. The activities that follow are designed to do just that. Students will use visual literacy skills to analyze propaganda in magazine advertisements; evaluate websites and photographs; interpret wordless picture books, signs, and body language; and communicate through sign language.

Classroom Vignette

Mr. Lewis asks his fifth graders to open their science books to page 134 and look at the large picture of a tomato plant found there. Students describe what they observe, while Mr. Lewis draws and labels plant parts on the chalkboard. As Mr. Lewis asks questions, student volunteers point to areas of the plant diagram depicted on the chalkboard. Students then view a brief video on how to plant and care for tomato plants before transplanting their own plants. They carefully follow directions depicted in simple sequential illustrations on a handout provided by Mr. Lewis. Mr. Lewis tells the class that they will be observing their plants over the next three weeks and recording the noticeable changes in their science learning logs.

DISCUSSION QUESTIONS

1. Which tasks described above require students to rely upon viewing to gain information?
2. Identify other areas of the curriculum, besides science, that require students to view in order to learn.
3. In addition to pictures, diagrams, and videos, name three other visual sources of information.
4. In what ways does technology promote learning by viewing?
5. Are you a visual learner? If so, what evidence can you provide to support this claim? If not, through which modality do you learn best? Supply supporting anecdotes.

References

Strickland, D., Galda, L., & Cullinan, B. (2004). *Language arts: Learning and teaching.* Belmont, CA: Wadsworth/Thomson Learning.

Yellin, D., Blake, M., & DeVries, B. (2004). *Integrating the language arts.* Scottsdale, AZ: Holcomb Hathaway.

ACTIVITY 6.1

Signs All Around the Town

GRADE LEVEL: **K–1**

OBJECTIVE

- To read non-print text, including environmental print, to build an understanding of the world

MATERIALS

- One copy of *Mr. Pine's Mixed-up Signs*, by Leonard Kessler (2001, Purple House Press)
- Clipboards (one per student)
- Signs All Around the Town Record Sheet (one per student)
- Crayons (one per student)

NCTE/IRA STANDARD

1 Students read a wide range of print and non-print texts to build an understanding of texts, of themselves, and of the cultures of the United States and the world; to acquire new information; to respond to the needs and demands of society and the workplace; and for personal fulfillment. Among these texts are fiction and nonfiction, classic and contemporary works.

PROCEDURES

1. Duplicate the Signs All Around the Town Record Sheet (Exhibit 6.1.A), making one per student. Attach each to a clipboard for student use.
2. Read the book *Mr. Pine's Mixed-up Signs*, by Leonard Kessler, to students. Another picture book with many examples of environmental print can be substituted. Focus students' attention on the street signs and other environmental print illustrated throughout the book. Discuss the meaning of each sign.
3. Ask students if they have ever seen these signs in their own neighborhoods. Allow time for students to respond.
4. Distribute a crayon to each student. English language learners may be paired with native English speakers. Tell students that they are going to take a walking tour of the neighborhood and look for the signs shown on the Signs All Around the Town Record Sheet (Exhibit 6.1.A). When they see a similar sign, they should mark an "X" next to the sign on the record sheet. In the two large boxes at the bottom of the sheet, the students should draw one or two other signs they see along the way.
5. When the class returns to the classroom, review the signs that were seen on the walking tour and their meanings. Have students tell about the signs they drew.

ASSESSMENT

You may use informal observation to assess students' level of participation during the walking tour and throughout discussion of the book and the signs.

INTEGRATING LANGUAGE ARTS ACROSS THE CURRICULUM

Further study of environmental print can be done in a social studies unit on the community and community helpers. In math, students can explore the shapes of various signs and count their sides and angles. Students can form the shapes with their bodies in the gymnasium during physical education. Students can use simple supplies such as craft sticks and yarn to create the shapes in art.

HOME-SCHOOL CONNECTION

Parents can play travel games with their children that include environmental print and road signs. For example, children can look for particular road signs, count the number of stop signs spotted throughout a journey, or look for the most unusual sign.

Signs All Around the Town

Record Sheet

Name ____ Date _______________

Directions: Place an "X" next to each sign that you see on the walking tour. Draw two other signs that you see.

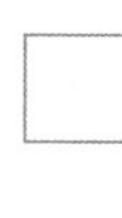

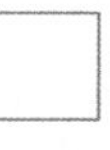

ACTIVITY 6.2

Reading the Pictures

Wordless Picture Book Interpretation

GRADE LEVEL: **K–1**

OBJECTIVES

- To read a wide range of print and non-print texts to build an understanding of texts, to acquire new information, and for personal fulfillment
- To apply a wide range of strategies to comprehend, interpret, evaluate, and appreciate texts

MATERIALS

- One copy of a wordless picture book such as *The Red Book*, by Barbara Lehman (See the Children's Literature section at the end of this activity for additional titles.)
- Magnifying glasses
- Paper, markers, and crayons

NCTE/IRA STANDARDS

1 Students read a wide range of print and non-print texts to build an understanding of texts, of themselves, and of the cultures of the United States and the world; to acquire new information; to respond to the needs and demands of society and the workplace; and for personal fulfillment. Among these texts are fiction and nonfiction, classic and contemporary works.

3 Students apply a wide range of strategies to comprehend, interpret, evaluate, and appreciate texts. They draw on their prior experience, their interactions with other readers and writers, their knowledge of word meaning and of other texts, their word identification strategies, and their understanding of textual features (e.g., sound–letter correspondence, sentence structure, context, graphics).

PROCEDURES

1. Introduce the picture book you have selected by showing students the cover. Ask them to guess what the book might be about. A book like *The Red Book*, which has detailed illustrations but no words on the cover, should elicit a variety of responses from students.

   Book Summary: A little girl finds a red book while she is walking in the snow. As she is looking at a map of some islands in the book, the illustrations begin to zoom in until she can see a little boy walking on the beach. The little boy finds a red book. In it are illustrations of a city that zoom in until he can see the little girl looking at him in her red book. The little girl buys a huge bunch of balloons and floats with her book out of the city. She drops the book but continues to float to the beach, where the boy is waiting.

2. Show page 1 of the story and ask students questions that will help them to interpret the pictures. For example, using *The Red Book*, you might ask:
   - Where does this story take place? How do you know?
   - What time of year is it? How do you know?
   - Where do you think this person is going?
   - What do we know about the story that we didn't know just by looking at the cover? Do we need to change any of our guesses about what this book is about?

3. Continue to share pages of the book and ask questions that require more in-depth interpretation. For example, you might want students to discuss what is happening to the pages in the book, and why the children are able to see each other through the pages of their books. On some pages, ask no questions, allowing for open discussion and interpretation by students. For example, it might be interesting to wait and see what students may say about the little girl floating off with the huge bunch of balloons. *The Red Book* offers a somewhat complex story line. For books like this, students may need multiple readings or extra time to analyze the illustrations before achieving adequate comprehension.
4. In *The Red Book*, consecutive illustrations are magnified until new details and surprises are evident. Discuss this technique with students, and have them take turns using magnifying glasses to enlarge objects and see details they couldn't otherwise see. Ask them to draw a picture of an object in the room before and after magnification.
5. Some students may need a simpler, more concrete story line than in *The Red Book*. Wordless picture books such as *Home*, by Jeannie Baker; *The Hunter and the Animals: A Wordless Picture Book*, by Tomie De Paola; *Little Star*, by Antonin Louchard; *Sidewalk Circus*, by Paul Fleischman; *Museum Trip*, by Barbara Lehman; and *Polar Slumber*, by Dennis Rockhill, are good choices for young children. Wordless picture books are an excellent tool for accommodating diversity. Students do not need to be able to read in order to enjoy the story, and they can create whatever story they like as they inspect the illustrations.

ASSESSMENT

You may observe students as they look at the illustrations and make predictions and interpretations of the story. Based on their responses, assess their comprehension of the story line. If you are using the extension activity for *The Red Book*, evaluate their artwork to determine whether students understand the concepts of magnification and perspective.

INTEGRATING LANGUAGE ARTS ACROSS THE CURRICULUM

Teachers who would like students to have more opportunities to interpret magnification and perspective can accompany the lesson using *The Red Book* with other wordless picture books, such as *Zoom* and *Re-Zoom*, by Istvan Banyai; and *Looking Down*, by Steve Jenkins. As in *The Red Book*, *Zoom* begins with pictures that are small and greatly magnified and moves gradually away until it ends with infinity. *Re-Zoom* shows just tiny pieces of objects and is perfect for encouraging students to guess what the picture might be. *Looking Down* does just the opposite of *Zoom* and *Re-Zoom*, by first showing the earth floating in outer space and then moving inward; the last picture is a ladybug.

HOME–SCHOOL CONNECTION

Wordless picture books are perfect for young children to take home and share with parents. These books foster creativity, and students enjoy "reading" them to family members. Family members might be encouraged to write or word process a child's story as they are "reading" the book, so that the story can be shared at school with the class.

CHILDREN'S LITERATURE

Baker, J. (2004). *Home.* Greenwillow.

Banyai, I. (1995). *Zoom.* Viking.

Banyai, I. (1998). *Re-Zoom.* Puffin.

De Paola, T. (1981). *The hunter and the animals: A wordless picture book.* Holiday House.

Fleischman, P. (2004). *Sidewalk circus.* Candlewick.

Jenkins, S. (2003). *Looking down.* Houghton Mifflin.

Lehman, B. (2004). *The red book.* Scholastic.

Lehman, B. (2006). *Museum trip.* Houghton Mifflin.

Louchard, A. (2003). *Little star.* Hyperion.

Rockhill, D. (2004). *Polar slumber.* Raven Tree Press.

ACTIVITY 6.3

I See What You Mean

Exploring Pantomime

GRADE LEVEL: **1–2**

OBJECTIVE

- To adjust use of visual language to communicate effectively

MATERIALS

- One copy of *Peck, Slither and Slide,* by Suse MacDonald (Gulliver Books, 1997)
- 25 plain index cards
- Marker
- Shoebox or paper bag

NCTE/IRA STANDARD

4 Students adjust their use of spoken, written, and visual language (e.g., conventions, style, vocabulary) to communicate effectively with a variety of audiences and for different purposes.

PROCEDURES

1. Neatly print one of the following verbs on each of the index cards:

jump	run	walk
dig	throw	slide
tip-toe	hop	skip
build	wave	sneeze
pound	wiggle	wink
swim	skate	slide
march	fly	snap
grab	pour	clap
cough		

   Fold each card to conceal the words, and place them in a shoebox or paper bag.
2. Read *Peck, Slither and Slide,* by Suse MacDonald. Call students' attention to the verbs, or action words, throughout the book. Another book with many action words can be substituted.
3. Tell students that verbs, or action words, show action or movement. Have students provide other examples of verbs. Discuss pantomime as a way to talk with your body without using words. Demonstrate how to pantomime several simple actions, and have students guess the action being pantomimed.
4. Reread *Peck, Slither and Slide,* and ask for student volunteers to pantomime the action words throughout the book.
5. Tell students they are going to play a game that involves pantomime. Call on student volunteers to choose an action word from the shoebox or bag previously prepared and pantomime the action. Encourage the rest of the students to guess the verb being pantomimed. You can provide support to

English language learners by providing a clip-art picture of the action verb along with the written word.

6. Continue until every student has had an opportunity to participate.

ASSESSMENT

Assess each student's ability to interpret visual language by pantomiming the following 10 verbs and noting how many of them the student identifies correctly:

run	jump
wave	smile
clap	dance
dig	sit
sneeze	cry

Students should be assessed individually during centers time or another available time throughout the school day.

INTEGRATING LANGUAGE ARTS ACROSS THE CURRICULUM

In math class, have students role-play story problems and have classmates identify the mathematical operations being depicted. For example, if the story problem was, "Johnny tried on three hats and Sophia tried on five hats. How many hats did they have in all?" Johnny and Sophia could stand in front of the class and put on all the hats at the same time, while you encourage students to discuss the operation depicted and the correct answer. Likewise, role-playing can be used appropriately in other areas of the curriculum.

HOME–SCHOOL CONNECTION

Allow students opportunities to take *Peck, Slither and Slide* home. Family members can take turns reading the book while others pantomime the action words.

Who Am I?

Making Predictions from Artifacts

GRADE LEVEL: **2–3**

OBJECTIVES

- To apply a wide range of strategies to comprehend, interpret, evaluate, and appreciate texts
- To develop an understanding of and respect for diversity in language use, patterns, and dialects across cultures, ethnic groups, geographic regions, and social roles

MATERIALS

- A picture book with diverse language usage, such as *Smoky Mountain Rose: An Appalachian Cinderella*, by Alan Schroeder (See the Children's Literature section at the end of this activity for additional titles.)
- Artifacts to represent the book
- A shoebox

NCTE/IRA STANDARDS

3 Students apply a wide range of strategies to comprehend, interpret, evaluate, and appreciate texts. They draw on their prior experience, their interactions with other readers and writers, their knowledge of word meaning and of other texts, their word identification strategies, and their understanding of textual features (e.g., sound–letter correspondence, sentence structure, context, graphics).

9 Students develop an understanding of and respect for diversity in language use, patterns, and dialects across cultures, ethnic groups, geographic regions, and social roles.

PROCEDURES

1. Cover the picture book you selected with brown paper, so students can't see the title or cover. Collect artifacts that represent the story and place them in a shoebox. For example, for *Smoky Mountain Rose: An Appalachian Cinderella*, you might place a fancy high-heeled shoe, a toy mouse or pig, a map of the Smoky Mountains, and a picture of a fiddle in the box.
2. Show students the wrapped book and ask them what they think the story might be about. Tell them that you will give them some hints. Show one artifact at a time from the shoebox and ask students to guess what it might represent in the story. Guesses can be documented on chart paper or the chalkboard.
3. After predictions have been made for each artifact, unwrap the book, read the title, and show the cover. Students can again make predictions about each of the artifacts. These guesses can be listed beside the first predictions.
4. Read the book, reminding students to listen for the way each artifact is used in the story. Discuss each artifact, documenting its actual purpose in a third list. Have students discuss how close their predictions were to the actual purpose of each item.
5. Discuss the history and people of the Appalachians, or the region or culture represented by the book you selected. Other picture books that could be used for a discussion of Appalachia include *Appalachia: The Voices of*

Sleeping Birds, by Cynthia Rylant; *A Is for Appalachia!: The Alphabet Book of the Appalachian Heritage*, by Linda Hager Pack; and *Granny Will Your Dog Bite and Other Mountain Rhymes*, by Gerald Milnes. Show the region on a map and discuss differences in language use.

6. Since students are participating in this activity as a group, few modifications would be necessary. The activity might be most challenging for English language learners, who may have difficulty understanding the dialect and diversity in language use. As an extension activity, write phrases in Appalachian dialect and the same phrases in standard English on sentence strips. Have students match the phrases with the same meaning.

ASSESSMENT

This activity gives teachers the opportunity to observe the quality of the predictions students are making in their attempts to comprehend the story. Take special note of those students who are able to make good predictions after the cover and title have been shared, and those who don't seem interested in making any predictions. You should also note students' comments that reflect what they've learned about the Appalachian culture from the artifacts and the book. Call on students randomly, rather than having students raise hands, to give everyone an opportunity to make guesses. You could also have students write down their predictions, to ensure the involvement of everyone.

INTEGRATING LANGUAGE ARTS ACROSS THE CURRICULUM

The use of artifacts to make predictions can be used in any subject area. *Snowflake Bentley*, by Jacqueline Briggs Martin, would be a good choice for the science classroom. Artifacts such as a camera, paper snowflakes, and a microscope could be used to prompt predictions. Diversity in dialect and culture can be seen in many picture books that would be appropriate for the social studies classroom. *Duke Ellington*, by Andrea Davis Pinkney; *Sam and the Tigers*, by Jerry Pinkney; and *Smoky Night*, by Eve Bunting, are just a few examples.

HOME-SCHOOL CONNECTION

The artifacts for the picture book you selected could be placed in a literacy bag along with the wrapped book. Students could take the bag home and have family members make predictions about the story. They could also choose another book from the classroom or school library and collect artifacts from school or home. After family members have made predictions, they could share the story.

CHILDREN'S LITERATURE

Bunting, E. (1994). *Smoky night.* Harcourt Brace.

Lester, J. (1996). *Sam and the tigers.* Dial.

Martin, J. B. (1998). *Snowflake Bentley.* Houghton Mifflin.

Milnes, G. (1990). *Granny will your dog bite and other mountain rhymes.* August House LittleFolk.

Pack, L. H. (2002). *A is for Appalachia! The alphabet book of Appalachian heritage.* Harmony House.

Pinkney, A. D. (1998). *Duke Ellington.* Hyperion.

Rylant, C. (1991). *Appalachia: The voices of sleeping birds.* Voyager.

Schroeder, A. (1997). *Smoky Mountain Rose: An Appalachian Cinderella.* Puffin.

ACTIVITY 6.5

Talking Hands

Understanding American Sign Language

GRADE LEVEL: **2–3**

OBJECTIVE

- To develop an understanding of and respect for American Sign Language (ASL) as a visual language and a way of communicating with others

MATERIALS

- One copy of *Moses Goes to School*, by Isaac Millman (See the Children's Literature section at the end of this activity for additional titles.)
- One copy of *Simple Signs*, by Cindy Wheeler
- American Sign Language websites for children

NCTE/IRA STANDARD

9 Students develop an understanding of and respect for diversity in language use, patterns, and dialects across cultures, ethnic groups, geographic regions, and social roles.

PROCEDURES

1. Ask students: Can people communicate with each other without using words? Explain.
2. Lead students in a discussion of how we use signs to communicate with others every day. Demonstrate a few simple signs that people use every day to communicate with others, such as waving to a friend to say hello or quieting another by placing an extended vertical index finger next to closed lips.
3. Discuss how the deaf and hearing impaired rely heavily on sign language to communicate with others, and then read *Moses Goes to School*, by Isaac Millman. Another picture book that familiarizes youngsters with the use of American Sign Language could be substituted.
4. After giving students an opportunity to respond to the book, introduce the book *Simple Signs*, by Cindy Wheeler. Have students observe the sign language depicted throughout the book. Demonstrate the various signs and have students replicate them. English language learners will be supported by the book's illustrations.
5. Many American Sign Language websites for children can be found at www.kidsdomain.com/kids/links/Sign_Language.html. Encourage students to explore these sites for extra practice in signing.
6. Call upon student volunteers to demonstrate their favorite sign, and have classmates view them and guess what is being signed. Provide enough time for every child to participate.

ASSESSMENT

Assess each student's ability to interpret American Sign Language by signing 8 to 10 simple signs depicted throughout the book and observing whether each student is able to interpret the signs correctly.

INTEGRATING LANGUAGE ARTS ACROSS THE CURRICULUM

Reinforce students' familiarity with American Sign Language in other content areas by occasionally signing key points. Introduce new signs from time to time. For example, Morning Meeting time is a perfect opportunity to introduce students to a new sign each day.

HOME-SCHOOL CONNECTION

Encourage students to teach their family members at home what they have learned about American Sign Language. Make other informational and picture books about ASL available for students to share at home.

CHILDREN'S LITERATURE

Addabbo, C. (2005). *Dina the deaf dinosaur.* Hannacroix Creek Books.

Collins, S. (2001). *An alphabet of animal signs.* Garlic Press.

Millman, I. (2003). *Moses goes to the circus.* Farrar, Straus & Giroux.

Millman, I. (2000). *Moses goes to school.* Farrar, Straus and Giroux.

Stuve-Bodeen, S. (2005). *The best worst brother.* Woodbine House.

Uhlberg, M. (2003). *The printer.* Peachtree Publishers.

INTERNET RESOURCE

www.kidsdomain.com/kids/links/Sign_Language.html

OTHER RESOURCES

Collins, S. (1995). *Songs in sign.* Garlic Press.

Collins, S. (1995). *Expanded songs in sign.* Garlic Press.

Collins, S. (1992). *Signing at school.* Garlic Press.

Flodin, M. (1991). *Signing for kids.* Perigee Trade.

Hafer, J. (1996). *Come sign with us: Sign language activities for children.* Gallaudet University Press.

Heller, L. (2004). *Sign language for kids: A fun and easy guide to American Sign Language.* Sterling.

Holub, J. (2004). My *first book of sign language.* Scholastic.

Kramer, J. (2004). *You can learn sign language!* Scholastic.

Wheeler, C. (1997). *Simple signs.* Puffin.

Wheeler, C. (1998). *More simple signs.* Viking Books.

ACTIVITY 6.6

A Picture Is Worth a Thousand Words

Analyzing Photographs

GRADE LEVEL: **3–4**

OBJECTIVES

- To use spoken, written, and visual language to learn and exchange information
- To analyze and interpret photographs
- To write a story based on visual images

MATERIALS

- Historical photographs, artwork, or postcards (portraying your community or a particular time period or geographic region pertinent to your units of study)
- Picture books with illustrations pertaining to your unit of study (See the Children's Literature section at the end of this activity for suggested titles.)
- Photograph Analysis Checklist (one per student)

NCTE/IRA STANDARD

12 Students use spoken, written, and visual language to accomplish their own purposes (e.g., for learning, enjoyment, persuasion, and the exchange of information).

PROCEDURES

1. Collect photographs from your local historical society or from websites. For example, photographs on the Wild West are available at many websites, including www.treasurenet.com/images, www.oldwesthistory.net, and www.iowalink.com/users/kbar/photos.htm. Print copies of those photographs that represent the time period or geographic region you have selected and, if possible, have them laminated. Wild West photographs may include cowboys, cowgirls, stagecoaches, covered wagons, saloons, lawmen, outlaws, ranches, Native Americans, and women of the Old West.
2. Select picture books on the same topic, so students can analyze the illustrations.
3. Design a set of questions to help students analyze the photographs and illustrations. Questions about Wild West photographs might include:
   - What types of transportation were available in the Wild West?
   - How do those methods of transportation differ from the transportation we have today?
   - What kinds of jobs did people have in the Wild West?
   - Were there any jobs that we no longer have?
   - What roles did women play in the Wild West?
   - What problems did communities have in the Wild West?

- What kinds of crimes were committed in the Wild West?
- What was the relationship between Native Americans and settlers?
- Why did people want to settle out West?
- How are things different in the time we live in today?

4. Introduce the topic you have selected by showing students artifacts from that time or place. Make a KWL chart on the chalkboard or chart paper. Ask students what they already know about the topic, and record their responses. Have students brainstorm things they would like to learn about the topic, and record their questions.
5. Display the photographs and picture books. Post the analysis questions beside the photographs. Discuss the questions with students. In small groups, have students inspect and analyze the photographs and picture books. Students who want to read the picture books may be encouraged to do so. Each small group can discuss the photographs and share ideas.
6. After all students have had an opportunity to analyze the photographs and illustrations, discuss their findings as a class. Discuss those questions whose answers are obvious from the photographs, as well as those questions whose answers would require more information. Pinpoint any misconceptions in students' previous knowledge of the topic. Refer back to the KWL chart and see how many of the students' questions have been answered. Have students brainstorm what they have learned about the topic and list those ideas in the KWL chart.
7. Ask students to choose one photograph and write a one- to two-paragraph story about the picture. Encourage them to use their imaginations in naming the characters, describing the setting, and creating the plot. Allow students to share stories. Students who have chosen the same photograph may want to compare stories to see how they are alike and different.
8. Small-group learning opportunities and large-group brainstorming will allow all students to participate and share ideas. Students who have difficulties with written expression may need assistance in paragraph writing. Modifications might include buddy work, dictation of the story to a peer or teacher, dictation of the story into a tape recorder, or the creation of artwork to represent the story.

ASSESSMENT

You may wish to use a Photograph Analysis Checklist (Exhibit 6.6.A) to assess students' participation, analysis skills, and paragraph writing. You can share checklists with students and parents during individual conferences and place them with the paragraphs in students' portfolios.

INTEGRATING LANGUAGE ARTS ACROSS THE CURRICULUM

The selection of topics can be based on particular units of study in science, social studies, or health. The Internet is a valuable resource for photographs on a multitude of topics. Students might analyze photographs on slavery, the Underground Railroad, the Dust Bowl of the 1930s, the Great Depression, space travel, or transportation from the 1800s to the present.

HOME–SCHOOL–COMMUNITY CONNECTION

You might ask family members or community representatives to share photographs for students to analyze. In some communities, students could also analyze historical photographs of homes and community buildings. They could follow up with a walking tour of the area to observe the ways in which the community has changed.

CHILDREN'S LITERATURE

Lester, J. (1998). *Black cowboy, wild horses.* Dial.

Thomas, J. C. (1998). *I have heard of a land.* HarperCollins.

Turner, A. (1999). *Red flower goes west.* Hyperion.

INTERNET RESOURCES

www.treasurenet.com/images

www.oldwesthistory.net

www.iowalink.com/users/kbar/photos.htm

EXHIBIT **6.6.A**

Photograph Analysis Checklist

Name ______________________________ Date ______________

	YES	NO	COMMENTS
Student participated in small-group photograph analysis and discussion.	☐	☐	
Student participated in large group discussion and brainstorming.	☐	☐	
Student was able to answer questions based on the photographs or other visual images.	☐	☐	
Student wrote a one- to two-paragraph story on the photograph of his/her choice.	☐	☐	
Student included characters' names and a description of setting and plot in the story.	☐	☐	
Student shared story with others and listened attentively as others shared their stories.	☐	☐	

Viewing and Understanding Comic Strips

GRADE LEVEL: **4–6**

OBJECTIVES

- To apply knowledge of media techniques to create and discuss print and non-print texts
- To use spoken, written, and visual language to enjoy comic strips and exchange information

MATERIALS

- Newspaper comic strips (one per pair of students)
- 5″ x $11^1/_2$″ strips of white drawing paper (one per pair of students)
- Glue sticks (one per pair of students)
- Plastic zip-lock sandwich bags
- Pencils

NCTE/IRA STANDARDS

6 Students apply knowledge of language structure, language conventions (e.g., spelling and punctuation), media techniques, figurative language, and genre to create, critique, and discuss print and non-print texts.

12 Students use spoken, written, and visual language to accomplish their own purposes (e.g., for learning, enjoyment, persuasion, and the exchange of information).

PROCEDURES

1. Collect a variety of simple comic strips from newspapers. Make a duplicate copy of each.
2. Cut apart each comic strip into individual frames. Cut out and discard the written text in each frame. Scramble the frames of each comic strip and place them into separate plastic zip-lock sandwich bags (one scrambled comic strip in each bag). Number the plastic bags to correspond with the matching copies of the original comic strips.
3. Pair students and give each pair a plastic bag containing a wordless scrambled comic strip, a glue stick, and a 5″ x $11^1/_2$″ strip of white drawing paper.
4. Have each pair study the frames in their bag and decide on a logical sequence for the frames. Have them glue the sequenced frames onto the paper strips.
5. Ask the pairs to work together to create appropriate text to go along with each frame.
6. When they have finished, give each pair the copy of the original comic strip. Have them compare their comic strip to the original.
7. Pairs can share their comic strips and the originals with the rest of the class.
8. Collect students' work and display on a classroom bulletin board.

ASSESSMENT

Informally assess students' interpretations. Consider whether the text is an appropriate fit for the illustrations. The captions need not match the originals as long as they fit the illustrations. You can assess individuals by giving them a cartoon and asking them to provide an original caption. Again, consider whether the text is an appropriate fit for the illustration.

INTEGRATING LANGUAGE ARTS ACROSS THE CURRICULUM

Students can view pictures and illustrations provided in content area textbooks, cover the caption, and predict what the caption states. Students can then compare their predictions to the actual caption.

HOME–SCHOOL CONNECTION

Encourage students to try the class activity with comic strips in newspapers found in their homes. Challenge family members to sequence them and rewrite the text. Students can even create their own comic strips, cut them apart, remove the text, and bring them to class to challenge classmates.

ACTIVITY 6.8

Don't Always Believe What You See

Website Evaluations

GRADE LEVEL: **5–6**

OBJECTIVES

- To use a variety of technological and information resources to gather and synthesize information and to create and communicate knowledge
- To allow English language learners to use their first language to develop competency in the English language arts and to develop understanding of content across the curriculum

MATERIALS

- Computer
- Internet access
- Website Evaluation Questionnaire (one per student)

NCTE/IRA STANDARDS

7 Students conduct research on issues and interests by generating ideas and questions, and by posing problems. They gather, evaluate, and synthesize data from a variety of sources (e.g., print and non-print texts, artifacts, people) to communicate their discoveries in ways that suit their purpose and audience.

8 Students use a variety of technological and information resources (e.g., libraries, databases, computer networks, video) to gather and synthesize information and to create and communicate knowledge.

10 Students whose first language is not English make use of their first language to develop competency in the English language arts and to develop understanding of content across the curriculum.

PROCEDURES

1. Discuss with students the need to evaluate websites. Anyone can create a website, and with more than 350 million documents online, students must be able to evaluate websites for accuracy, authorship, user-friendliness, and usefulness.
2. Select a website to demonstrate evaluation methods to students. You could choose to evaluate one that students might access to gather information for a report or project. If your school has the capability to project the computer screen onto a large wall screen, use this technology so that all students can view the evaluation at the same time.
3. Give each student a Website Evaluation Questionnaire (Exhibit 6.8.A). Use the questionnaire to demonstrate an evaluation with the website you have chosen. Allow students to participate in the evaluation, and answer any questions they might have about the evaluation questionnaire.
4. Discuss other websites that might be appropriate for evaluation. If students have a report or project assigned for which they must gather information, they can search for a website on that topic. Have students get the website they have chosen approved before they begin their evaluation. Students can complete their evaluations in the classroom, at home, or in the computer lab.
5. After students have completed their evaluations, have them get in groups to share their websites and evaluations. If the computer lab is available, students can sit at a computer with one or two other students, so the sharing

can be more interactive. They can share the name of their website, information about the author, their opinion of the user-friendliness of their site, and whether the information they found was accurate and useful.

6. English language learners can evaluate a website written in their first language. They may need to pair up with another student or the teacher to receive assistance in reading and comprehending the evaluation questions. They can share their website in either their first language or in English.

ASSESSMENT

Check the students' Website Evaluation Questionnaires (Exhibit 6.8.A) to determine if students completed their evaluations. The brief summaries should contain pertinent information on the accuracy and usefulness of the website. During sharing, circulate in the computer lab to observe the ways in which students are sharing important information about their websites.

INTEGRATING LANGUAGE ARTS ACROSS THE CURRICULUM

This activity is integrated across the curriculum, as students can choose a website from any subject area. You may modify this lesson by having all students select a website on a particular topic, such as the Civil War, a historical figure, or a sport. Students can then compare and contrast the information they find.

HOME-SCHOOL CONNECTION

Students who have a home computer and Internet access can share their website with family members. They can explain the purpose of the assignment; why they chose a particular website; and what they discovered about its accuracy, user-friendliness, and usefulness. Students who do not have a home computer can take their Website Evaluation Questionnaire home to share pertinent information, or invite their family members to school or a community library site.

Website Evaluation Questionnaire

Name ______________________________ Date ______________

Name of Website ______________________________

Website address ______________________________

Directions: Circle the most appropriate response for each question.

USER-FRIENDLINESS

1. Does the website load quickly?	YES	NO
2. Can you move easily from one page to another?	YES	NO
3. Are there links to take you to other pages in the website or to related websites?	YES	NO
4. Does the website's home page tell you what the website is about?	YES	NO
5. Are there graphics that make the website attractive?	YES	NO

AUTHORSHIP

1. Is the author's name on the page?	YES	NO
2. Is there contact information for the author?	YES	NO
3. Does the author give you information about his/her education, experience, profession, or workplace?	YES	NO
4. Does the author's education, experience, or profession make him/her a credible source for the information on the site?	YES	NO
5. Does the author work for an organization or company that you have heard of?	YES	NO
6. Is the website trying to sell you something?	YES	NO

ACCURACY AND USEFULNESS

1. Do you believe the information presented in the website is correct?	YES	NO
2. Did you compare information in this website with other sources, such as books or encyclopedias, to check for accuracy?	YES	NO
3. Does the website present any information that you disagree with?	YES	NO
4. Does the website include information that you were looking for?	YES	NO
5. Do the links lead you to any information you find useful?	YES	NO

SUMMARY

1. Overall, did you find this website useful?	YES	NO
2. Would you use this website again or recommend it to others?	YES	NO

Write a one-paragraph summary of your website. Include the name of the website, the website address, information about the author, and your opinion of the accuracy, usefulness, and user-friendliness of the site.

ACTIVITY 6.9

Eyewitness

Did You Really See What You Thought You Saw?

GRADE LEVEL: **5–6**

OBJECTIVE

- To participate as knowledgeable, reflective, and critical members of a literacy community

MATERIALS

- Brief video clip from a popular TV crime show
- Television set or computer
- VCR or DVD player
- Screen
- Eyewitness to the Crime handout (one per student)

NCTE/IRA STANDARD

11 Students participate as knowledgeable, reflective, creative, and critical members of a variety of literacy communities.

PROCEDURES

1. Videotape a 5- to 10-minute scene from a popular televised crime show depicting a non-violent crime in progress, such as two men entering a jewelry story to steal diamonds. Make sure that the program is rated appropriately for children.
2. Duplicate the Eyewitness to the Crime handout (Exhibit 6.9.A).
3. Show students the video clip and ask them to watch carefully. Play the clip only once.
4. When the video is over, tell students they have just witnessed a crime and are being called to testify in court as eyewitnesses. As witnesses, they may not discuss their testimony with anyone else.
5. Distribute the Eyewitness to the Crime handout (Exhibit 6.9.A) and ask students to record their responses based on what they viewed in the video.
6. When students are done, discuss their answers and call attention to the differences in their responses. Also discuss the fact that eyewitnesses often view the same event, as they did, and give very different accounts of what they witnessed. Ask: Why does this occur? What other kinds of evidence do courts reply on?
7. Show the video clip again and have students check the accuracy of their original accounts.

ASSESSMENT

Collect student papers and informally assess their ability to view and recall details accurately.

INTEGRATING LANGUAGE ARTS ACROSS THE CURRICULUM

After reading novels in class, have the class watch the video versions and compare and contrast the two.

HOME–SCHOOL CONNECTION

Encourage students to view age-appropriate mystery videos with family members at home and pause the video occasionally to discuss their observations and guess "who done it."

EXHIBIT **6.9.A**

Eyewitness to the Crime

Name ______________________________ Date ______________

Directions: After viewing the video clip, answer the following questions about the scene you viewed.

1. Describe in detail where the crime took place.

2. When did the crime take place?

3. How many people were involved?

4. Describe the physical characteristics of the people involved.

5. Describe what the people were wearing.

6. Describe how the crime occurred.

7. Summarize what you heard.

ACTIVITY 6.10

Propaganda Alert!

Analyzing Magazine Advertisements

GRADE LEVEL: **5–6**

OBJECTIVE

- To conduct research by gathering, evaluating, and synthesizing data from a variety of sources and to communicate their discoveries in ways that suit their purpose and audience

MATERIALS

- Children's magazines such as *Girl's Life, Boy's Life, Nickelodeon, National Geographic for Kids*, and *Sports Illustrated for Kids*
- Magazine Advertisement Data Collection Form (one per student)
- Analyzing Advertisements Evaluation Rubric (one per student)
- Poster board, markers, and crayons

NCTE/IRA STANDARD

7 Students conduct research on issues and interests by generating ideas and questions, and by posing problems. They gather, evaluate, and synthesize data from a variety of sources (e.g., print and non-print texts, artifacts, people) to communicate their discoveries in ways that suit their purpose and audience.

PROCEDURES

1. Ask students if what they read and see has an influence on what they think, feel, and do. Show students advertisements from a familiar magazine, such as *Popular Science.* Have students discuss what the ads are designed to do and what techniques advertisers use to get people to buy their products. Discuss common advertising techniques such as beauty promises, celebrity endorsement, promises of friendship or acceptance, and appeals to intelligence. Give each student a Magazine Advertisement Data Collection Form (Exhibit 6.10.A). Guide students through the analysis of one or two advertisements in the magazine you have selected. For example, many magazines now have advertisements for milk in which celebrities are shown with "milk mustaches." Students would record "milk" as the product, "people of all ages who wish to be healthy" as the target audience, and "celebrity endorsement" as the advertising technique used.
2. Divide students into the same number of groups as there are different types of children's magazines. Have each group choose a magazine, and give each group one issue. Ask students to work together to study the magazine's advertisements, choose 10 advertisements to analyze, and record their findings on the Magazine Advertisement Data Collection Form (Exhibit 6.10.A).
3. After each group has recorded data for the 10 advertisements they have selected, have them analyze their results. They should identify:
   - The kinds of products promoted in the magazine

- Reasons why products were chosen by advertisers
- The target audience
- The kinds of advertising techniques being used (beauty promises, celebrities endorsements, other promises, and so on)
- Whether all of the advertisements are clearly labeled as ads, or if some magazine articles are designed to sell products
- Whether the advertisements appeal to your emotions, and if so, what emotions
- Which advertisement uses the most effective advertising techniques and why
- Whether the advertisements influence what you think, feel, and do, and if so, why

4. Allow each group an opportunity to share their results with the class. Students can create visuals such as posters, collages, or graphs to represent their findings. Encourage students to be creative in designing their visuals and to discuss factors that might make a visual suitable for this purpose and audience (e.g., visuals must be easily understood, free of mechanical errors, and visible to the audience).
5. Small-group learning opportunities offer all students the chance to participate and use their skills. This activity requires skills in oral language, decision making, critical analysis, social interaction, and creativity. Students can participate to the best of their ability. The teacher may need to give further guidance to some groups, including additional examples of the types of advertising techniques used.

ASSESSMENT

You can use the Analyzing Advertisements Evaluation Rubric (Exhibit 6.10.B) to assess the extent to which students are able to conduct research and analyze the data they have collected, follow directions, identify the target audience and techniques in advertisements, and create visuals that represent their findings.

INTEGRATING LANGUAGE ARTS ACROSS THE CURRICULUM

This activity could be integrated into the teaching of mathematics. Students could communicate their results through percentages, charts, and graphs. For example, they might determine the percentage of advertisements in a magazine that are designed to sell video games. They could graph the results and compare them to the percentage of advertisements for food or beauty products. The results for each magazine could then be compared to the results for other magazines, to determine which have the most ads for each product or the most total ads per magazine pages. Students with technology skills can create their charts and graphs on the computer.

HOME-SCHOOL CONNECTION

Students can take one issue of their magazine home to share with family members. They can explain the advertising techniques, the most common products marketed to children, and why the advertisements are effective in getting people to buy products.

Magazine Advertisement

Data Collection Form

Name ______________________________ Date ______________

PRODUCT	TARGET AUDIENCE (AGE, GENDER, LIFESTYLE)	ADVERTISING TECHNIQUES USED

EXHIBIT **6.10.B**

Analyzing Advertisements Evaluation Rubric

Name ______________________________ Date ____________

QUALITY POINTS

Criteria	5	3	1
Conducting research and analyzing data collected	Student effectively conducts research and analyzes the data collected.	Student conducts research but has difficulty analyzing the data collected.	Student fails to conduct research and/or is unable to analyze the data collected.
Identifying target audience and advertising techniques	Student correctly identifies target audience and advertising techniques in most advertisements.	Student correctly identifies target audience and advertising techniques in at least half of advertisements.	Student fails to identify target audience and advertising techniques in advertisements.
Creating visuals	Student creates visuals that are creative and suit the purpose and audience.	Student creates visuals that meet some of the requirements for creativity and suitability.	Student fails to create visuals that are creative and suit the purpose and audience.

Total points ______ / 15

Teacher comments: ______________________________

VISUALLY REPRESENTING

Conveying Meaning Through Visual Representation

INTRODUCTION

Visual literacy has increased in importance since the advent of the World Wide Web, cellular phones with video and photography capabilities, animation, DVDs, and computer programs. Because today's students are bombarded with visual images, it is imperative that they be able to interpret and construct them. However, in most school settings, students receive very little training in visual literacy, and the power of visual learning tools is often lost (Hobbs, 1997).

Visual representation is the ability of a student to create visuals that convey meaning to others. Graphs, charts, diagrams, photographs, maps, artwork, videos, and computer programs are just a few of the visuals students can produce to share their knowledge (Heinich, Molenda, Russell, & Smaldino, 1999; Valmont, 2003).

Drawings are perhaps the most common form of visual representation found in classrooms. Students can use drawings and artwork to convey ideas before they are able to write, and later they include illustrations as an accompaniment to stories or poetry. Photographs have also found widespread use, as students incorporate them into collages, posters, and montages.

However, visual representation goes well beyond drawings and photographs to include the creation of graphs, charts, diagrams, multimedia presentations, and word processed documents and web pages. Thus, visual literacy and technological literacy are strongly linked as students learn to use technology to enhance their learning capability (Roe & Ross, 2006).

The activities in this chapter give students opportunities to represent their knowledge visually in a variety of ways. Students will be engaged in plotting profile graphs; charting math results; using Venn diagrams; constructing human graphs; and creating quilt squares, paper plate timelines, and media print advertisements.

Classroom Vignette

Mr. Johnson's fourth grade students have been involved in a unit on the American Revolution for the past three weeks. They are now investigating the role of women during the war and are reading books such as *They Called Her Molly Pitcher, Sybil's Night Ride,* and *The Scarlet Stockings Spy.* Mr. Johnson has asked his students to work in small groups and visually represent their knowledge of women in the Revolutionary War. One group is constructing a Venn diagram comparing and contrasting Sybil Ludington, the main character in *Sybil's Night Ride,* with Maddy Rose, the protagonist in *The Scarlet Stockings Spy.* Another group is tracking Sybil's midnight journey, marking the route on a map of New York State, and graphing the time required for the journey and the distance traveled. A third group is creating a diorama of Molly Pitcher and her efforts during the war. After the projects are completed, Mr. Johnson will encourage each group to assess how and what they've learned, display their project, and explain their visual representations to the class.

DISCUSSION QUESTIONS

1. What are the benefits of asking students to visually represent their knowledge of women in the American Revolution?
2. What other types of visual representations would complement this study?
3. What kinds of support do students need in order to represent their work visually?
4. How would visual representations enhance other subjects, such as math or science?
5. How do you think that visual representations benefit English language learners or those with learning difficulties?

CHILDREN'S LITERATURE

Noble, T. (2004). *The scarlet stockings spy.* Sleeping Bear Press.

Rockwell, A. (2002). *They called her Molly Pitcher.* Random House.

Winnick, K. (2000). *Sybil's night ride.* Boyds Mills Press.

REFERENCES

Heinich, R., Molenda, M., Russell, J., & Smaldino, S. (1999). *Instructional media and technologies for learning.* Upper Saddle River, NJ: Merrill/Prentice Hall.

Hobbs, R. (1997). Literacy for the information age. In J. Flood, S. Heath, & D. Lapp (Eds.), *Research on teaching literacy through the communication and visual arts* (pp. 7–13). New York: Simon & Schuster.

Roe, B., & Ross, E. (2006). *Integrating language arts through literature and thematic units.* New York: Pearson.

Valmont, W. (2003). *Technology for literacy teaching and learning.* Boston: Houghton Mifflin.

ACTIVITY 7.1

See How I Feel

Expressing Feelings with Others

GRADE LEVEL: **K–1**

OBJECTIVE

- To use visual language to communicate feelings to others

MATERIALS

- One copy of *The Feelings Book,* by Todd Parr (2000, Megan Tingley)
- Paper plates (one per student)
- Colored markers

NCTE/IRA STANDARD

12 Students use spoken, written, and visual language to accomplish their own purposes (e.g., for learning, enjoyment, persuasion, and the exchange of information).

PROCEDURES

1. Begin by discussing feelings and emotions with students. Ask them to discuss things that make them feel happy, sad, surprised, angry, scared, silly, lonely, cranky, brave, and so forth. As students share experiences, have them demonstrate what they look like when they are experiencing each feeling or emotion.
2. Introduce *The Feelings Book,* by Todd Parr. Point to the four faces depicted on the book's cover and have students identify and pantomime each emotion. As you read the book aloud, pause and have students pantomime the emotions being discussed.
3. After reading and discussing the book, play a version of the game "Simon Says," with emotions. Have children stand in a circle. Ask if anyone has ever played "Simon Says" before and explain that they are going to play a pantomime version of the game. If the teacher says, "Simon says feel happy," students are to pantomime what it looks like to be happy by silently smiling or pantomiming clapping hands. Students continue pantomiming the emotion until the teacher gives another direction beginning with the words, "Simon says feel . . ." Explain that students do not pantomime any emotion that is not preceded by these words.
4. After playing the game, have students return to their seats. Distribute a paper plate and markers to each student. Ask them to use the plate to draw a picture of their face expressing an emotion. Tell them only to draw their face on the paper plate.
5. When students are done, have them share their paper plate faces with the class, and have classmates guess what emotion is being expressed.
6. Collect the paper plate faces and use them to create a bulletin board entitled *Today I Feel . . . .* Print the names of the emotions on cards and place them under each corresponding face.

ASSESSMENT

You can use informal teacher observation to assess students throughout the discussion of the book, the pantomime game, and the drawing activity.

INTEGRATING LANGUAGE ARTS ACROSS THE CURRICULUM

Call students' attention to different feelings and emotions as they are encountered in other reading materials. Students can also pantomime short skits or scenes from books to reinforce their skill in using their bodies to visually represent and communicate with others.

HOME–SCHOOL CONNECTION

Have students practice talking using their bodies through pantomime at home. They might pantomime scenes from favorite books and have family members guess what they are depicting.

ACTIVITY 7.2

Beginning–Middle–End Folktale Retellings

GRADE LEVEL: **K–1**

OBJECTIVES

- To adjust spoken, written, and visual language to communicate effectively
- To apply a wide range of strategies to comprehend, interpret, evaluate, and appreciate texts

MATERIALS

- Manila file folders (one per student)
- $8^1/_2$″ x 11″ white drawing paper (one sheet per student)
- Transparent tape
- Scissors
- Colored markers and crayons
- A favorite fairytale from a book or website (See the Children's Literature section at the end of this activity for suggested titles.)

NCTE/IRA STANDARDS

3 Students apply a wide range of strategies to comprehend, interpret, evaluate, and appreciate texts. They draw on their prior experience, their interactions with other readers and writers, their knowledge of word meaning and of other texts, their word identification strategies, and their understanding of textual features (e.g., sound–letter correspondence, sentence structure, context, graphics).

4 Students adjust their use of spoken, written, and visual language (e.g., conventions, style, vocabulary) to communicate effectively with a variety of audiences and for different purposes.

PROCEDURES

1. Prepare flip folders for students in advance. Place the closed folder on a desk so that the open side is nearest you and the closed side is at the top. Cut the top flap of the folder from the open bottom to the fold into three equal sections. Tape a piece of white drawing paper inside the folder.
2. Read a favorite fairytale to students and discuss the concept that stories have a beginning, a middle, and an end. In addition to fairytales from books, you can find interactive, narrated, and animated Grimm fairytales at www.grimmfairytales.com/en/main.
3. On the chalkboard draw three story panels. Label the first "B" for beginning, the second "M" for middle, and the third "E" for end.
4. Have students talk about what happened at the beginning of the story they heard. Make sure that students identify the setting and characters. Ask a student volunteer to draw on the chalkboard, in the first panel, what happened at the beginning of the story.
5. Then discuss what happened in the middle of the story, and have a student draw this in the middle panel on the chalkboard. Make sure that students illustrate the problem or conflict in the story.
6. Do the same for the end of the story, making sure that students discuss and illustrate the resolution of the story.

7. Choose and read another fairytale and ask students to listen carefully to the story and be ready to draw what happened at the beginning, middle, and end.
8. After reading the story, talk about the story.
9. Distribute the folders and have students label the three flip panels "B," "M," and "E." Have them draw what happened during each part of the story on the white drawing paper inside the flip folder.
10. When done, ask individuals to share their drawings and retell the story aloud.

ASSESSMENT

You can use informal teacher observation to assess students' understanding. Consider the following:

- Was the child able to visually represent the beginning of the story correctly?
- Was the child able to visually represent the middle of the story correctly?
- Was the child able to visually represent the end of the story correctly?

INTEGRATING LANGUAGE ARTS ACROSS THE CURRICULUM

Students can use tri-cut flip folders in other areas of the curriculum. For example, students could illustrate three-step directions in science or a sequence of three events in social studies. Students can use folders for practicing the reading of one-, two-, and three-digit numerals.

HOME-SCHOOL CONNECTION

Encourage students to share their story folders at home with parents. They can insert a clean sheet of white drawing paper inside the folder and illustrate the beginnings, middles, and ends of other stories shared at home.

CHILDREN'S LITERATURE

Andersen, H. (2006). *Hans Christian Andersen's fairytales.* Minedition.

Andersen, H. (1993). *The complete Hans Christian Andersen Fairy Tales.* Gramercy.

Comfort, L. (2005). *Fairytale princess stories.* Campbell Books.

EnTechneVision. (2006). *Kidoons: Welcome to Grimm fairytales.* Available at www.grimmfairytales.com/en/main.

Grimm, B. (1993). *The complete Brothers Grimm fairy tales.* Gramercy.

Impey, R. (1994). *The Orchard book of fairytales.* Orchard Books.

Krutop, L. (2005). My *first book of fairytales.* Gardners Books.

Lacome, S. (2005). *Bedtime stories: 4 well-loved fairytales to read aloud and share.* Silver Dolphin.

Middleton, H. (2002). *Grimm's last fairytale.* St. Martin's Griffin.

Segur, A. (1999). *The golden book of fairytales.* Golden Books.

INTERNET RESOURCE

www.grimm-fairytales.com/en/main

Shoebox Theaters

GRADE LEVEL: **1–2**

OBJECTIVES

- To read a wide range of print and non-print texts to build an understanding of texts, of themselves, and of the cultures of the United States and the world
- To allow students whose first language is not English to make use of their first language to develop competency in the English language arts
- To retell a story through spoken and visual language

MATERIALS

- Shoeboxes (one per student)
- Craft sticks (five or six per student)
- Construction paper in a variety of colors
- Scissors
- Glue sticks
- Markers, crayons, or colored pencils
- Scraps of other materials that could be used for creating the shoebox theaters and stick puppets (for example, pieces of material, craft eyes, pipe cleaners, cellophane)
- Shoebox Retellings Checklist (one per student)

NCTE/IRA STANDARDS

1 Students read a wide range of print and non-print texts to build an understanding of texts, of themselves, and of the cultures of the United States and the world; to acquire new information; to respond to the needs and demands of society and the workplace; and for personal fulfillment. Among these texts are fiction and nonfiction, classic and contemporary works.

10 Students whose first language is not English make use of their first language to develop competency in the English language arts and to develop understanding of content across the curriculum.

12 Students use spoken, written, and visual language to accomplish their own purposes (e.g., for learning, enjoyment, persuasion, and the exchange of information).

PROCEDURES

1. Students can creatively retell stories through the construction and use of shoebox theaters and craft stick puppets. Begin by having each student bring a shoebox from home.
2. Prepare the boxes in advance for student use. Place the shoebox on a table in front of you so that the longer part of the box is resting on the table and the outside bottom of the box is facing you. With a pair of scissors or a box cutter, cut a 3/4" slit into the bottom back of the box as it faces you. Students will insert stick puppet characters through this opening.
3. Once boxes have been prepared, have each student choose a favorite picture book. (See the Children's Literature section at the end of this activity for suggested picture books and additional multilingual titles.) The book should have a simple plot line and a limited number of characters. Offer

students picture books that are bilingual, and those that are written in languages other than English, as well as those written in English.

4. Students should decorate the inside of the box to replicate the setting of the book or an important scene with construction paper, markers, and other available materials. Make sure that students do not cover up the opening that was cut into the box at the bottom of the stage.
5. Once students have the shoebox theaters prepared, they may work on creating stick puppet characters with the craft sticks and other available materials. Caution students that the characters must fit through the opening.
6. When the theaters and characters are complete, encourage students to practice retelling the story with their newly created props. Students might be paired up for practice before they present their retellings to the class. English language learners might choose to tell their story in their first language and then in English.

ASSESSMENT

You can use the Shoebox Retellings Checklist (Exhibit 7.3.A) to assess student performance.

INTEGRATING LANGUAGE ARTS ACROSS THE CURRICULUM

Students can prepare shoebox theaters and stick puppets to reenact social studies and science concepts. In studying different kinds of communities and habitats, shoeboxes could be transformed into the communities or habitats and displayed together in an area of the classroom. In science, students can portray the stages of development in a butterfly's life cycle or growth of a plant starting with a seed.

HOME–SCHOOL CONNECTION

Encourage students to retell their stories at home with the props created in school. Parents and family members can take on the roles of characters and collaboratively retell the story, or they could create another shoebox theater and puppets together.

CHILDREN'S LITERATURE

Brown, M. (1971). *Cinderella.* Atheneum.

Craft, K. Y. (2000). *Cinderella.* Seastar Books.

Grimm, J., & Grimm, W. (1997). *Rapunzel.* North-South Books.

Howe, J. (1998). *Jack and the beanstalk.* Little, Brown & Co.

Hyman, T. (2000). *The sleeping beauty.* Little, Brown & Co.

Hyman, T. (1983). *Little Red Riding Hood.* Holiday House.

Jarrell, R. (1972). *Snow-White and the seven dwarfs.* Farrar, Straus & Giroux.

Kellogg, S. (1991). *Jack and the beanstalk.* William Morrow and Company.

Lesser, R. (1999). *Hansel and Gretel.* Dutton Children's Books.

Mayer, M. (2000). *Beauty and the beast.* Sea Star Books.

McCaughrean, G. (2000). *Beauty and the beast.* Carolrhoda Books.

Reins, P. (2000). *Snow White.* Little, Brown & Co.

Rogasky, B. (1987). *Rapunzel.* Holiday House.

The Brothers Grimm. (1995). *Little Red-Cap.* North-South Books.

Zelinsky, P. (1986). *Rumpelstiltskin.* Dutton Children's Books.

BILINGUAL AND MULTILINGUAL VERSIONS OF CHILDREN'S PICTURE BOOKS

Chinese

Bateson-Hill, M. (1996). *Lao-Lao of Dragon Mountain.* De Agostini Editions.

Lee, J. (1995). *Song of Mu Lan.* Front Street Publishing.

Wyndham, R. (1998). *Chinese Mother Goose rhyme.* PaperStar Books.

Young, E. (1997). *Mouse match.* Harcourt.

Hopi

Coyote and little turtle: Iisaw Niqw Yongosonhoya: A traditional Hopi tale. (1994). Based on a story told by Herschel Talashoema. Clearlight.

Inuktitut

Ekoomiak, N. (1990). *Artic memories.* Henry Holt & Co.

Khmer

Spagnoli, C. (1991). *Judge Rabbit and the tree spirit: A folktale from Cambodia.* Children's Book Press.

Korean

Han, S. (1995). *The rabbit's escape./Kusa ilsaenghan tooki.* Henry Holt.

Holt, D. (1998). *Tigers, frogs, and rice cakes: A book of Korean proverbs.* Shen's Books.

Multilingual

Fedor, J. (1995). *Table, chair, bear: A book in many languages.* Ticknor/Houghton.

Spanish

Ada, A. F. (1997). *Gathering the sun: An alphabet in Spanish and English.* Lothrop, Lee & Shepard.

Ada, A. F. (1997). *The lizard and the sun/La lagartija y el sol.* Doubleday.

Ada, A. F. (1997). *Mediopollito/Half-chicken.* Doubleday.

Beinstein, P. (2003). *Dora's book of words/Libro de palabras de Dora: A bilingual pull tab adventure!* Simon Spotlight.

Bertrand, D. G. (1999). *Family.* Pinata Books.

Bofill, F. (1998). *Jack and the beanstalk/Juan y los frijoles magicos.* Chronicle.

Brusca, C. M., & Wilson, T. (1995). *Three friends: A counting book/Tres amigos: Un cuento para contar.* Henry Holt.

Bruzzone, C. (2005). *Lucy the cat at the farm: La gatita Lucia en la granja.* Bilingual Picture Strip Books.

Bruzzone, C. (2005). *Lucy the cat in town: La gatita Lucia en la cuidad.* Bilingual Picture Strip Books.

Corpi, L. (1997). *Where fireflies dance/Ahi, donde bailan las luciernagas.* Children's Book Press.

Delgado, M. I. (1996). *Chaves's memories/Los recuerdos de Chave.* Pinata Books.

Ehlert, L. (1997). *Cuckoo/Cucu: A Mexican folktale/Un Cuento folklorico Mexicano.* Harcourt.

Eversole, R. (1995). *The flute player/La flautista.* Orchard Books.

Facklam, M. (2002). *Bugs for lunch/Insectos para el almuerzo.* Ten Speed Press.

Foster, K. S. (1997). *Good night my little chicks/Buenas noches mis pollitos.* First Story Press.

Garza Lomas, C. (1996). *In my family/En mi familia.* Children's Book Press.

Garza Lomas, C. (1999). *Magic windows: Ventanas magicas.* Children's Book Press.

Guy, G. F. (1996). *Fiesta!* Greenwillow.

Herrera, J. F. (1995). *Calling the doves/El canto de las palomas.* Children's Book Press.

Keister, D. (1995). *Fernando's gift/El regalo de Fernando.* Sierra Club Books for Children.

Lainez, R. C. (2005). *I am Rene, the boy/ Soy Rene, el nino.* Pinata Books.

Lowell, S. (1996). *Los tres pequenos jabalies/The three javelinas.* Northland.

Luenn, N. (1998). *A gift for Abuelita: Celebrating the day of the dead/Un regalo para Abuelita: En celebracion del dia de los muertos.* Rising Moon.

McCunn, R. L. (1998). *Pie-biter/Compasteles.* Shen's Books.

Mora, P. (1999). *Delicious hullabaloo: Pachanga deliciosa.* Arte Publico.

Olivas, D. (2005). *Benjamin and the word/Benjamin y la palabra.* Pinata Books.

Reiser, L. (1998). *Tortillas and lullabies/Tortillas y cancioncitas.* Greenwillow.

Rockhill, D. (2005). *Ocean whisper/Susurro del oceano.* Eida De LA Vega.

Saenz, B. A. (1998). *A gift from papa Diego/Un regalo de papa Diego.* Cinco Puntos Press.

Saenz, B. A. (1999). *Grandma Fina and her wonderful umbrellas/La abuelita Fina y sus sombrillas mara villosas.* Cinco Puntos Press.

Stevens, J. (1995). *Carlos and the cornfield/Carlos y la milpa de maiz.* Northland.

Swahili

Kitsao, J. (1995). McHeshi *goes to the market.* Jacaranda Designs.

Thai

MacDonald, M. R. (1998). *The girl who wore too much: A folktale from Thailand.* August House.

Tibetan

Halpern, G. Translated by Ngawang Jorden. (1991). *Where is Tibet—Bod ga pa yod red-Poo Kabah yoreh: A story in Tibetan and English.* Snow Lion Publications.

Vietnamese

Cowcher, H. (1997). *Tigress.* Millet.

Waddell, M. (1995). *Owl babies.* Magi Publications.

Zhang, S. N. (1998). *The ballad of Mulan. Bai Ca Moc Lau.* Pan Asian Publications.

EXHIBIT **7.3.A**

Shoebox Retellings Checklist

Name ______________________________ Date __________

	HIGH PROFICIENCY	MODERATE PROFICIENCY	LOW PROFICIENCY
1. Appropriate setting for story	3	2	1
2. Main characters represented	3	2	1
3. Accurate story details	3	2	1
4. Appropriate sequence of events	3	2	1
5. Used expression	3	2	1
6. Fluid and smooth story retelling	3	2	1
7. Varied vocal intonations	3	2	1
8. Neat and attractive props	3	2	1

Total points ______ / 24

Comments and any modifications:

ACTIVITY 7.4

Discovering Women's History

Constructing a Baggy Quilt

GRADE LEVEL: **2–3**

OBJECTIVES

- To read a wide range of literature from many periods in many genres to build an understanding of human experiences
- To allow students whose first language is not English to make use of their first language to develop competency in the English language arts
- To use written and visual language to learn and exchange information

MATERIALS

- A wide range of biographies and historical picture books, including fiction and nonfiction, that detail the experiences and accomplishments of women (See the Children's Literature section following this activity for suggestions.)
- Children's websites on women in history
- Gallon size zip-lock freezer bags (without labeling) (one per student)
- Colored duct tape
- 8 1/2″ x 11″ paper (one sheet per student)
- Markers and crayons
- Self-Assessment Questionnaire (one per student)

NCTE/IRA STANDARDS

2 Students read a wide range of literature from many periods in many genres to build an understanding of the many dimensions (e.g., philosophical, ethical, aesthetic) of human experience.

10 Students whose first language is not English make use of their first language to develop competency in the English language arts and to develop understanding of content across the curriculum.

12 Students use spoken, written, and visual language to accomplish their own purposes (e.g., for learning, enjoyment, persuasion, and the exchange of information).

PROCEDURES

1. Make a quilt from gallon zip-lock freezer bags and duct tape. Generic bags work well because they typically do not have writing on them. Lay the bags out on the floor in a 5 x 5 or 5 x 6 pattern, depending on the number of students in your classroom. Use long strips of duct tape to connect the bags along all the borders. When the quilt is turned over, you should be able to open each zip-lock bag from the back to insert an 8 1/2″ x 11″ sheet of paper. (The construction of the quilt can be a little tricky, and you may need to complete it before students become involved in the lesson.)
2. Share with students a variety of biographies and historical picture books on the experiences and accomplishments of women. Some books can be read aloud, while others might be read individually or with a buddy. Also, have students investigate websites such as www.timeforkids.com/TFK/specials/whm/0,8805,101044,00.html and www.pocanticohills.org/womenenc/womenenc.htm.

3. Discuss the accomplishments of women throughout history and involve students in a grand conversation about issues such as:
   - The number of men and women in history that are well known
   - The reasons why fewer women are known
   - The rights of women throughout history (voting, owning property, securing a patent, etc.)
4. Have each student choose a woman that they believe has done great things in history. Using paper, markers, and crayons, have students design a quilt square that visually represents the accomplishments of that woman. Students can use both words and pictures. A drawing of the woman is optional, but the square should be labeled so that the women can be easily identified. Encourage students to use available trade books as resources as they design their quilt squares.
5. As the quilt squares are completed, place them inside the zip-lock bags in the quilt. Students may benefit from an opportunity to share the accomplishments of the woman they represented, either in a small or large group setting. The quilt can be displayed in the classroom or in the hallway, so other classes might benefit from this tribute to women in history.
6. Students with reading difficulties can read with a buddy or have books read aloud. Those students might also benefit from a brainstormed list of words that describe the woman they've chosen, to use as a resource as they design their quilt squares. English language learners might choose a woman from their own culture to represent on their quilt square. You can encourage them to design their squares in both their first language and in English.

ASSESSMENT

The design of quilt squares is considered to be a performance-based method of assessment. Students are demonstrating what they know about a woman in history through the design of their square. A Self-Assessment Questionnaire (Exhibit 7.4.A) can allow students to evaluate their learning and their finished products. You may choose to have an individual conference with each student to document further details of this learning experience. Students can discuss the experiences and accomplishments of the woman they chose, the design of their quilt square, what they like best about the square, and what might improve its design. Conference notes, along with the Self-Assessment Questionnaire, serve as documentation of student learning and can be shared with family members.

INTEGRATING LANGUAGE ARTS ACROSS THE CURRICULUM

In this activity, language arts and social studies are integrated. However, the baggy quilt can be used to represent student work in any subject area. The quilt might be used in math to represent geometric figures and in science to show examples of different kinds of plants.

HOME–SCHOOL CONNECTION

You can invite family members to school to view the quilt and review their child's self-assessment. Students can take a book home that features the woman they chose, to read and share with others. A book such as *Girls Think of Everything: Stories of Ingenious Inventions by Women*, by Catherine Thimmesh, might also be fun for students to take home. Family members could try to guess what each woman invented.

CHILDREN'S LITERATURE

Adler, D. (2003). *A picture book of Harriet Beecher Stowe.* Holiday House.

Adler, D. (2001). *A picture book of remarkable women.* Live Oak Media.

Adler, D. (2000). *A picture book of Sacagawea.* Scholastic.

Adler, D. (1998). *A picture book of Amelia Earhart.* Holiday House.

Adler, D. (1995). *A picture book of Eleanor Roosevelt.* Scholastic.

Adler, D. (1994). *A picture book of Sojourner Truth.* Scholastic.

Adler, D. (1993). *A picture book of Anne Frank.* Holiday House.

Adler, D. (1993). *A picture book of Rosa Parks.* Scholastic.

Adler, D. (1992). *A picture book of Florence Nightingale.* Holiday House.

Adler, D. (1992). *A picture book of Helen Keller.* Scott Foresman.

Allen, D. (2000). *Dancing in the wings.* Dial Books for Young Readers.

Amstel, M. (2000). *Sybil Ludington's midnight ride.* First Avenue Editions.

Ashby, R., & Ohrn, D. (1995). *Her story: Women who changed the world.* Viking.

Atkins, J. (1999). *Mary Anning and the sea dragon.* Farrar, Straus & Giroux.

Bains, R. (1982). *Clara Barton: Angel of the battlefield.* Troll.

Blue, R. (1998). *Madeleine Albright: U.S. Secretary of State.* Blackbirch Marketing.

Borden, L. (2001). *Fly high!: The story of Bessie Coleman.* Margaret K. McElderry.

Bridges, R. (1999). *Through my eyes.* Scholastic.

Brown, D. (1997). *Alice Ramsey's grand adventure.* Houghton Mifflin.

Casey, S. (1997). *Women invent! Two centuries of discoveries that have shaped our world.* Chicago Review Press.

Cheney, L. (2003). *A is for Abigail: An almanac of amazing American women.* Simon & Schuster Children's Publishing.

Coleman, E. (1996). *White socks only.* Albert Whitman.

Coles, R. (1995). *The story of Ruby Bridges.* Scholastic.

Conant, C. (1994). *Georgia O'Keeffe: Painter of the desert.* Blackbirch Marketing.

Cooney, B. (1996). *Eleanor.* Puffin.

Corey, S. (2000). *You forgot your skirt, Amelia Bloomer: A very improper story.* Scholastic.

Dahl, M. (2003). *Keep on sewing, Betsy Ross! A fun song about the American flag.* Picture Window Books.

Dungworth, R., & Wingate, P. (1996). *Famous women from Nefertiti to Diana.* Scholastic.

Ehrlich, A. (2003). *Rachel: The story of Rachel Carson.* Silver Whistle.

Ford, C. (2002). *Amelia Earhart: Meet the pilot.* Enslow.

Ford, C. (2002). *Helen Keller: Meet a woman of courage.* Enslow.

Ford, C. (2003). *Sacagawea: Meet an American legend.* Enslow.

Gelletly, L. (2001). *Harriet Beecher Stowe: Author of Uncle Tom's Cabin.* Chelsea House.

Grimes, N. (2002). *Talkin' about Bessie: The story of aviator Elizabeth Coleman.* Orchard Books.

Guiteras, G. (2001). *Famous American women.* Dover Publications.

Hurwitz, J. (1988). *Anne Frank: Life in hiding.* Avon Books.

Johnson, L. (1994). *Barbara Jordan: Congresswoman.* Blackbirch Marketing.

Johnson, L. (1994). *Mother Teresa: Protector of the sick.* Blackbirch Marketing.

Jones, B. (2003). *Learning about achievement from the life of Maya Angelou.* Powerkids Press.

Katz, W. (1995). *Black women of the Old West.* Atheneum.

King, S. (1994). *Maya Angelou.* Millbrook Press.

Knight, A. (1993). *The way west: Journal of a pioneer woman.* Simon & Schuster.

Krull, K. (2000). *Lives of extraordinary women: Rulers, rebels (and what the neighbors thought).* Harcourt.

Krull, K. (2000). *Wilma unlimited: How Wilma Rudolph became the world's fastest woman.* Voyager Books.

Kucharczyk, E. (2002). *Wilma Mankiller: Native American leader.* Blackbirch Marketing.

LaFontaine, B. (2001). *Famous American aviators.* Dover.

Langley, A. (1998). *Amelia Earhart: The pioneering pilot.* Oxford University Press Children's Books.

Lasky, K. (2000). *Vision of beauty: The story of Sarah Breedlove Walker.* Candlewick.

Lindbergh, R. (1998). *Nobody owns the sky: The story of "Brave Bessie" Coleman.* Candlewick Press.

Massey, C. (2002). *Famous African-American women.* Dover.

McDonough, Y. (2000). *Sisters in strength: American women who made a difference.* Henry Holt.

McKissack, P. (1994). *Sojourner Truth: Ain't I a woman?* Scholastic.

Noble, T. (2004). *The scarlet stockings spy.* Sleeping Bear Press.

Otfinoski, S. (1994). *Marian Wright Edelman: Defender of children's rights.* Blackbirch Marketing.

Paul, A. (1999). *All by herself: 14 girls who made a difference.* Harcourt.

Plowden, M. (2001). *Famous firsts of black women.* Pelican.

Polette, N. (2003). *Mae Jemison.* Children's Press.

Polette, N. (2003). *Pocahontas.* Children's Press.

Ransom, C. (2003). *Martha Washington.* Carolrhoda Books.

Ringgold, F. (1999). *If a bus could talk: The story of Rosa Parks.* Simon & Schuster Children's Publishing.

Rockwell, A. (2000). *They called her Molly Pitcher.* Knopf Books for Young Readers.

Roehm, M. (2000). *Girls who rocked the world 2: Heroines from Harriet Tubman to Mia Hamm.* Beyond Words Publishing.

Ryan, P. (2002). *When Marian sang.* Scholastic.

Sabin, F. (1982). *Amelia Earhart: Adventure in the sky.* Troll.

Sabin, F. (1982). *The courage of Helen Keller.* Troll.

Silcox-Jarrett, D. (1998). *Heroines of the American Revolution: America's founding mothers.* Scholastic.

Tallchief, M., & Wells, R. (1999). *Tallchief: America's prima ballerina.* Viking.

Thimmesh, C. (2000). *Girls think of everything: Stories of ingenious inventions by women.* Houghton Mifflin.

Thimmesh, C. (2002). *The sky's the limit: Stories of discovery by women and girls.* Houghton Mifflin.

Thomas, J. (1998). *I have heard of a land.* HarperCollins.

Wallner, A. (1994). *Betsy Ross.* Scholastic.

Wallner, A. (1997). *Laura Ingalls Wilder.* Scholastic.

Welden, A. (1998). *Girls who rocked the world: Heroines from Sacagawea to Sheryl Swoopes.* Scholastic.

Wheeler, J. (1991). *Nancy Reagan.* Abdo & Daughters.

Winnick, K. (2000). *Sybil's night ride.* Boyds Mill Press.

Zeldis, M. (2000). *Sisters in strength: American women who made a difference.* Henry Holt.

INTERNET RESOURCES

Pocantico Hills School. (2006). *Children's encyclopedia of women.* Available at www.pocantico-hills.org/womenenc/womenenc.htm.

Time for Kids. (2006). *Women's history month.* Available at www.timeforkids.com/TFK/specials/whm/0,8805,101044,00.html.

OTHER RESOURCES

Bolden, T. (2002). *33 things every girl should know about women's history.* Crown.

Haven, K. (1995). *Amazing American women: 40 fascinating 5-minute reads.* Libraries Unlimited.

Keenan, S. (1996). *Scholastic Encyclopedia of women in the United States.* Scholastic.

Kent, D. (1995). *The Vietnam Women's Memorial.* Children's Press.

Smith, C. (2003). *Extraordinary women from U.S. History: Readers theatre for grades 4–8.* Teacher Ideas Press.

Women in History Quilt

Self-Assessment Questionnaire

Name ______________________________ Date ______________

1. What is the most important thing you learned about the woman you chose?

2. What do you like best about your quilt square?

3. What would you like to change or improve on your quilt square?

4. Does your quilt square show your very best work? Why or why not?

5. How might you share the information you learned about this woman?

ACTIVITY 7.5

Kate and Jack Climb Up the Beanstalk

Using Venn Diagrams to Compare and Contrast

GRADE LEVEL: **3–4**

OBJECTIVES

- To apply a variety of strategies to comprehend, interpret, evaluate, and appreciate texts
- To use visual language to learn about literature and exchange information

MATERIALS

- Books suitable for comparison, such as *Kate and the Beanstalk*, by Mary Pope Osborne, and *Jack and the Beanstalk*, illustrated by Matt Faulkner. Other choices might include:
  1. *The Fourth Little Pig*, by Teresa Celsi; *The Three Little Wolves and the Big Bad Pig*, by Eugene Trivizas; *The Three Pigs*, by David Wiesner; and *The True Story of the 3 Little Pigs!*, by Jon Scieszka
  2. *Rumpelstiltskin's Daughter*, by Diane Stanley, and *Rumpelstiltskin*, by Jacob Grimm
  3. The Cinderella stories, such as *Cinderella*, by Barbara McClintock; *The Egyptian Cinderella*, by Shirley Climo; *Cendrillon: A Caribbean Cinderella*, by Robert San Souci; and *The Irish Cinderlad*, by Shirley Climo. Variations of the Cinderella story can also be found online at wneo.org/WebQuests/TeacherWebQuests/Cinderella/The_Cinderella_Project.htm and www.ucalgary. ca/~dkbrown/cinderella.html.
- Venn Diagram handout (one per student)

NCTE/IRA STANDARDS

3 Students apply a wide range of strategies to comprehend, interpret, evaluate, and appreciate texts. They draw on their prior experience, their interactions with other readers and writers, their knowledge of word meaning and of other texts, their word identification strategies, and their understanding of textual features (e.g., sound–letter correspondence, sentence structure, context, graphics).

12 Students use spoken, written, and visual language to accomplish their own purposes (e.g., for learning, enjoyment, persuasion, and the exchange of information).

PROCEDURES

1. Read *Kate and the Beanstalk* and *Jack and the Beanstalk*. Ask students to consider questions such as:
   - How are the main characters alike? How are they different?
   - How are Kate's and Jack's experiences alike and different?
   - How are the settings alike and different?
   - How are the illustrations alike and different?
   - Compare the end of each story. How are the endings alike or different?
   - Why do you think Mary Pope Osborne rewrote the story to include a female main character? How do you feel about this change and why?

2. Give each student a Venn Diagram handout (Exhibit 7.5.A). Have students label one circle "Kate" and another circle "Jack." Ask students to compare and contrast the two books, using words and pictures. List students' responses on the chalkboard. Students who have difficulty with written expression may choose to use only pictures on their Venn diagrams.
3. Have students consider what a modern-day version of the beanstalk story might be like. They will label the third circle with the name of the main character of their modern-day story. Using words and pictures, students can compare and contrast their story with the other two versions. If they wish, students could write and illustrate their stories.
4. Ask students to form groups of three or four. Students will take turns using their Venn diagrams to retell their story to the others in their group. They should point out the ways their story is similar to and different from the other stories.

ASSESSMENT

You can use a Children's Literature Comparison Rubric (Exhibit 7.5.B) to assess the Venn diagrams and the modern-day story retelling. You can make anecdotal records on the rubric to document strengths, weaknesses, small-group interaction, and support offered.

INTEGRATING LANGUAGE ARTS ACROSS THE CURRICULUM

Students can use Venn diagrams to make comparisons throughout the elementary curriculum. In social studies, students can compare and contrast topics and concepts such as types of government, small towns versus large cities, and the impact of various wars. In science, they can compare plant and animal cells, types of recycling, and mammals and fish.

HOME-SCHOOL CONNECTION

Students can take their Venn diagrams home and explain their purpose to family members. They might also retell their modern-day beanstalk story and explain how it is like and different from the original versions.

CHILDREN'S LITERATURE

Celsi, T. (1992). *The fourth little pig.* Raintree Steck-Vaughn.

Climo, S. (1991). *The Egyptian Cinderella.* HarperTrophy.

Climo, S. (2000). *The Irish Cinderlad.* HarperTrophy.

Faulkner, M. (1986). *Jack and the beanstalk.* Scholastic.

Grimm, J., & Zelinsky, P. (ill.) (1996). *Rumpelstiltskin.* Puffin.

McClintock, B. (2005). *Cinderella.* Scholastic.

Osborne, M. (2000). *Kate and the beanstalk.* Atheneum.

San Souci, R. (2002). *Cendrillon: A Caribbean Cinderella.* Aladdin.

Scieszka, J. (1989). *The true story of the 3 little pigs!* Scholastic.

Stanley, D. (1997). *Rumpelstiltskin's daughter.* Morrow.

Trivizas, E. (1993). *The three little wolves and the big bad pig.* Aladdin.

Wiesner, D. (2001). *The three pigs.* Scholastic.

INTERNET RESOURCES

Dougherty, L. (2006). *The Cinderella Project.* Available at wnea.org/WebQuests/TeacherWebQuests/Cinderella/The_Cinderella_Project.htm.

Martin, K. (2006). *Cinderella stories.* Available at www.ucalgary.ca/~dkbrown/cinderella.html.

EXHIBIT **7.5.A**

Venn Diagram

Name

Date

EXHIBIT **7.5.B**

Children's Literature Comparison Rubric

Name ______________________________ Date ______________

5 = Strongly agree   3 = Agree   1 = Disagree

CRITERIA	POINT VALUE
Student identified ways in which stories were alike.	5 3 1 *Comments:*
Student identified ways in which stories were different.	5 3 1 *Comments:*
Student created a modern-day beanstalk story and identified ways in which it was like and different from the original versions.	5 3 1 *Comments:*
Student used the Venn diagram to retell his/her modern-day beanstalk story and explain how it is like and different from the original versions.	5 3 1 *Comments:*

Total points ______ / 20

Depicting the Past

Paper Plate Timelines

GRADE LEVEL: **3–4**

OBJECTIVES

- To read a variety of print texts to build an understanding of texts and the cultures of the United States
- To use spoken, written, and visual language to accomplish their own purposes

MATERIALS

- Paper plates (six per student)
- Markers, crayons, or colored pencils
- Hole punch
- 12″ lengths of yarn (six per student)
- A selection of biographical picture books (at least one per student) (See the Biographical Picture Books section at the end of this activity for suggestions.)
- Paper Plate Timeline Rubric (one per student)

NCTE/IRA STANDARDS

1 Students read a wide range of print and non-print texts to build an understanding of texts, of themselves, and of the cultures of the United States and the world; to acquire new information; to respond to the needs and demands of society and the workplace; and for personal fulfillment. Among these texts are fiction and nonfiction, classic and contemporary works.

12 Students use spoken, written, and visual language to accomplish their own purposes (e.g., for learning, enjoyment, persuasion, and the exchange of information).

PROCEDURES

1. Begin by selecting a biographical picture book to share with students.
2. After previewing the book, create a sample paper plate timeline that depicts important events in the life of the person highlighted in the book. The timeline will serve as an example for students.
3. With a hole punch, punch a hole at the top and bottom of six paper plates. Lay the plates in a vertical line with holes aligned. Connect the plates with 12-inch pieces of yarn. Tie a piece of yarn to the top plate. This piece of yarn will be used to hang the timeline from the ceiling or a bulletin board.
4. On the first plate, write the name of the person, and then visually depict five sequential events from the person's life on the remaining plates. Beneath each picture, write a sentence that summarizes the event.
5. Prepare six paper plates for each student with holes (leave them separate).
6. Discuss the genre of biography with students, and then read the selected story. Tell students to listen for important events in the person's life.
7. After discussing the story, show students the sample timeline and describe the steps you took to create it.
8. Allow students to choose a biographical picture book from a selection of books and have them create timelines. English language learners can be paired with a native English speaker or assisted by an aide. Distribute six paper plates and pieces of yarn to each student.

9. When complete, have students share their timelines. Display them by suspending them from the classroom ceiling, from a bulletin board, or on the walls around the classroom. English language learners can share their timelines in their first language or in English.

ASSESSMENT

You can assess students' timelines with the Paper Plate Timeline Rubric (Exhibit 7.6.A).

INTEGRATING LANGUAGE ARTS ACROSS THE CURRICULUM

Students can use timelines to represent events in the lives of well-known scientists in science class, mathematicians in math class, explorers in social studies, musicians in music class, artists in art class, and athletes in physical education.

HOME–SCHOOL CONNECTION

Encourage students to create personal timelines at home with family members that depict important events in their own lives. They can attach family photographs to the paper plates, instead of illustrations. The timeline can be displayed in the child's bedroom.

BIOGRAPHICAL PICTURE BOOKS

Adler, D. (2003). *A picture book of Harriet Beecher Stowe.* Holiday House.
Adler, D. (2003). *A picture book of Lewis and Clark.* Holiday House.
Adler, D. (2001). *Lou Gehrig: The luckiest man.* Voyager Books.
Adler, D. (2000). *A picture book of Sacagawea.* Scholastic.
Adler, D. (1998). *A picture book of Amelia Earhart.* Holiday House.
Adler, D. (1995). *A picture book of Eleanor Roosevelt.* Scholastic.
Adler, D. (1994). *A picture book of Sojourner Truth.* Scholastic.
Adler, D. (1993). *A picture book of Anne Frank.* Holiday House.
Adler, D. (1993). *A picture book of Rosa Parks.* Scholastic.
Adler, D. (1992). *A picture book of Florence Nightingale.* Holiday House.
Adler, D. (1992). *A picture book of Helen Keller.* Scott Foresman.
Adler, D. (1992). *A picture book of Harriet Tubman.* Scholastic.
Adler, D. (1992). *A picture book of Jesse Owens.* Holiday House.
Adler, D., & Wallner, A. (1991). *A picture book of Christopher Columbus.* Scholastic.
Allen, D. (2000). *Dancing in the wings.* Dial Books for Young Readers.
Amstel, M. (2000). *Sybil Ludington's midnight ride.* First Avenue Editions.
Anholt, L. (1998). *Picasso and the girl with the ponytail.* Barron's Educational Series.
Borden, L. (2001). *Fly high!: The story of Bessie Coleman.* Margaret K. McElderry.
Bridges, R. (1999). *Through my eyes.* Scholastic.
Brown, D. (2004). *Odd boy out: Young Albert Einstein.* Houghton Mifflin.
Burleigh, R. (2003). *Home run: The story of Babe Ruth.* Voyager.
Coles, R. (1995). *The story of Ruby Bridges.* Scholastic.
Conant, C. (1994). *Georgia O'Keeffe: Painter of the desert.* Blackbirch Marketing.
Cooney, B. (1996). *Eleanor.* Puffin.
Corey, S. (2000). *You forgot your skirt, Amelia Bloomer: A very improper story.* Scholastic.
Dahl, M. (2003). *Keep on sewing, Betsy Ross! A fun song about the American flag.* Picture Window Books.

Ford, C. (2003). *Sacagawea: Meet an American legend.* Enslow.

Fritz, J. (1996). *And then what happened, Paul Revere?* Putnam Juvenile.

Giovanni, N. (2005). *Rosa.* Henry Holt.

Grimes, N. (2002). *Talkin' about Bessie: The Story of aviator Elizabeth Coleman.* Orchard Books.

Johnston, L. (2006). *Ellen Ochoa: Pioneering astronaut.* Fact Finders.

Krull, K. (2003). *Harvesting hope: The story of Cesar Chavez.* Harcourt Children's Books.

Krull, K. (2000). *Wilma unlimited: How Wilma Rudolph became the world's fastest woman.* Voyager.

Mara, W. (2006). *Betsy Ross.* Children's Press.

Mara, W. (2004). *Henry Ford.* Children's Press.

Mara, W. (2004). *Clara Barton.* Children's Press.

Martin, J. (1998). *Snowflake Bentley.* Houghton Mifflin.

Mattern, J. (1992). *Young Martin Luther King, Jr.: I have a dream.* Troll.

Oppenheim, J. (2006). *Dear Miss Breed.* Scholastic.

Pinkney, A. (1994). *Dear Benjamin Banneker.* Harcourt Brace.

Rodriquez, R. (2006). *Through Georgia's eyes.* Henry Holt.

Ryan, P. (2002). *When Marian sang.* Scholastic.

Tallchief, M., & Wells, R. (1999). *Tallchief: America's prima ballerina.* Viking.

Venezia, M. (1989). *Van Gogh.* Children's Press.

Walker, S. (2003). *Bessie Colman: Daring to fly.* Lerner Publishing Group.

Wallner, A. (1994). *Betsy Ross.* Scholastic.

Winnick, K. (2000). *Sybil's night ride.* Boyds Mill Press.

Zannos, S. (2004). *The life and times of Archimedes.* Mitchell Lane Publishers.

Paper Plate Timeline Rubric

Student ____ Date ____________

Book Title ____

____

3 = Excellent 2 = Good 1 = Satisfactory 0 = Unacceptable

EVALUATION CRITERIA				
1. Five major events represented	3	2	1	0
2. Events correctly sequenced	3	2	1	0
3. Sentences accurately describe events	3	2	1	0
4. Illustrations and text are neat	3	2	1	0
5. Presentation of timeline	3	2	1	0

Total score _______ / 15

Comments and modifications: ____

ACTIVITY 7.7

Plotting the Story

Developing Plot Profile Graphs

GRADE LEVEL: **3–4**

OBJECTIVES

- To apply a wide range of strategies to comprehend, interpret, evaluate, and appreciate texts
- To use visual language to represent the degree of excitement in the story related to each story element or event

MATERIALS

- A picture book with significant events that lead to a resolution of suspense or excitement, such as *The Three Billy Goats Gruff,* by Janet Stevens (See the Children's Literature section at the end of this activity for additional titles.)
- Sample Plot Profile Graph for *The Three Billy Goats Gruff*
- Plot Profile Graph handouts (one per student) or a large sheet of graph paper with a plot profile drawn
- Plot Profile Graph Checklist (one per student)

NCTE/IRA STANDARDS

3 Students apply a wide range of strategies to comprehend, interpret, evaluate, and appreciate texts. They draw on their prior experience, their interactions with other readers and writers, their knowledge of word meaning and of other texts, their word identification strategies, and their understanding of textual features (e.g., sound–letter correspondence, sentence structure, context, graphics).

12 Students use spoken, written, and visual language to accomplish their own purposes (e.g., for learning, enjoyment, persuasion, and the exchange of information).

PROCEDURES

1. Read the story to the students. Ask them to list the significant events in the story and write them on the chalkboard, numbering their sequence. After the events are listed, discuss with students the degree of excitement, suspense, or tension each event brought to them as readers. Help students to understand that that degree of excitement is what keeps readers interested in the story and curious about the story's resolution. For the book *The Three Billy Goats Gruff,* the story events might include:
    1. The three billy goats were hungry.
    2. They wanted to eat the sweet, green grass on the other side of the hill, but they would have to cross the bridge.
    3. Under the bridge lived a mean troll, and he was hungry.
    4. The tiniest billy goat started across the bridge, but the troll caught him and threatened to eat him.
    5. The littlest billy goat told the troll to wait for a bigger billy goat, and the troll let him go.
    6. The second billy goat started across the bridge, but the troll caught him and threatened to eat him.

7. The second billy goat told the troll to wait for the big billy goat, and the troll let him go.
8. The big billy goat started across the bridge, and the troll threatened to eat him.
9. The big billy goat told the troll to come ahead, but that he would get knocked off the bridge.
10. The big billy goat knocked the troll off the bridge into the river.
11. The three billy goats ate the sweet, green grass on the other side of the bridge.

2. Draw a plot profile with an *x* and a *y* axis on a large sheet of graph paper. The numbers for each story element or event will go along the horizontal *x* axis and the degree of excitement will go along the vertical *y* axis. Assist students in discussing each story event listed on the chalkboard and the level of suspense or excitement created by each event. Plot the level of excitement for each event. Allow students to go back and change their ratings for a particular event as they discuss and examine the relationship between events in the story. See Exhibit 7.7.A for a Sample Plot Profile Graph for this story.
3. When the Plot Profile Graph is complete, discuss with students the changes in suspense throughout the story. Have students identify when there was the least excitement and the most excitement, and how and why the suspense ended.
4. Plot profiles can be done with the entire class, in small groups, or independently, depending on the level of assistance and support that students need. As students become more experienced with plot profiles, they can use the Plot Profile Graph handouts (Exhibit 7.7.B) to graph the events of a story independently (Johnson & Louis, 1987).

ASSESSMENT

You can use the Plot Profile Graph Checklist (Exhibit 7.7.C) to assess students' skill in comprehending the story, determining the level of suspense for each story event, and plotting the level of suspense. You can also document whether students are able to perform these tasks independently, or whether they need assistance and support.

INTEGRATING LANGUAGE ARTS ACROSS THE CURRICULUM

Plot profiles can enhance the teaching of social studies with books that include historical fiction and nonfiction. Books such as *Sybil's Night Ride*, by Karen Winnick; *The Scarlet Stockings Spy*, by Trinka Noble; and *They Called Her Molly Pitcher*, by Anne Rockwell, could add depth and human interest to studies of the American Revolution. *Rose Blanche*, by Roberto Innocenti, the story of a young girl in Germany who helped those held in Jewish prison camps, and *Cecil's Story*, by George Ella Lyon, could help students to understand the impact of war from a child's perspective.

HOME-SCHOOL CONNECTION

Students could take Plot Profile Graphs home and explain their purpose to family members. Students could also use the plot profiles as prompts for story retellings.

CHILDREN'S LITERATURE

Innocenti, R. (1985). *Rose Blanche.* Harcourt Brace.

Lyon, G. (1995). *Cecil's story.* Scholastic.

Noble, T. (2004). *The scarlet stockings spy.* Sleeping Bear Press.

Rockwell, A. (2002). *They called her Molly Pitcher.* Random House.

Stevens, J. (1987). *The three billy goats gruff.* Harcourt Brace.

Winnick, K. (2000). *Sybil's night ride.* Boyds Mills Press.

REFERENCE

Johnson, T., & Louis, D. (1987). *Literacy through literature.* Portsmouth, NH: Heinemann.

Sample Plot Profile Graph

Name ______________________________ Date ____________

Book The Three Billy Goats Gruff

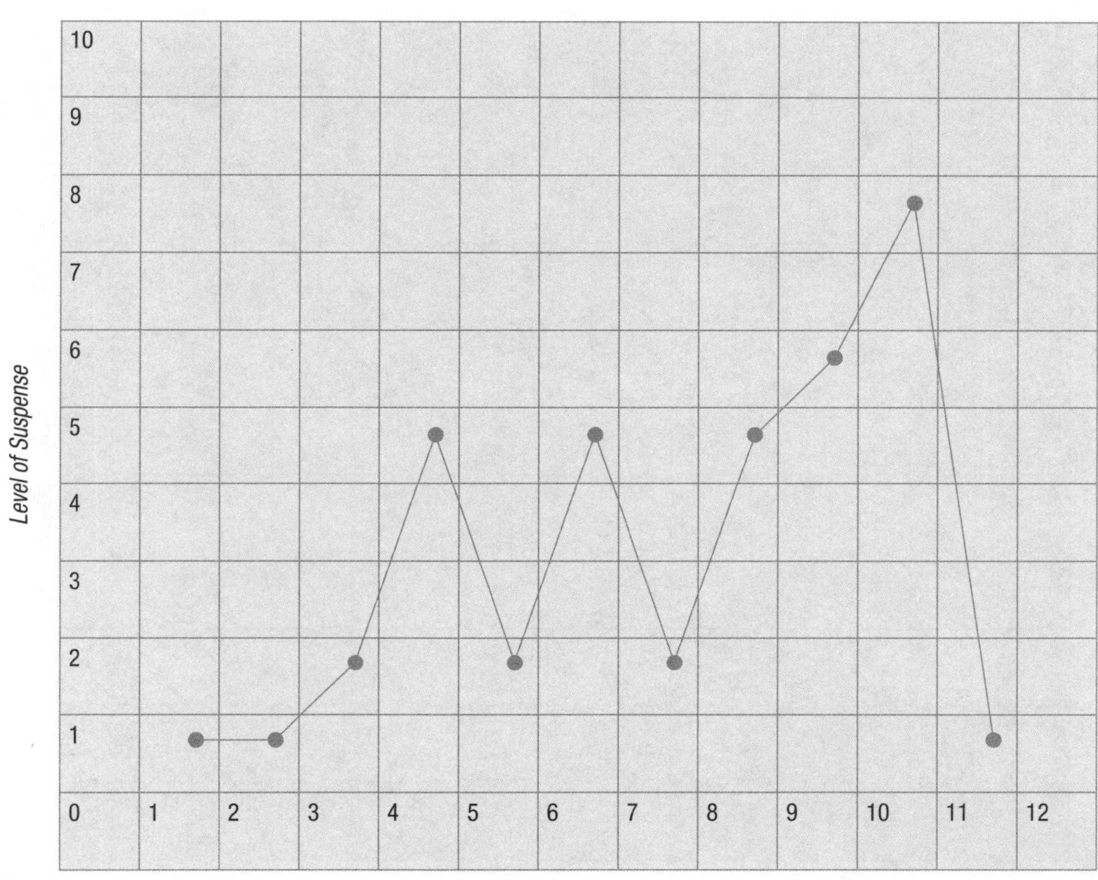

EXHIBIT **7.7.B**

Plot Profile Graph

Name ______________________________ Date ______________

Book ______________________________

Level of Suspense

10												
9												
8												
7												
6												
5												
4												
3												
2												
1												
0	1	2	3	4	5	6	7	8	9	10	11	12

Story Events

EXHIBIT **7.7.C**

Plot Profile Graph Checklist

CRITERIA	INDEPENDENTLY	WITH ASSISTANCE FROM TEACHER AND/OR PEERS	NOT YET MASTERED
Student listens to story and participates in discussion and identification of story events.			
Student understands the concept of "suspense" and is able to identify the level of suspense of story events.			
Student correctly plots the level of suspense for story events on the graph, creating a visual profile.			

Teacher comments:

ACTIVITY 7.8

Constructing a Human Bar Graph

GRADE LEVEL: **4–5**

OBJECTIVES

- To read literature from many periods to build an understanding of the many dimensions of human experience
- To use spoken and visual language to learn, persuade, and exchange information

MATERIALS

- A book that encourages students to form their own opinions and contemplate controversial issues, such as *Let Them Play*, by Margot Raven (See the Children's Literature section at the end of this activity for an additional title.)
- Masking tape

NCTE/IRA STANDARDS

2 Students read a wide range of literature from many periods in many genres to build an understanding of the many dimensions (e.g., philosophical, ethical, aesthetic) of human experience.

12 Students use spoken, written, and visual language to accomplish their own purposes (e.g., for learning, enjoyment, persuasion, and the exchange of information).

PROCEDURES

1. Read and discuss *Let Them Play*, and give students other examples of prejudice and segregated practices. Help students understand the segregated South during the 1950s and 1960s and the impact prejudice had on children.

   Book Summary: Let Them Play is the true story of the Cannon Street All-Stars, an all-black Little League baseball team of 1955. All the white teams refused to play them, so by default they won all their games and were invited to the Little League World Series in Williamsport, Pennsylvania. However, the team made the trip knowing that they would not be allowed to play. In 2002, fourteen members of the Cannon Street All-Stars were honored at the Little League World Series.

2. Have students assess their own beliefs and prejudices by participating in a human bar graph. Students form a human bar graph by lining up at various positions along a line to represent how they feel about a particular statement. Place a piece of masking tape across the front of the room from one wall to another. Label the left side of the tape "disagree," the middle section of the tape "I don't know," and the right side of the tape "agree." Explain to students that you will read a statement related to the story. They must individually decide what they believe about the statement and move to the "agree," "I don't know," or "disagree" sections of the tape. Emphasize to students that there are no correct answers, and they should make their own decisions and try not to be influenced by the opinions of their peers. Students at each section of the tape stand directly behind one another, forming a straight line. The resulting bar graph allows students to see how many people agree with each statement.

3. After students have made a decision and are in a line, have them look at the bar graph that is formed and interpret the graph. Then ask them to turn to someone else in the same line and share why they made the decision they did. Allow three to four minutes for discussion. Then ask each student to turn to someone in a different line and share the reasons for their decision. Explain to students that they are not trying to change a person's opinion or beliefs, but instead are listening to attempt to understand how others feel. During the discussion portion of this activity, some students may change their opinions and should be permitted to move to a different line. They can then explain why they decided to move. Discussion statements for *Let Them Play* might include:
   - I would like to be on the team with the Cannon Street All-Stars.
   - If I had been on one of the other teams, I would have agreed to play the Cannon Street All-Stars.
   - If I were on the Cannon Street All-Stars, I would have been disappointed that I didn't get to play in the World Series.
   - Other teams did not want to play the Cannon Street All-Stars because they were afraid they would lose.
   - We don't have to worry about racism and prejudice like people did in 1955.
   - There is racism and prejudice in sports today.
   - I would have liked to see the Cannon Street All-Stars honored at the Little League World Series in 2002.
4. Additional details about the team, the honor they were bestowed in 2002, and pictures then and now can be found in abundance at websites such as www.littleleague.org/media/archive/cannonstreet.htm, www.blackathlete.net/Blackbox/blackbox080705.html, and www.sptimes.com/2002/08/16/Sports/Banned_team_to_be_hon.shtml. Encourage students to view these websites and discuss how things have changed since the 1950s.
5. Students who don't have a full understanding of "agree" and "disagree" may feel more comfortable with "yes" and "no" on the masking tape. Others may have difficulty comprehending terms such as "racism" and "prejudice," and will require clear, concrete explanations of these terms.

ASSESSMENT

Students' placement on the human bar graph is based on their own opinions. Therefore, limit your evaluation to peer discussions, and assess whether students are able to defend their positions as well as consider others' points of view. You might choose to circulate during discussions and take anecdotal records of students' interactions.

INTEGRATING LANGUAGE ARTS ACROSS THE CURRICULUM

The human bar graph is an effective tool to encourage discussion of controversial issues in science. For example, *Genetic Engineering*, by Ray Spangenburg and Kit Moser, can help children to consider and discuss the social and ethical issues surrounding genetic engineering.

HOME-SCHOOL CONNECTION

Create a literacy bag with *Let Them Play* or another book of your choice, discussion statements to consider, and masking tape. Have students read the book with family members and/or friends and participate in the human bar graph activity. Remind students that it is all right to have differences of opinion on significant issues, even within a family.

CHILDREN'S LITERATURE

Raven, M. (2005). *Let them play.* Sleeping Bear Press.

Spangenburg, R., & Moser, K. (2004). *Genetic engineering.* Benchmark.

INTERNET RESOURCES

Black Athlete Sports Network. (2002, Aug. 7). New kids book for all of us. Available at www.blackathlete.net/Blackbox/blackbox080705.html.

Little League Online. (2002, Aug. 6). 1955 Little League team from Charleston, SC to be honored at Little League baseball World Series. Available at www.littleleague.org/media/archive/cannonstreet.htm.

St. Petersburg Times Online Sports. (2002, Aug. 16). Banned team to be honored at Little League ceremony. Available at www.sptimes.com/2002/08/16/Sports/Banned_team_to_be_hon.shtml.

Sell that Product!

Creating Media Print Ads

GRADE LEVEL: **5–6**

OBJECTIVE

- To use spoken, written, and visual language to inform and persuade others

MATERIALS

- A variety of print ads for popular, well-known products
- Internet access
- $8^1/_2$″ x 11″ white drawing paper (one per student)
- Colored markers or colored pencils
- Video camera and cassette tape
- Sell That Product! Scoring Rubric (one per group)

NCTE/IRA STANDARD

12 Students use spoken, written, and visual language to accomplish their own purposes (e.g., for learning, enjoyment, persuasion, and the exchange of information).

PROCEDURES

1. Collect print ads from magazines, newspapers, or the Internet for a variety of popular, well-known products, including food, beverages, clothing, and automobiles. A variety of magazine advertisements can be found at www.magazine-ads.com/index.php.
2. Share a few ads with the class and have them react to each. Possible discussion questions include:

   What does the ad promote?

   What is depicted in the print ad?

   Are there any words in the ad or a product slogan?

   To what audience does the ad appeal?

   Would you want to purchase the product? Explain why or why not.
3. Divide students into groups of three or four students. Give each group a print ad, or have them access one on the Internet, and ask them to examine it carefully. Groups can trade ads with other groups after five minutes and continue trading until all of the groups have seen all of the ads.
4. Tell groups to pretend that they have just been hired to create a print ad for a new product. As a group, they must decide the following:
   - To whom their ad will appeal—children, teenagers, young adults, adults, or senior citizens
   - How they wish to advertise the product—seriously, humorously, or in some other way
   - What images the ad will include

- What advertising slogan the ad will contain
- What colors will be used in the illustrations

5. Distribute drawing paper to each group and randomly assign one of the following imaginary products to each group:

Jumpin' Jupiter Juice Bars	Big Bob's Country Biscuits
Darrel's Doughnut Holes	Bright and White Laundry Detergent
Crispy, Crumbly Crackers	Fresh Scent Alpine Deodorant
Peachy Keen Hand Cream	Tangy, Tingly Tangerine Toothpaste
Eat-on-the-Go Breakfast Bars	Captain Charley's Chewing Gum

6. Have each group create a print ad for the product and prepare to present it to the class. Rather than hand drawing, groups may also create their print ads on the computer to reinforce technology skills. Presentations can be videotaped so that students can view and self-critique their own performances.

ASSESSMENT

You can use the Sell That Product! Scoring Rubric (Exhibit 7.9.A) to assess students. Provide groups with a copy of the evaluation criteria before they begin working.

INTEGRATING LANGUAGE ARTS ACROSS THE CURRICULUM

Students can research print ads for popular products throughout time. They can also research improvements made in specific products over the years.

HOME-SCHOOL CONNECTION

Have students find interesting print ads for products in magazines at home. Encourage them to bring them to class to share.

Scoring Rubric

Sell That Product!

Name ______________________________ Date ____________

Group # ____________ Product Name ______________________________

5 = Outstanding   4 = Very Good   3 = Good   2 = Fair   1 = Poor

EVALUATION CRITERIA	SCORE				
Intended audience was clear.	5	4	3	2	1
Tone of ad was apparent.	5	4	3	2	1
Images captured attention.	5	4	3	2	1
Ad contained a slogan or catch-phrase.	5	4	3	2	1
Ad was creative and original.	5	4	3	2	1
Illustrations and text were neat and attractive.	5	4	3	2	1
Student worked well as a team member.	5	4	3	2	1
Presentation was well prepared and delivered.	5	4	3	2	1

Total Score ______ / 40

Comments:

ACTIVITY 7.10

Charting Math Results

Discovering Pi

GRADE LEVEL: **5–6**

OBJECTIVES

- To gather, evaluate, and synthesize data from a variety of sources and communicate findings
- To use visual language to learn and exchange information

MATERIALS

- String
- Tape measures and yardsticks
- Circle Measurement Data Collection Sheet (one per student)
- One copy of *Sir Cumference and the Dragon of Pi: A Math Adventure*, by Cindy Neuschwander (Charlesbridge, 1999)
- Construction paper, scissors, glue, and any other materials needed for bulletin board creation

NCTE/IRA STANDARDS

7 Students conduct research on issues and interests by generating ideas and questions, and by posing problems. They gather, evaluate, and synthesize data from a variety of sources (e.g., print and non-print texts, artifacts, people) to communicate their discoveries in ways that suit their purpose and audience.

12 Students use spoken, written, and visual language to accomplish their own purposes (e.g., for learning, enjoyment, persuasion, and the exchange of information).

Activity adapted from C. Funk, 2003.

PROCEDURES

1. Ask students to explore their environment, both at school and at home, and find things that are circles. The circles can be as small (a dime) or as large (a spinning wheel) as they wish. Ask students to take two measurements for each circle: the distance across the circle in inches and the distance around the circle in inches. If students do not have a tape measure at home, they can use a piece of string to measure the distance and then lay the string on a yardstick.
2. Students should record the measurements for each circle on their Circle Measurement Data Collection Sheet (Exhibit 7.10.A). The number of inches across the circle will go in the first column and the number of inches around the circle in the second column. Students should measure as many circles as they can over a period of several days. When they bring the measurements to class, have them choose three of the items they've measured. Using graph paper, ask students to make a bar graph to show the measurement for the distance across and the distance around each of the three items. Demonstrations on the chalkboard might be helpful.
3. Ask students to examine their graphs and the numbers they have recorded in the two columns. Ask questions such as:
   - What is interesting about your graphs?

- What is interesting about the numbers in the two columns?
- Is one column of numbers bigger than the other column?
- How much bigger are the numbers in the second column than the numbers in the first column?
- How much bigger are the bar graphs representing the distance around circles than the distance across circles?
- How can we find out how much bigger the numbers are in the second column than the numbers in the first column?

4. For each circle, have students divide the bigger number by the smaller one. Students may come up with this idea on their own after class discussion. Students record their answers for each calculation in the third column. They should soon discover that all of their answers are a little more than 3, or about 3.14.
5. Read aloud *Sir Cumference and the Dragon of Pi: A Math Adventure.* Discuss Sir Cumference's adventures and the concept of pi.
6. Involve students in the construction of a bulletin board that explains the concept and uses of pi. They might include their data collection sheets, bar graphs showing distances across circles and distances around circles, and any other creative visuals that represent their knowledge of pi.
7. Some students may need repeated demonstrations and support to learn how to measure the distance across and around circles accurately. Calculators should be available for division calculations.

ASSESSMENT

Throughout classroom discussion, calculations, graphing, and bulletin board construction, observe student performance. Take anecdotal records noting which students have mastered the concept of pi, those who have a basic understanding, and those who are having difficulty grasping the concept.

INTEGRATING LANGUAGE ARTS ACROSS THE CURRICULUM

This activity is based on the integration of the language arts into mathematics. Creating visual representations during the learning process through graphing and charting can assist young students' comprehension of math concepts. Comprehension is also aided by the incorporation of children's literature, as students are able to see math concepts portrayed throughout the text. Graphs, charts, and data collection records would also be useful when integrating language arts into the sciences.

HOME–SCHOOL CONNECTION

Explaining concepts to others improves students' own comprehension of math concepts. Students can take their graphs and data collection sheets home and explain pi to family members. Many adults and siblings may have only a vague understanding of the concept, so a student's role as teacher may prove to be very valuable.

REFERENCE

Funk, C. (2003). James Otto and the pi man: A constructivist tale. *Phi Delta Kappan*, 85(3), 212.

EXHIBIT **7.10.A**

Circle Measurement Data Collection Sheet

Name ______________________________ Date ______________

ITEM MEASURED	DISTANCE ACROSS CIRCLE (IN INCHES)	DISTANCE AROUND CIRCLE (IN INCHES)	
1.			
2.			
3.			
4.			
5.			
6.			
7.			
8.			
9.			
10.			
11.			
12.			
13.			
14.			
15.			
16.			
17.			
18.			
19.			

AUTHOR & TITLE INDEX

(This list includes only those titles discussed within Activities. See lists of Children's Literature and other resource lists at the ends of activities for other books and resources.)

SUBJECT INDEX